The Joint Military Intelligence College supports and encourages research on intelligence issues that distills lessons and improves Intelligence Community capabilities for policy-level and operational consumers

Y: The Sources of Islamic Revolutionary Conduct, Major Stephen P. Lambert, U.S. Air Force

This product has been reviewed by senior experts from academia and government, and has been approved for unrestricted distribution by the Directorate for Freedom of Information and Security Review, Washington Headquarters Services. It is available to the public through the National Technical Information Service (www.ntis.gov).

The author has also arranged for publication of this study through the Hoover Institution at Stanford University. The projected publication date is 2005. The Hoover Institution book includes commentaries on Major Lambert's work by an even greater variety of scholars than included in the present book.

Russell.Swenson@dia.mil, Editor and Director
Center for Strategic Intelligence Research

The Sources of Islamic Revolutionary Conduct

Major Stephen P. Lambert, U.S. Air Force
Research Fellow

JOINT MILITARY
INTELLIGENCE COLLEGE

WASHINGTON, DC
April 2005

With the cooperation and support of the

Institute for National Security Studies (INSS)
USAF Academy, Colorado Springs

CONTENTS

Acknowledgments

I take this opportunity to express my appreciation to those who provided insight, advice, and encouragement and who made this work possible.

I would like to thank the Institute for National Security Studies (INSS) in Colorado Springs and the Center for Strategic Intelligence Research (CSIR) in Washington, DC. for providing the funding and administrative support to make my travels possible. I sincerely appreciate the strong commitment by the Institute for National Security Studies to actively support research in the public policy and national security fields—and, in particular, the efforts of Dr. Jim Smith and Mrs. Diana Heerdt. In addition, much of the research would have been impossible without the helpful attitudes of the staffs at the research libraries of the Oxford Centre for Islamic Studies and the Middle East Centre at Oxford University, as well as the Oriental Institute at Oxford University. The research libraries at Oxford University contain many rare editions and limited-release books, particularly ones from non-Western Islamic publishers. I also need to acknowledge the kind support for research that I received from the World Council of Churches in Geneva, Switzerland, as well as from the Fuller Theological Seminary in Pasadena, California. In addition, the access provided by the University of Rabat, Morocco; the American University in Cairo, Egypt; and Baku State University in Azerbaijan facilitated close contacts with a diverse group of Islamic experts.

I am most grateful to Drs. Russell G. Swenson, David S. Yost, James M. Smith, and Jeffrey A. Larsen for the detailed and careful reviews of successive drafts of this work. Their patient and deliberate criticisms helped sharpen my focus and were tremendously valuable in providing detailed peer reviews. Along similar lines, I would like to thank Dr. Mark Dever and Dr. Bill Anderson for many hours of thoughtful and provocative probing as I grappled with ways to structure and write this work. I also appreciate Dr. Carl Haselbach's careful reading of the final manuscript and his uniquely European perspectives. Dr. Fares Braizat, at the University of Jordan's Center for Strategic Studies, graciously spent many hours scrutinizing my ideas, and presented a diverse set of considerations applicable to understanding the broader Islamic phenomenon. Finally, I would be remiss without also thanking two individuals for their faithful commitment: Bill Ruddell, for his tireless support, and in particular his exhaustive review of the final draft; and David Miller, for being a patient sounding board during innumerable discussions on the core themes of this book.

The author with Vasim Mamedaliev, Chairman of the Religious Council of the Caucasus Muslim region and Chairman of the Department of Arabic Philology/Dean of the Theological Faculty at the University of Baku in Azerbaijan

Commentaries

The title of this book naturally brings to mind the renowned diplomatic telegram from 1946, composed by "X" to explain "The Sources of Soviet Conduct." The anonymous George Kennan grasped the essence of the Soviet challenge, and the subsequent Containment Strategy became the foundation for strategic thought and action by the U.S. and its allies. The relatively brief "Cold War" of the late 20th century, we can now see, ironically carried the very name given in 13th century Spain to the ancient and ongoing conflict between Christians and Moors (Maghreb Moslems), a point underscored by Adda Bozeman. In the present work, Stephen Lambert convincingly argues that an effective, strategic appreciation of our present, worldwide contest, especially as it reflects the historic conflict between religious ideologies, cannot be achieved without public discussion of the religious foundations of individual and collective belief and action, whatever the label we choose to apply to the struggle. He captures the metaphysical foundation of a struggle that is at the same time entirely physical and real for those in the arena. Ideas are in conflict, and ideas rule the world.

— Dr. Russell G. Swenson
Center for Strategic Intelligence Research, Washington, D.C.

The gulf between the radicalized elements of the Islamic world and typical Americans who desire an expansion of personal freedom and political democracy seems vast. To many, it seems unbridgeable. In *Y: The Sources of Islamic Revolutionary Conduct*, Stephen Lambert deftly leads the reader through worlds that are normally kept quite separate: political theory, social history, even a detailed account of theology. In so doing, Lambert does make some eye-opening suggestions on why the West faces an enemy that seems intractable. The book is marked throughout by carefully considered questions and concise summaries.

Though this book has been written with the care of an academic, Lambert isn't reluctant to give the reader clear, even bold analysis. So, for example, early on Lambert tells us that we in the West find it difficult to understand these "enemies" (Lambert uses the word) because of the Enlightenment, our "anti-Socratism" and Wilsonian idealism. These three themes he weaves together in the first chapter simply to help us better understand the tint of the windows through which we view the world. That should give any prospective reader a sense of the sweep of factors considered in this brief, but weighty, volume.

Part 2 is in many ways the heart of Lambert's argument. I say this not because I am a theologian, but because Lambert's thesis is that our enemy is deeply theological. Part of our problem, he argues, is that though our *language* about religion is neutral, Western *ideas* about it are not—we naively and probably unwittingly assume that other religions are like Christianity, when, in some very important ways, they are not. So with our heritage of John Owen, John Locke and Thomas Jefferson, we have assumed that all religions are equally, or at least substantially, able to co-exist with a society committed to the freedoms that we enjoy in America and the West. But this is not so, according to Lambert. It's not psychologically abnormal people, but rather committed Muslims, who refuse to separate the political from the religious. In fact, Lambert's long and sometimes difficult message—especially in Part 2—leads us to the conclusion that Islam may well be closer to an ideology than it is to what most Westerners imagine when we say the word "religion." A privatized religion is an oxymoron to a faithful Muslim, as much so as privatized politics would be to a Marxist.

One more thing about theology: I think Mr. Lambert has it right. He has carefully interviewed numerous theologians—Muslim and Christian—and has gone to great pains to understand and to express their faith and worldviews in ways that the proponents themselves would recognize. He has not crammed them into a secular box in which all religious motivations are simply place-holders for some economic, political or sexual drive which is then taken to be the real reason for their actions. He has treated the self-understandings of both Christians and Muslims with unusual self-restraint and respect. And yet this has led not to an undigested recapitulation, but to a sensitive and provocative description and analysis of the current situation.

Part 3 convincingly applies the idea of *ressentiment* to the "Muslim trauma" and Part 4 gives a succinct summary of how revolutionary violence comes out of the very core of Islam and is not a strange distortion of it. It is this thesis, of course, that will outrage and embarrass, and it is for this very thesis that this book must be read, digested, understood and discussed. If Lambert is right, the world looks very different than the idealistic one often presented in even the most "realistic" of books on diplomacy and foreign relations. And it is Lambert's care in understanding the theologies that gives his argument such force.

Many will undoubtedly turn to the conclusion first, to see what "school" Lambert is arguing from and for. Here is found no easy solution, but rather help in terms of better analysis. Palestinians and Sufis are distinguished from what Lambert sees as the core of the challenge to the West. Lambert disturbingly concludes that we are already engaged in a religious war, whether we recognize it or not, and that success in it is compromised by our not recognizing it.

In short, this is a book to outrage the faithful, disturb the academic, provoke the analyst and help to secure freedoms for us and for our posterity that we have so long enjoyed. Brief, but weighty, this book exposes us to a world in which religion entails political ideology and unwitting secularism is a fatal blindness.

— Dr. Mark Dever, Washington, DC.
Author and Speaker, PhD in
Theological History (Cambridge University)

This is a work of fundamental strategic importance. It will serve as a starting point in understanding of the nature of the enemy we face in the war on Islamofascism. Habits of thought developed during the ideological wars of the 20th century are not sufficient cognitive models for prosecution of the current conflict. Deeply ingrained Western assumptions on the nature of religion must be reexamined in the light of the current challenge. Stephen Lambert here provides us with a strategic plan for correcting this deficiency. Just as we needed a deep understanding of Communist ideology for victory in the Cold War, so we must now face up to the task of investigating the philosophical and religious underpinnings of our current adversaries.

This will require reevaluation of assumptions long cherished by Americans, such as the idea that all religions are the same in their essentials, or at least sufficiently similar that deep study is not required. The United States has never fought a religious war, and the very idea makes us cringe. We prefer to assume that religion is essentially a private matter, and that its various manifestations are uniformly compatible with peace and freedom. Unfortunately, our adversaries utterly reject this view. We now confront a religious, political, and social belief system that at its core resists Western understanding of pluralism, tolerance, and individual freedom. Islam as understood and practiced by our enemies is an expanding and absorbing worldview destined by Divine command to become the universal perspective of mankind.

This manuscript is a seminal work of wide-ranging scholarship. Many a doctoral dissertation could spring from its well-crafted arguments. It begins the Socratic debate which will be necessary for policymakers and the public in order to sustain the war effort to a successful conclusion.

— Dr. William Henry Anderson, Harvard University

Stephen Lambert has written a great, superbly organized and intellectually demanding book. His comparison between the theology of Islam and Christendom seems to be an exhaustive treatment of the subject. Lambert's conclusions are instructive—his description of the phenomenon of Ressentiment is especially insightful—even if some of his concluding propositions are too tame.

Lambert's attempt to write a parallel to George Kennan's *The Sources of Soviet Conduct* is smart and apt, and one especially appreciates the haunting similarities of the "transformed" quotations from Kennan's original work. However, there remain some differences. Though the Communist ideology was generally known to the larger public, especially since 1917, the threat of Soviet Communism was a relatively new concept in 1945. The Soviet Union, a key WWII ally, was one of the victorious powers, had gained international respectability, was a founding and veto-level member of the United Nations, had dramatically enhanced its influence in Eastern Europe, and thus was ready to embark on a geopolitical expansion that it could only dream about before WWII. It was Kennan's great merit to clearly explain all of this.

On the other hand, the religious dimension that is identified in Lambert's work is nothing fundamentally new. The book is an excellent compilation and synthesis on Islamic and Christian identity, the Islamic trauma and the Islamic revolutionary ideology, but others—and Lambert names a lot of them—have addressed and emphasized this context in the past. Furthermore, the puristic (excellent descriptive used by Lambert and much more insightful than fundamentalist or radical) revival of Islam is a phenomenon known at the latest since the 1978/9 Iranian revolution and the theocracy of the Tehran ayatollahs.

Lambert is correct in attributing the blindness of U.S. policymakers and of intelligence to the three factors—the "Enlightenment" pedigree, an "Anti-Socratic Mentality" and "Wilsonian Idealism"—which he presents in the book's first part. It would, however have been challenging to go a step further and to try to also explain—and in my European view this is the true problem—why the available knowledge about the "Why?" has not yet reached the policymakers. In other words, to explain why scholars and educated people perceive the motives of Islamic conduct, whereas politicians "seem hobbled by (...) myopia" as the author puts it. And it would also have been fascinating—though a bit delicate, I admit—if the author would have tried to unravel the (seeming?) contradiction in his statement that "in the realm of American policy and academic elites, religion is *persona non grata*. To those elites, religion seems antiquated." A contradiction seems to lie in the Bush administration's difficulty in grasping the "Why?" though constantly referring to God.

In his conclusions, Lambert gets right to the heart of the issue in his Proposition # 4: The United States is engaged in a religious war. Though troublesome and highly unsettling, this is an essential point and one could not say it more clearly. When, in Proposition # 5, Lambert calls for the United States to "move away from supporting corrupt police states," he makes an honest, yet difficult point. Is this really feasible when, for example, Saudi Arabia is a key energy supplier to the natural-resource consuming American way of life? Proposition # 6 should be formulated in a blunter way. The goal of "one day attaining Palestinian statehood" is not only "relatively realistic and pragmatic" as Lambert puts it, it is legitimate! Israel owes its existence to the 1947 UN partition plan. This plan also foresaw a Palestinian state. Why accord statehood to one side but not the other? The United States would not only do right but also tremendously defuse the Islamic Ressentiment phenomenon if it would uncompromisingly tame Israel and work toward the implementation of either the Oslo Agreement, the so-called Road Map, or maybe the Geneva Initiative on a fair basis. This alone would, as Lambert writes, "remove the Palestinian rallying cry from the propaganda toolbox of corrupt [Arab] regimes, as well as from the recruitment rhetoric of the Islamic revolutionaries."

— Dr. Carl Haselbach, Puidoux, Switzerland

An important component that one should note in this book is the overarching concept of Establishment Principles. These principles consist of four institutions, each with its own authority source, to provide for the preservation of the human race. R.B. Thieme Jr. sets forth these four institutions: "God ordained four divine institutions through which the laws of divine establishment function: the individual, marriage, family, and the national entity. God delegated a primary authority within each institution…," and Mr. Lambert's book deals with two of those authority sources: the volition of the individual, and the government of the national entity. Thieme continues: "Authority protects self-determination, privacy, property, human life—the basic components of freedom." The religion of Islam, however, rejects the authority of the individual's volition as well as the government of a national entity, thus rejecting freedom in detail. The Islamic concept of freedom seems to involve world domination and extermination or forced conversion of all non-Muslims. As Mr. Lambert states in this book, investigating this current conflict truthfully will be difficult; choosing conciliation or failing to decide at all in this situation will prove fatal.

This situation of being unwilling or unable to decide or choosing conciliation is exacerbated by a relatively new trend in this country. The 1960s era engendered the affirmative action movement that lost favor in the late 1970s and early 1980s mainly because the original ideal of having equal opportunity for all was hijacked to mean special privileges for some. Peter Wood, in his book *Diversity, the Invention of a Concept*, describes a new trend that has gained momentum in the U.S. called "diversity." Diversity has several definitions. Some proponents claim diversity celebrates the differences in culture, skin color, gender, sexual orientation, religion, etc. These proponents say solely because a difference exists it is to be celebrated and not judged. A former secretary of the Air Force emphasized the doctrine of "Strength Through Diversity" for the USAF in 1995. Colleges and universities trumpet their strong support of diversity in their catalogues and brochures. However, in practice, diversity does not celebrate the individual's mind but his background, skin color, orientation, etc. The proponents of diversity have in effect created an environment, even an ideology, which suppresses freedom of expression and debate. Peter Wood states: "The other word that I have used over and over to characterize diversity is ideology. The word is not neutral; it registers my judgment that diversity offers a closed loop of thought and experience. Like other ideologies, diversity seeks to explain away rather than to explain inconvenient facts. It invests its position with emotional commitments and usually attacks the critic rather than answer the criticism. It sets itself up as a way of viewing the world in predetermined categories rather than exploring the world with the possibility of finding new understanding."

In breaking the collective use of categories, Howard Roark, a character in *The Fountainhead* states: "Independence is the only gauge of human virtue and value. There is no substitute for personal dignity." This dignified, thinking individual must be allowed to pursue that Jeffersonian concept of "free argument and debate." The proponent of diversity would silence debate on the current conflict by stating that Muslims are a protected diversity group, and that it does not matter what beliefs they hold. From our nation's very inception, virulent debate in order to find Truth has been the order of the day. Mr. Lambert finds that our society is now based on opinion rather than truth. The devoted adherents to Truth must persevere.

— *Major William Ruddell, USAFR*

Written in the shadow of the events of 9/11, Stephen Lambert's "Y" is a treatise that delves not only into the question of who our enemy is, but also provides grist for the greater question—why does the enemy of the United States hate us? Lambert believes that the key to answering these basic questions can only be found by our first knowing ourselves. And to know ourselves, we must begin with a greater understanding of the cultural and larger metaphysical belief structures inherent in America's Judeo-Christian foundation. In addition, while from Lambert's perspective, Americans capably grasp the answers to "who-what-when-where-how" questions in the current conflict, that same understanding does not extend to "why" America's enemy thinks the way it does or acts the way it does.

Who is America's enemy? Lambert's treatise doesn't mince words—the enemy is a revolutionary fundamental purist movement whose aim is nothing less than a world-wide Islamic Theocracy, the likes of which will stop at nothing short of demanding total and complete adherence to Islamic practice by the people of the world—or alternately death. Lambert is careful to lay out his premise by comparing the tenets of Islam and its antithesis with Christianity, by identifying the root causes in the Muslim world for its apparent sympathies for a transnational Islamic revival, by delving into the universal resentment of America harbored by the greater Muslim community of believers, and most importantly, by attempting to delve into the workings of the enemy's mind itself. In his final sections, Lambert extends his thesis of who our enemy is by attempting to answer why our enemy acts in the manner it does. He offers some propositions—Islamic theocratic expansionism, a revolutionist enemy and not a terrorist bogeyman, a universal Islamic resentment against Western culture, a religious war—and the strategic approaches that Americans might consider in the theater of debate. Most importantly, it is in honest debate that we must address these important propositions so that we can apply our findings in the policy-making process surrounding this most important matter of state.

Whether one agrees or disagrees with the thrust of Lambert's argument, his well-documented materials research, interviews with Islamic and Christian leaders and experts, and his concluding propositions for re-establishing a strategic purpose, can only result in furthering beneficial dialogue on this most important "Y" question. This treatise makes for thoughtful reading.

— Mr. Edward Adair, RPE
Chief Operating Officer, CSA Engineering, and
strategic analyst, Scottsdale, Arizona

Author's Preface

In 632 A.D. the Prophet Mohammad died on the Arabian Peninsula.

One hundred years later, in 732 A.D., Muslim Armies were defeated in Frankish Europe at the Battle of Poitiers. The Battle of Poitiers represented a zenith in the advance of the Islamic Caliphate and was the first time that the peoples of the European Peninsula united to collectively defend themselves against an expanding Muslim empire.

On 11 September 1683, Ottoman armies reached a second zenith when they foundered at the siege of Vienna and were driven back by the Hapsburg defenders, with support from Polish, Venetian, and Russian allies.

On 11 September 2001, Islamic Revolutionaries achieved a third zenith when they successfully attacked one of the greatest symbols of the economically powerful Western Hemisphere—the World Trade Center in New York.

The United States has been conditioned to believe that it faces a threat of terrorism, that Islam is a religion of peace, and that Islam as religion has been hijacked and perverted by fundamentalist radicals. Furthermore, it seems to be conventional wisdom that the conditions for so-called terrorism will be ameliorated by a renewed emphasis on education, more equitable resource distribution, and an infusion of democratic values.

Yet nowhere has the following question been satisfactorily answered: Why were 19 Muslim hijackers driven to kill themselves and thousands of innocent civilians . . . when many of the hijackers were educated in the West, owned profitable business enterprises, and had access to modern Western resources and conveniences? Furthermore . . . why the repeated chant of *Allahu akbar* . . . and even more fundamentally, what is Islam?

These are deeply metaphysical questions.

They are at once religious and anthropological, and require that one critically examine culturally foreign systems of thought. The probing generated by this type of analysis tends to assault the current *Zeitgeist*, which above all else, credits itself as tolerant and universally accepting of all things and all ideas. This, in turn, begs the following question: How can a society like that of the United States, one conditioned by these philosophies of the secular age, be brought to consider fundamental questions of a religious nature? It can do so by first rediscovering its own intellectual pedigrees and coming to terms with its own foundations. It does so, secondly, by penetrating the religious ideology of the enemy in an attempt to decipher the answer to why the religion of peace seems to perpetually produce passionate warriors for Allah.

This journey will be profoundly uncomfortable.

Introduction

Asking Strategic Questions

Democracy refuses to think strategically unless and until compelled to do so for the purposes of defense.

—**Halford J. Mackinder,** British Strategist and Geographer[1]

In a time of drastic change, it is the learners who inherit the future. The learned usually find themselves equipped to live in a world that no longer exists.

—**Eric Hoffer**, Philosopher and Author[2]

Truth is great and will prevail if left to herself; that she is the proper and sufficient antagonist to error, and has nothing to fear from the conflict unless by human interposition disarmed of her natural weapons, free argument and debate—errors ceasing to be dangerous when it is permitted freely to contradict them.

—**Thomas Jefferson**,
from A Bill for Establishing Religious Freedom[3]

Why? This is the key question that has so far gone unanswered in the current struggle, the United States' so-called global war on terrorism. It is the "why" questions that can be notoriously difficult to answer. It used to be the case in American secondary education, when pupils were taught how to write, that they were prompted to consider answering the traditional battery of basic questions: who, what, when, where, how, and why. In a general sense, the "who-what-when-where-how" questions seem rather straightforward; they involve description, characterization, classification, or basic fact-finding. But the "why" question is in a category all of its own. It can pose the thorny challenge of uncovering more than just superficial reality. In terms of human behavior, it probes deeper and requires the writer to explore such concepts as meaning, truth, falsehood, intent, passion, and belief. It demands a completely different scope and level of reasoning. Over and above description, classification, or characterization, it requires analysis. In the fields of

---

[1]Halford J. Mackinder, *Democratic Ideals and Reality*, NDU Press Defense Classic Edition (Washington D.C.: National Defense University Press, 1996), 17.

[2]Eric Hoffer cited in *The Columbia World of Quotations* (New York: Columbia University Press, 1996), at URL:<*www.bartleby.com/66/76/28576.html*, accessed 10 December 2004.

[3]Thomas Jefferson, "A Bill for Establishing Religious Freedom," in *Thomas Jefferson: Writings, ed.* Merril D. Peterson (New York: Library of America, 1984).

study that address human interaction—for example in ethics, politics, international affairs, or warfare—answering "why" questions involves penetrating the underlying cultural and metaphysical belief structures that serve to guide both individual and collective behavior. While "who-what-when-where-how" questions more often lend themselves to measurement, "why" questions inevitably reach beyond the scope of data collection and processing. The latter explore the strategic high ground that forms the basis for understanding humanity in all its shades, customs, cultures, and conflicts.

Policy and academic elites in the United States seem very skilled at answering the "who-what-when-where-how" questions. In the current conflict, apparently inaugurated by the shocking events of 9/11, policy and academic elites have meticulously researched the answers to this standard battery of questions. Yet few thoughtful analyses have emerged that rise to the strategic scope of explaining why the collective enemies of the United States continue to perpetuate their violence. Many pundits have contributed their thirty-second made-for-television ideological and political sound bites. What is lacking, however, is a robust and rugged exchange of ideas, or a substantive Lincoln-Douglas style debate about the "why" questions. One primary reason for the absence of this strategic debate is that today's policy and academic elites are intimidated by passionate religious faith—and the current war is unavoidably connected to religion. Whatever one thinks of the metaphysical realm, one cannot escape the fact that one side clothes itself in religious rhetoric, and often seems driven by metaphysical passion. But in the realm of American policy and academic elites, religion is *persona non grata*. To these elites, religion seems antiquated, troublesome, pedestrian, and unsophisticated. Their *Zeitgeist* is defined by the empirical rather than by metaphysical phenomena.

Though some claim to see strong evidence of Christian dogmatism in American political culture, David Brooks correctly appraises the current American ethos. "Our general problem is not that we're too dogmatic," he writes. "Our more common problems come from the other end of the continuum. Americans in the 21st century are more likely to be divorced from any sense of a creedal order, ignorant of the moral traditions that have come down to us through the ages and detached from the sense that we all owe obligations to a higher authority."[4] Instead, academic and policy elites studiously search for so-called "root" causes to explain the violence in our current struggle. But modern secular approaches, and their focus on materialism—whether in the form of inequalities in resource distribution, education, or income—are less than satisfying in answering "why" our avowed enemies continue to attempt to revolutionize the world we live in. Thus, in the words of one

---

[4]David Brooks, "Hooked on Heaven Lite," *New York Times*, 9 March 2004, A27.

commentator, in the "two and a half years after the Twin Towers fell, our nation and its friends fight on, but in those two and a half years this great semantic fudge [the "terrorist" label] has allowed our enemies to remain ill-defined." Perhaps the alternatives are too terrifying. The thought of being engaged in a war with an enemy whose ideology is born of a religion triggers, at best, a sense of revulsion in some, at worst, a sense of panic in others. American observers seem to incredulously wonder how a religion could possibly be used to inspire anything but individual worship and collective good will in its adherents.

George Kennan asked himself the "why" question when he considered the threat the United States faced in the aftermath of World War II. His groundbreaking answer to "why" the Soviets behaved the way they did would form the foundation for American foreign and defense policy for the next half century. His strategic analysis, entitled "The Sources of Soviet Conduct," published in 1947 in *Foreign Affairs* magazine under the pseudonym "X," penetrated deeply into the Soviet Communist ideology and explained their political philosophy and fundamental assumptions about how society was to be organized. Instead of so-called materialistic "root" causes, Kennan uncovered the core ethos of the Soviet statist belief system. It was an unvarnished and penetrating strategic analysis.

The United States needs to renew Kennan's spirit of strategic analysis if it is to successfully defend itself against today's new threats. A strategic consensus will only emerge as a result of what Jefferson called "free argument and debate." The notion that the core ethos of our opponents' ideology—Islam—is officially shelved and protected from public debate flies in the face of all classical or Socratic approaches to public discourse and debate. American policy and academic elites seem generally ignorant about religion, and even more so about the comprehensive system of religious and political beliefs called Islam. If, as Jefferson wrote, in the course of human dialogue truth is disarmed of its natural allies—free argument and debate—then the strategic errors that are likely to result from the lack of free argument and debate will grow increasingly dangerous. Today, we live in times of instability and drastic change. Eric Hoffer, the "common-sense" political philosopher, adds that in such times, "it is the learners who inherit the future. The learned usually find themselves equipped to live in a world that no longer exists."

The conditions of the present world demand a fresh debate that seeks to answer the strategic "why" questions that will determine the course of future events. In light of these questions, the present analysis first attempts to outline the sources of American strategic blindness. To paraphrase Sun Tzu's often quoted maxim, if you know yourself and your enemy, then you will be successful in war. Strategic insight will only be achieved if we first "know ourselves." In Part I, I explore the American intellectual pedigree and why it tends to constrain strategic analysis. I argue that the present strategic malaise is the result of three main factors: (1) the Enlightenment and its influence on American policymaking; (2) a hardening anti-Socratic mentality within American society; and (3) the ethos of 20th century Wilsonian idealism. Not only has this three-fold pedigree substantively shaped our worldview, but it has also constrained our analytical tool set. Our cognitive processes are shaped and focused by an inherited myopia that would have been viewed as ignorance by our classical Greek predecessors. We are in peril because we do not know ourselves.

One of the primary conclusions of Part I is that policy and academic elites are blinded by their bias against qualitative analysis, and especially against the study of religion. I attempt to rectify this deficiency in Part II, where I compare and contrast the core doctrines of Christianity and Islam. The rich theological doctrines of these two religions have yielded undeniable political and historical imperatives. My aim is to show *why* those imperatives result in significantly different outcomes and that those outcomes have strategic consequences. In fairness to the reader, I must apologize if Part II seems too lengthy. Let me take this opportunity to encourage readers to persevere—Part II contains the raw data that form the essential foundation upon which Parts III and IV are based. After establishing this working understanding of Islamic doctrine and its political and historical imperatives, I then attempt to capture the mindset of the broader Islamic faithful in Part III. Islamic identity is plagued by the fourfold trauma of (1) the impact of European colonialism, (2) the pressures of modern secularism, (3) the blunt reality of military and scientific impotency vis-à-vis the West, and (4) the distorting influences of modern Arab successes. The impact of this trauma has yielded a contrarian reaction, best described as the collective phenomenon of *ressentiment*. Max Scheler's concept of ressentiment brings us toward an explanation and understanding of *why* the so-called "Arab street" often erupts in voyeuristic fits of celebration at the news of events like 9/11. After analyzing the collective mind of the broader Islamic faithful, I then focus on the mind of our avowed enemies in Part IV. Understanding *why* they think the way they do is strategically vital. But before I attempt to address their thinking, I first define who these enemies are. Unfortunately, they remain ill-defined in today's politically charged arena. They are not terrorists and we are not waging a "Global War Against Terrorism." As one observer has cogently stated,

> I think it is utterly naïve to think this is a fight about "terrorism." I am willing to say that the distinction between a good Muslim and terrorists is politically a good or necessary move, a kind of "noble lie." But we should not be naïve about what we are up against. The reason that we cannot see that there may be a more dangerous problem is because we are mostly all relativists today. Our relativism blinds us and does not

allow us to say that there is someone so passionately interested in what he believes, that he does not care about his own life and death.[5]

Indeed, while our enemy may sometimes deploy terrorism as a tactic, he is not a terrorist. Instead, the enemy is collectively a revolutionary Islamic vanguard, with a goal nothing less than the complete transformation of the global status quo as we know it.

Finally in Part V, I offer some ideas about how to return to strategic insight. I conclude with seven propositions that are aimed at achieving strategic clarity—a more resolute but also more refined approach to fighting the current war in which we are engaged. The United States stands once again at odds with an enemy that calls for complete revolutionary change to the international order. While today's revolutionary Islamic vanguard is different from the threat posed by Soviet Communism, it will nonetheless require a strategic vision to successfully propagate a war against this religious and ideological threat. The following pages are intended to encourage that type of strategic thought.

Largest mosque in Central Caucasus region, Baku, Azerbaijan.
Photo by author.

---

[5]Fr. James V. Schall quoted in Ken Masugi, "Interview with James V. Schall on Reason and Faith," *The Claremont Institute*, 23 December 2002, URL: www.claremont.org/writings/021223masugi_b.html, accessed 13 June 2004.

I. Our Intellectual Pedigree

The Search for Strategic Insight

If ignorant both of your enemy and yourself, you are certain to be in peril. Know your enemy and know yourself and you can fight a hundred battles without disaster.

- **Sun Tzu** in The Art of War[6]

Lord Acton once said that few discoveries are more irritating than those which expose the pedigree of one's own ideas.[7] In order to come to terms with the challenges posed by the world abroad, we must first begin to understand ourselves; and more specifically, we must examine the intellectual pedigree of the lenses through which the American national security and foreign policy communities view that world. Most political or policy journals either concentrate on trying to make sense of the world *abroad* or attempt to diagnose the failures of American foreign policy, yet few—if any—have truly explored what Sun Tzu meant by "knowing yourself." Increasingly, our profound lack of self-understanding is proving to be a crippling obstacle toward achieving a strategic understanding of the current world crisis. Because we do not appreciate the core and pedigree of our own philosophy and worldview, we fail to comprehend the complexities of the world around us. In the words of one outsider looking in, "the American melting pot results in a kind of obliviousness to the world . . . a multicultural unilateralism. The result is a paradox: a fantastically tolerant and flexible society that has absorbed the whole world, yet has difficulty comprehending the world beyond its borders."[8]

One manifestation of this problem occurs within the U.S. Intelligence Community. The Intelligence Community seems hobbled by a strategic myopia—one which it does not perceive or self-detect. Even as it consumes itself with the crucial task of "knowing the enemy," it fails to recognize the historical, philosophical pedigrees that prevent it from achieving that elusive strategic clarity. In the meantime, the Intelligence Community is under increasing scrutiny because of public and political perceptions that it failed to anticipate adequately and forecast the difficulties encountered in the current crisis. The myopia that resides not only within the Intelligence Community, but also in the policymaking community as a

---

[6]Sun Tzu in The Art of War, as presented and compiled by Michael I. Handel in *Masters of War: Classical Strategic Thought*, 2nd rev. ed. (London: Frank Cass & Co Ltd, 1996), 139.

[7]Acton quoted in F. A. Hayek, *The Road to Serfdom* (Chicago: University of Chicago Press, 1994), 3.

[8]Peter Schneider, "Separated by Civilization," *International Herald Tribune*, 7 April 2004, 6.

whole, stems from three primary sources: (1) the intellectual underpinnings of Enlightenment and post-Enlightenment political philosophy, (2) a hardening anti-Socratic mentality against open public discourse, and (3) the 20th-century inheritance of Wilsonian idealism. The deep entrenchment of these three cognitive components is obscuring from American decisionmakers what should have been a *clear and present danger*—in the words of former CIA director James Woolsey, "Al Qaeda has been at war with us for the better part of a decade. What's new is that we finally noticed."[9]

The Enlightenment and its Influence on American Policymaking

The first component of the American intellectual pedigree is the Enlightenment, which centered on a struggle to deny man's metaphysical or religious orientation and rebuild society based on reason and the pursuit of empiricism. Charles Hodge, the well-known Princeton professor and theologian, aptly characterized the struggle between Enlightenment rationalism and the influence of the Divine in man's affairs. "From an early period in the history of the Church," Hodge wrote,

> there have been two great systems of doctrine in perpetual conflict. The one begins with God, the other with man. The one has for its object the vindication of the Divine supremacy and sovereignty in the salvation of men; the other has for its characteristic aim the assertion of the rights of human nature . . . The latter is characteristically rational. It seeks to explain every thing so as to be intelligible to the speculative understanding. The former is confessedly mysterious.[10]

The political philosophies that emerged from this conflicted period fathered the modern thought systems that are internalized in today's policymaking community. The Enlightenment eventually gave birth to secular humanism, which in turn developed into what is now often called postmodernism. The core of these movements revolved around a focus on rationalism and science. In the social sciences, this eventually manifested itself in the form of a swing away from classical, qualitative methodologies toward a concentrated effort to master quantitative methodologies.

---

[9] James Woolsey quoted in Parag Khanna, "Terrorism as War," *Policy Review* 121 (October/November 2003), URL: www.policyreview.org/oct03/khanna_print.html, accessed 23 March 2003.

[10] Hodge, cited in Edwin Gaustad, *A Documentary History of Religion in America: To the Civil War,* 2d ed. (Grand Rapids: Eerdmans Publishing Company, 1993), 420-22.

The Doctrines of the Enlightenment. The battle between religion and the secular elements of society was not a new phenomenon in late-eighteenth century Europe. In 1517, Martin Luther's epoch-making 95 theses had initiated a period of religious tension that evolved into 130 years of on-and-off again warfare and bloodshed, ultimately culminating in the pivotal 1648 Peace of Westphalia. Men of letters and intellectual giants like Leonardo da Vinci and Sir Isaac Newton had nudged Western European civilization toward a renaissance of scientific and rational thought. But the spirit of the French revolution and the Enlightenment raised the conflict to a new intellectual intensity. The depth of the societal struggle against religion is revealed in a 1792 spectacle when the French revolutionaries held a festival in honor of the goddess of Reason in Notre-Dame Cathedral in Paris: "the goddess was personified by an actress, Demoiselle Candeille, carried shoulder-high into the cathedral by men dressed in Roman costumes."[11] "[I]n the enthusiasm of revolution, the cathedral had been renamed the Temple of Reason. A papier-mâché mountain with Greco-Roman motifs stood in the nave."[12] In the throes of the conflict, the French philosopher Voltaire wrote that "we have witnessed the development of a new doctrine which is to deliver the final blow to the already tottering structure of prejudice [the church and religion]. It is the idea of the limitless perfectibility of the human species."[13] If man was perfectible, and man's capacity for reason and science was infinite, then there was no need for God, church, or religion. The rejection of the divine occurred not only in the fields of science; philosophy also reoriented man's search for meaning away from God and toward the secular realm.

Man's efforts to understand the world and its surroundings would henceforth be based on scientific rationalism. In 1843, Karl Marx outlined the future direction of society: "We no longer translate worldly questions into theological ones; rather, we translate theological questions into earthly questions." Indeed, the "final version of the Christian state is the democratic one, where religion is subordinated beneath all other elements of common society. Religion will become nothing more than a developmental phase of the human experience," he wrote, "just as a snake in its development sheds its skin, so mankind sheds its religion as it grows and develops." Marx argued that "democracy does not need religion for its political completion. Rather, democracy can be abstracted from religion, because the basis of religion is fulfilled in the establishment of the secular state." He concluded that "mankind does not unite any longer based on religion, but

---

[11]Francis A. Schaeffer, *How Should We Then Live?* (Wheaton: Crossway Books, 1995), 122.

[12]Mark A. Noll, *Turning Points* (Grand Rapids: Baker Academic Books, 1997), 246.

[13]Voltaire quoted in Schaeffer, 121.

rather based on science, secularism, and critical thinking." "Science," he declared, "becomes man's unifying principle."[14]

Mainstream political philosophy agreed with Marx's judgment. The privatization and ultimate demise of religion was forecast as unavoidable and irreversible as a product of industrialization, increased education, the urbanization of society, and the growing wealth of capitalism. As Marx revealed his faith in the absolute perfectibility of human nature under the influence of appropriate economic conditions—the essence of dialectic materialism—he also concluded that eventually, political life and religion must vanish to be replaced by an uncoerced, rational society.[15] Alexis de Tocqueville described the prevailing mood when he wrote that the reigning philosophers "explained in a very simple manner the gradual decay of religious faith. Religious zeal, said they, must necessarily fail the more generally liberty is established and knowledge diffused."[16]

The quest by scientists and philosophers to claim that life itself could be understood with reference to *itself*—rather than with any references at all to God or the teaching of the church—is what C.S. Lewis once called "the greatest of all divisions in the history of the West."[17] The Western intellectual world's momentous shift away from religion was carried forward by the philosophical influences of men like Immanuel Kant, G. W. F. Hegel, and John Stuart Mill as they worked to replace the religious with the rational. Charles Darwin's *The Origin of Species* (1859) became a celebrated work of science, carried forth without any reference to a divine creator. As one author notes, "by the middle of the nineteenth century, even the instinctive deference to Scripture as a divinely given book, a deference that had played a central role in European self-consciousness since time immemorial, was fading away."[18] The promises of science and technology brought tangible benefits to the life and welfare of the Western world. Broad demographic changes encouraged by the urbanization of society changed the way people thought about themselves. Man was becoming the center of the newly modern world. Whittaker Chambers notes that it was

> the vision of man's mind displacing God as the creative intelligence of
> the world . . . the vision of man's liberated mind, by the sole force of its

---

[14]Marx quoted in Karl Peter Schwarz, "Der Engel der Nationen," trans. by the author, *Frankfurter Allgemeine Zeitung*, 7 April 2004, 8.

[15]Joseph Cropsey, "Karl Marx," in *History of Political Philosophy*, 3d ed., eds. Leo Strauss and Joseph Cropsey (Chicago: University of Chicago Press, 1987), 826. Cited hereafter as *History*.

[16]Alexis de Tocqueville, *Democracy in America* (London: David Campbell Publishers, 1994), 308.

[17]C.S. Lewis quoted in Noll, 253.

[18]Noll, 255.

rational intelligence, redirecting man's destiny and reorganizing life and the world . . . the vision of man, once more the central figure of the Creation, not because God made man in His image, but because man's mind makes him the most intelligent of the animals.[19]

In short, as the American patriot Thomas Paine once famously quipped, "[M]y mind is my church."

Humanistic Philosophies. The scientific and philosophical rejection of divine influence would have a more subtle impact on cognitive development, one that would eventually lead to the development of secular humanistic philosophy. Inevitably, the drive to remove the divine influence in mankind led philosophers to discount the value of divine love for mankind—which resulted in a focus on the love of man, that is, modern humanism. The German philosopher and social scientist Max Scheler accurately described this new intellectual reality. "Modern humanism," he wrote, "is in every respect a polemical and protesting concept. It protests against divine love, and consequently against the Christian unity and harmony of divine love, self-love, and love of one's neighbor which is the 'highest commandment' of the Gospel. Love is not to be directed at the 'divine' essence in man, but only at man as such, outwardly recognizable as a member of his species." [20] The effect of this emphasis on the love of man was to detach and isolate man from the divine creation. This great divorce—the isolation of man from God and the resulting focus on humanitarian love—was not without its consequences. Modern philosophy no longer allowed man to hold up a transcendent, ascetic, ideal love in the form of a divine creator, but instead was forced to rely upon satisfying the search for meaning and love based on the human ethos. Perceptive observers soon discovered, however, that mankind was unable to satisfy its own desires. As Scheler writes, "the pathos of modern humanitarianism, its clamor for greater sensuous happiness, its subterraneously smoldering passion, its revolutionary protest against all institutions, traditions, and customs which it considers as obstacles to the increase of sensuous happiness, its revolutionary spirit—all this is in characteristic contrast to the luminous, almost cool *spiritual enthusiasm* of Christian love [italics in the original]."[21]

Postmodernism. This intellectual focus on humanistic love and on the secular ethos bore with it an unintended side effect. By the late nineteenth century,

---

[19]Whittaker Chambers, "Letter to my Children from Witness," in *American Heritage: A Reader*, 2d rev. ed., ed. History Department Hillsdale College (Acton: Tapestry Press, 2001), 501.

[20]Max Scheler, *Ressentiment,* trans. Lewis Coser and William Holdheim, ed. and introduced by Manfred Frings (Milwaukee: Marquette University Press, 2003), 79.

[21]Scheler, 81.

Western philosophers were resolving a crisis in self-understanding, a crisis in understanding ordinary man and his tasks, standards, purposes, and reason for being. Without a divine influence to undergird man's moral comprehension and to provide suppositional guidance in the study of knowledge—what the ancient Greeks called *episteme* (knowledge)—the philosophers of the day attempted to extract meaning from their social and political surroundings. The rejection of divine meaning uprooted most traditional foundations of political and moral society. It was in this new search for meaning that the roots of postmodernism were born. Edmund Husserl, one of the founders of postmodern thought, reasoned that "[N]ot only philosophy but our civilization as a whole can no longer take for granted the validity of the starting points and the results of established sciences."[22] Instead, in mankind's search for meaning, there could ultimately be no presuppositions, since these would corrupt the very process of science and philosophy itself. Husserl, in arguing for the ideal of a rigorously scientific phenomenology, explained that science must be absolutely presuppositionless, that is, it must be able to base any assumptions or concepts in the absolute self-evidence of the scientist or philosopher's own inspecting consciousness.[23] In this manner, postmodernism presents itself as the ultimate manifestation of Enlightenment philosophy, because Husserl's phenomenology is ultimately an attempt to make reason itself the sole source of meaning and value and to set up the true essence of reason as being able to provide for itself all meaning, value, and ends.[24] Thus, Husserl concluded that "man must look to rigorous science for the satisfaction of the highest theoretical needs and of the needs for norms of an ethical, even religious, nature."[25]

However, the suppositionless nature of Husserl's phenomenology and its radical search for pure, unobstructed science and reason proved to be less than logically satisfying. Man's cognitive processes were always, in one form or another, forced to make assumptions—this was part of the scientific process in itself. Ultimately, even Newtonian thought and mathematics had to start with basic assumptions about the universe. Thus, early postmodernism was hamstrung by its own paradox—a skepticism that originated from the scientific process itself. Husserl attempted to bridge this gap by introducing the notion that all of philosophy or science is really ultimately based on a particular *doxa* (or opinion), thus arguing against the ancient Platonic elevation of *episteme* (or knowledge)—the implication being that there really cannot be a pure system of

---

[22]Richard Velkley, "Edmund Husserl," in *History*, 872.
[23]Velkley, 872.
[24]Velkley, 873.
[25]Velkley, 878.

knowledge because *doxa*, or opinion, is really the starting point for all philosophical and scientific processes.[26]

The consequence of this chain of reasoning is that nothing can be fundamentally true, which means that as both Dostoevsky and Nietzsche recognized, "everything is permitted," the end result of which is nihilism—the doctrine that denies objective truth, and especially moral truth.[27] Martin Heidegger, the German philosopher who is widely credited as the father of postmodernism, attempted to grapple with this problem. He believed that modern Western society was the realm of ultimate freedom, and that this predominant subjectivity freed man from the theocentric structures of traditional Christian society and established man as a being based on himself alone—this an ongoing manifestation of the Enlightenment philosophy characterized by a pervasive faith in the progress of reason and science.[28] While this was essentially a worthy condition, according to Heidegger, there remained a serious problem. The predominant and alienating focus of Western individualism left a gaping hole in man's existence, for it left man without an anchor "within the ordered cosmos of traditional society."[29] Western modernity was unable to provide a satisfying answer regarding man's existence—and so in order to combat nihilism and fulfill the search for meaning, Heidegger argued that man needed to be liberated from all metaphysical categories in the history of Western thought and instead be vaulted back to a primordial destiny in a time before modernity. He advocated an almost violent rejection of modern, Western society in his efforts to overcome nihilism and its problem of no fixed standard or eternal truth.[30] But Heidegger was ultimately unsuccessful in articulating a successful escape from nihilism, and he died before he was able to adequately satisfy his thirst for meaning. In the meantime, he bequeathed a set of ideas that are as diffused throughout the philosophies of the modern age, as are the roots of his ideas—with their origins in the Enlightenment.

Implications. The intellectual revolution brought about by the Enlightenment thus sent shock waves through science and philosophy for centuries to come. Originating as a rejection of divine influence in the sciences, it spilled over into

---

[26]Knowledge assumes that there is a right and a wrong, and even as the ancients (for example, Socrates) argued that vigorous public debate is required to determine what will hold up as *episteme*, Husserl seemed to believe that the very idea that one can assume that there is an episteme is repugnant. Velkley, 885-86.

[27]Michael Gillespie, "Martin Heidegger," in *History*, 889.

[28]Gillespie, 889, 897.

[29]Gillespie, 897.

[30]Concepts in Waller R. Newell, "Postmodern Jihad," *The Weekly Standard 7*, no. 11 (11 November 2001). URL:<www.weeklystandard.com/Content/Public/Articles/000/000/000/553fragu.asp >, accessed 26 April 2004.

cognitive development and philosophy, moving toward secular humanism and subsequently developing into its progeny, postmodernism. These philosophies formed the broad framework for America's intellectual elite throughout the late nineteenth and twentieth centuries. They are the basis for the scholarly literature of international relations and policymaking today, and form the core intellectual philosophical foundation for most institutions of higher learning throughout the Western world. They also constitute the subconscious intellectual foundation of America's policymaking community and shape the lenses through which that community views the world abroad.

Modern international relations theory, in the words of Stanton Burnett, "extends from the Enlightenment and Auguste Comte through Max Weber and the school's arrival on the scene as a reaction to the lack of scientific rigor in earlier commentaries on international relations."[31] Its focus, according to Burnett, is dogmatically and unflinchingly secular. Its denial of human factors—including religious and spiritual aspects—is carried forth in an ongoing attempt to imitate the physical sciences and to gain, therefore, the success and prestige that these sciences have gained in our society.[32] Significantly, in denying the religious and spiritual elements of human behavior, it also denies most other cultural factors as being significant in shaping the behavior of states. As Burnett concludes, "American diplomats, raised in the Enlightenment secularism of the Realist school, are unprepared to see spiritual aspects of problems and possible solutions or, for that matter, to cope . . . with the whole cultural richness, including the intellectual life and structure of belief of the *people* (not just the institutions) with whom they deal abroad [italics in the original]."[33]

Instead, modern international relations theory and social science focus primarily on quantitative methodologies, which in many ways gained credence with efforts to rationalize, or put the "science" into social science. Simultaneously, the classical qualitative disciplines receded in their prestige and acceptance. In the modern Western world, academia increasingly marginalized the study of theology, history, and anthropology, as models, variables, and causality became the accepted vocabulary of social science. David Brooks points to a concrete example of how this mentality resides in our policymaking community today. "The misconception that may be the most damaging is seen in the social science, quantitative, cost-benefit mindset of our intelligence and foreign pol-

---

[31] Stanton Burnett, "Implications for the Foreign Policy Community," in R*eligion, The Missing Dimension of Statecraft*, eds. Douglas Johnston and Cynthia Sampson (New York: Oxford University Press, 1994), 293.
[32] Burnett, 293.
[33] Burnett, 293.

icy agencies. The CIA's published assessment of world trends to 2015 says almost nothing about religion. Globalization is the focus. Religious motives escape the CIA's rationalistic categories, and so they leave it out."[34] It is this kind of analysis, with its systematic, quantitative nature, that "neglects those aspects of human behavior which are not economic, but which are 'heroic,' or more accurately, identity-originating . . . [It] cannot penetrate into the mind of the dedicated individual or understand what it is in the way of experiences and views of the world that produces dedication."[35] Dedication on this level is often produced by religious loyalty and commitment. But this type of dedication is almost impossible to measure quantitatively—and our intellectual pedigree tells us that it is not important. Brooks accurately diagnoses the challenge. "Religion," he argues, "is too abstract, too hard to define and measure, too hard to standardize. Religious yearnings just don't compute, and we haven't learned to study and assess religious forces intelligently as part of our policymaking. Our foreign policy community, in short, is backward when it comes to understanding religion."[36] Religious passions and motives escape the policymaking community's rationalistic categories, so they are disregarded—or even worse, studiously avoided. As a result, American scholars, diplomats, and national security experts are often ill prepared to see the religious component of problems that dominate today's strategic landscape.

Even while the intellectual pedigree of modern elites has taught them to disregard the religious variable, they are being challenged by a resurgence of religion and creedal violence. Religion has, since the collapse of the bipolar world order, unavoidably thrust itself back into the public spotlight. Yet, in the words of one observer, our public discourse reveals a "deep need to avoid the entire subject of creedal contradictions" and "our public discourse gropes uneasily, even desperately, to assign materialistic causes to 9/11 and other shockingly violent acts."[37] After all, Suzanne Rudolph explains that "Modern social science did not warn us that this would happen. Instead it asserted that religion would fade, then disappear, with the triumph of science and rationalism."[38] A resurgence of religion

[34]David Brooks, "The Rise of Global Christianity: A Conversation with Philip Jenkins and David Brooks," *Center Conversations*, no. 23 (Washington D.C.: Ethics and Public Policy Center, July 2003), 6.

[35]Nathan Leites and Charles Wolf, Jr., *Rebellion and Authority: An Analytic Essay on Insurgent Conflicts* (Chicago: Markham, 1970), reviewed by Kenneth E. Boulding. In *The Annals of the American Academy*, 392, November 1970, 185.

[36]Brooks, 13.

[37]Brooks, 5.

[38]Susanne Hoeber Rudolph, "Introduction: Religion, States, and Transnational Civil Society" in *Transnational Religion and Fading States*, eds. Susanne Hoeber Rudolph and James Piscatori (Boulder: Westview Press, 1997), 1.

does not conform to—indeed cannot be explained by—our intellectual pedigree. "The educated classes of the West have been taught all their lives that history moves in one direction: toward even greater pluralism and ever more profound liberal secularism. In the master narrative that has come down to them from the Enlightenment, religions are supposed to move inevitably from fundamentalism to pluralism, and people are supposed to become more secular as they become wealthier and better educated."[39] As Rudolph cogently explains,

> We must remind ourselves that Enlightenment rationalism gave religion a bad name. Religion was false knowledge, the kind of knowledge that Voltaire, Condorcet, and Comte foresaw as disappearing from human consciousness. For Marx, the lingering effects of religions were actively negative, shoring up exploitation and repression. Modernist social scientists cannot imagine religion as a positive force, a practice and worldview that contributes to order, provides meaning, and promotes justice.[40]

But the rejection of religion as an explaining, contributing, or even causal variable does not mean that, as Marx believed, mankind has shed religion as the snake molts its skin. Instead, religion has expanded explosively. Ironically, in many ways this expansion has been stimulated as much by secular globalization (migration, multinational capital formation, media revolution) as by proselytizing activities. Contrary to prevailing Western philosophy and its expectations, the expansion of religion has been an answer to (and driven by) modernity. A century of material progress and scientific discovery has generated unforeseen social challenges. The rapidity of change has broken down traditional social ties, and this has been amplified by a secular, scientific worldview that has marginalized traditional faith and meaning. In short, it has led to a crisis of identity and meaning.[41] As Rudolph explains, "In response to the deracination and threats of cultural extinction associated with modernization processes, religious experience seeks to restore meaning to life."[42] In many parts of the world, the appeal to religious identity resonates powerfully, since "religion is perhaps the most compelling force that motivates and mobilizes people."[43] The implications of religion as a contributing, if not causal variable—to use modern social science jargon—are profound. In the words of John Voll, a contemporary scholar at Georgetown Uni-

---

[39]Brooks, 5.

[40]Rudolph, 6.

[41]Subhash C. Inamdar, *Muhammad and the Rise of Islam: The Creation of Group Identity* (Madison: Psychosocial Press, 2001), xvii.

[42]Rudolph, 1.

[43]Inamdar, xix.

versity, "if one starts with a position of faith in an almighty God, your conclusions about the ultimate destiny of religion in the world are going to be different from a person whose starting assumptions are basically secular and who hypothesizes the ultimate disappearance of religion."[44]

To summarize, the intellectual assumptions of Enlightenment and post-Enlightenment philosophies constitute one of the three components of the intellectual pedigree of the American academic and policymaking elites. This pedigree clouds their vision of strategic and social realities. The Enlightenment philosophies, which gave birth to modern humanism, postmodernism, and social science's overwhelming focus on quantitative disciplines, all but completely disregarded religion as a component of human nature. The metaphysical realm was ignored as science and philosophy were attracted to the allure of empiricism, technology, and the scientific method. According to Harvey Cox and his co-authors,

> A century ago, forecasters often predicted the disappearance or increased marginalization of religions in the modern era, but this has hardly turned out to be the case. Those who in the late nineteenth and early twentieth centuries foresaw the triumph of scientific rationality or of various secular and humanistic ideologies did not, it turns out, read the tea leaves very accurately. Instead, the twentieth century has witnessed a phenomenal renaissance of religious traditions in virtually every part of the globe.[45]

Perhaps the biases of our Enlightenment intellectual pedigree are slowly beginning to reveal themselves. The *Financial Times* recently reported that the Foreign and Commonwealth Office in London has concluded that, "Religious belief is coming back to the fore as the motivating force in international relations." As Philip Stephens, a *Financial Times* columnist, recently commented, "Many of us had imagined religious wars ended with the Treaty of Westphalia."[46] One wonders if Sun Tzu would be as mild in his criticism toward our lack of self-understanding. Indeed, as David Brooks points out, "Future historians looking back at us will wonder how so many highly schooled people could be so ignorant of religion."[47]

---

[44]John Obert Voll, I*slam: Continuity and Change in the Modern World*, 2d ed. (Syracuse: Syracuse University Press, 1994), 385.

[45]Harvey Cox and others, "World Religions and Conflict Resolution," in *Religion, The Missing Dimension of Statecraft*, eds. Douglas Johnston and Cynthia Sampson (New York: Oxford University Press, 1994), 266.

[46]Philip Stephens, "The unwitting wisdom of Rumsfeld's unknowns," *Financial Times*, 12 December 2003, 19.

[47]David Brooks, "The Rise of Global Christianity: A Conversation with Philip Jenkins and David Brooks," 5.

A Hardening Anti-Socratism: *Episteme* versus *Doxa*

The second major component of the American intellectual pedigree is a hardening anti-Socratic mentality which is opposed to rigorous public discourse about values and matters of ultimate meaning. The leveling mechanisms inherited from Enlightenment philosophy tend to stifle open public debate, largely because of the assumption that there are no indisputable presuppositions, no universal truths, and correspondingly, no possible errors in religion, philosophy, or metaphysics. Modern relativism discourages rigorous debate in such areas because the very notion of "taking a position" is deemed to be myopic and narrow minded. This can be destructive in the public policy arena, where healthy debate is essential for three primary reasons: (1) it serves to educate and engage the democratic public at large; (2) it tends to produce the most refined solutions to thorny and difficult questions by shedding light on alternatives; and (3) it helps to guard against error by exposing the implications of the presuppositions of the parties engaged in the debate.

***Episteme*, Socrates, and the Ancient Greeks**. To understand this component and its implications, we must first look at how the ancient Greeks dealt with the study of ideas and knowledge. Socrates bequeathed a legacy of thoughtful questioning and public debate to Western civilization. He believed that the unexamined life is not worth living—the study of ideas, the "searching out of one thing," and the discerning between good and evil were all critical to the human experience.[48] Socrates irritated a number of his contemporaries with what would probably be perceived in today's world as a most annoying habit: he was always conversing about things, raising the question "what is?" about everything he studied, aiming at bringing to light the nature, form, or character of that thing or concept.[49] In the words of Xenophon, he

> was always conversing about the human things, investigating what is pious, what impious, what is noble, what base, what is just, what unjust, what is moderation, what madness, what is courage, what cowardice, what is a state, what a statesman, what is rule of human beings, what a fit ruler of human beings, and about the other things as to which he considered those who knew them to be noble and good, and those ignorant of them to be justly called slavish.[50]

---

[48]Victor Davis Hanson and John Heath, *Who Killed Homer?* (San Francisco: Encounter Books, 2001), 44.

[49]Leo Strauss, "Introduction" in *History*, 5.

[50]Xenophon quoted in Christopher Bruell, "Xenophon," in *History*, 108.

Why were Socrates and other ancient Greeks concerned with discovering these truths? Because, as one observer notes, "Classical authors such as Plato, Aristotle, and Xenophon believed that the question of what is good and bad, 'values' as we imprecise moderns label it, was too serious to be shrugged off."[51] Instead, the ancients believed that, through vigorous public debate, the ultimate truths (as they related to the benefit of the *polis*—or city state) would begin to emerge. Thus, they held that truth, though imperfectly known, could be more thoroughly revealed through a deliberate and interactive public process. "The method is that of a dialogue in which two or more parties, each with imperfect knowledge, engage in a joint inquiry that raises all of them to a higher level of knowledge."[52] Note that the goal was to discover *the truth*—which they called *episteme* (or knowledge)—about the larger, more fundamental issues of life. Implicit in this is the assumption that there is in fact a concept of *episteme*—truth and knowledge—and that therefore there is also a concept of error and falsehood. Knowledge—or truth—was to be discovered about principles, values, and ways of life. For Socrates and other ancient Greeks, discovering the truth and knowledge was important because it would reveal to them how they should live within the *polis*, and how the *polis* should relate with the surrounding world. One of the preeminent virtues Leo Strauss found in the ancient and medieval rationalism inspired by Socrates was its "openness and tenacity in engaging major alternative outlooks—including not only antagonistic ancient philosophic positions but, above all, the claims to divine inspiration advanced in such different ways by the Greek poets and the biblical prophets."[53] Indeed, as Strauss puts it, "Socratic skepticism [is] a way of life devoted to inquiry into the most comprehensive questions regarding the human situation."[54]

Significantly, this ancient Socratic skepticism incorporated a certain sense of humility—of understanding that the corpus of knowledge was not complete, and that juxtaposed against the entire universe, mankind understood only a very small part of the whole. The thought process goes something like this: "[W]e possess insight, but an incomplete insight, into the 'natures,' that is, the kinds or class characteristics or 'ideas' of things, as perceived by senses and expressed in ordinary speech; and we grasp, but only dimly grasp, the whole that is articulated by these natures as parts."[55] Above all else, the Greeks approached what they considered the most important and urgent question very cautiously: "whether our lives

---

[51]Burnett, 300.

[52]Burnett, 300.

[53]Nathan Tarcov and Thomas Pangle, "Epilogue: Leo Strauss and the History of Political Philosophy," in *History*, 919.

[54]Tarcov and Pangle, 919-20.

[55]Tarcov and Pangle, 921.

can and should be guided by human reason alone, or whether the God or gods revealed by the Scripture or the poets exist—and therefore demand from us that we follow their laws and piously seek illumination from them."[56]

***Doxa* and Modern Philosophy**. These perspectives stand in contrast to the philosophies of secular humanism and postmodernism's nihilistic leveling mechanisms. That is to say, when the prevailing philosophy holds that there is no ultimate truth, then the debate about what constitutes the ultimate truth is no longer necessary or even desirable. Modern relativism claims that truth—and even the pursuit of truth or knowledge—can only accurately be seen as one person or group's belief relative to a particular frame of reference. In other words, truth is relative to one's *doxa*, or opinion. Indeed, modern philosophy denies the possibility of a corpus of rational knowledge with universal validity, purpose or principle. This can be directly linked to Husserl's secular humanism. "Social science restricted its competence to facts as distinguished from moral and fundamental choices and principles, which it understood as 'values' or irrational preferences."[57] As articulated by two of Leo Strauss' students, the inevitable outcome of this anti-Socratic approach is the following: "The practical consequences included not only vulnerability to external danger but, more important, an internal tendency for liberal democracy, deprived of belief in the rationality of its purpose and standards, to degenerate into permissiveness or conformism and philistinism."[58]

Thus the leveling relativism bequeathed by post-Enlightenment philosophies fosters a lack of concern for discovering true knowledge, or *episteme*. And if *episteme* is no longer a reality, then vigorous public debate is not required to discover it. This is, as Tarcov and Pangle have observed, the "insidious and hence more corrosive . . . tendency of democratic tolerance to degenerate, first into the easygoing belief that all points of view are equal (hence none really worth passionate argument, deep analysis, or stalwart defense), and then into the strident belief that anyone who argues for the superiority of a distinctive moral insight, way of life, or human type is somehow 'elitist' or antidemocratic—and hence immoral."[59] When this is the case, *doxa* (or opinion) becomes the leveling mechanism by which all is accepted, nothing is debated, and ideas are not exposed to the rigorous analysis that should show them to be beneficial, true, and good for society, or false, incorrect, and destructive to society. De Tocqueville once referred to this phenomenon in democracies as the tyranny of the majority—a

---

[56]Tarcov and Pangle, 921.
[57]Tarcov and Pangle, 908.
[58]Tarcov and Pangle, 909.
[59]Tarcov and Pangle, 929.

"subtle, unorganized, but all-pervasive pressure for egalitarian conformity arising from the psychologically chastened and intimidated individual's incapacity to resist the moral authority of mass 'public opinion.'"[60] Another scholar's condemnation of this anti-Socratic mentality is even sterner:

> Under these conditions man's mind more and more depends on the "climate" produced by these creations: man no longer knows how to judge as a man, in function, that is to say, of an absolute which is the very substance of intelligence; losing himself in a relativism that leads nowhere, he is judged, determined and classified by the contingencies of science and technology; no longer able to escape from the dizzy fatality they impose on him and unwilling to admit his mistake [that] the only course left to him is to abdicate his human dignity and freedom.[61]

When one eschews the pursuit of the truth because one considers the very concepts of truth, knowledge, right, and wrong as noxious to one's intellect, then one is left with the rudderless drift described above. The most dangerous feature of that drift is that it is antagonistic to the concept of questioning, discovery, and debate itself. Ideas and knowledge are no longer valuable because their validity is tenaciously debated; instead, they are based merely on the doxa of the individual.

Implications. To be consistent with Socratic principles, the study of ideas and the pursuit of knowledge and truth should be balanced with a healthy sense of skepticism. It

> would attempt to be neither value-neutral (relativistic) nor "committed" (in the fashion of so-called "postbehavioral" efforts to muster theoretical or empirical evidence for left or right ideological programs); rooted in Socrates' conversational transcendence of common sense, a theoretically sound political science would begin from and never leave off critical engagement with the perspective of actively involved citizens arguing in defense of various persuasions.[62]

Thus and in sharp contrast to today's social science, this approach "would be less obsessed with trying to make predictions, on the basis of pseudo-universal laws or abstract models." Instead, it "would devote itself more to guiding genuine

---

[60]For a full description of this problem, see chapters 15 and 16 in volume 1 of Alexis de Tocqueville, *Democracy in America* (London: David Campbell Publishers, 1994), 254-288; Tarcov and Pangle, 929.

[61]Frithjof Schuon, *Understanding Islam*, trans. D. M. Matheson (London: George Allen and Unwin, 1965), 32.

[62]Tarcov and Pangle, 931.

deliberation by enriching the citizenry's awareness of the range, weight, and validity of the factors and principles involved in major decisions."[63]

The objective is to advance beyond the type of "political reasoning" prevalent in today's policy arena—that which never really transcends the level of dogma and ideology, because instead of being a debate, it tends to be a confrontation of mutual ignorance in which participants are neither actively listening to, let alone carefully considering, the opposing arguments. Most fundamentally, this approach understands that all ideas are not created equal nor do they have equal merit; that some are more beneficial to society than others; that in the pursuit of episteme and what is best for society, *all* alternative ideas should be aggressively and publicly debated, and not avoided because of their political difficulty or social sensitivity; and that the end result of this process is not another *doxa*—but *episteme*, the product of a rigorous process of discovery about what policy alternative is truly the best for the welfare of society and the nation.

20th Century Wilsonian Idealism

The third major component of the American intellectual pedigree is best referred to as Wilsonian idealism. It could be said that the presidency of Woodrow Wilson gave classic expression to many of the ideas that cause some observers to label the twentieth century as the American century. Wilson's own ideas were broadly based on the democratic, progressive, and secular movements of the previous two centuries, including the ideals of the Enlightenment and of the French Revolution. But their roots also have a uniquely American component. In 1630, John Winthrop stood on the pitching deck of the *Arbella*. He was on his way to the New World and he addressed his fellow Puritans with these famous words: "We shall be as a city upon a hill." But then he added the following warning: "The eyes of all people are upon us. So that if we shall deal falsely with our God in this work we have undertaken, and so cause Him to withdraw His present help from us, we shall be made a story and a by-word through the world." Winthrop's vision was narrowly and spiritually conceived. The "city upon a hill" was based on the Christian concept of a covenantal relationship with the divine Creator, and the divine blessings[64] that would result from staying faithful in that relationship. The "city upon the hill" has since been transformed into a broadly secularized concept that speaks to America's destiny as the example of democracy to the rest of the world.

---

[63]Tarcov and Pangle, 931.

[64]Dr. David Yost notes that the "city on a hill" metaphor comes from Matthew 5:14, and the interpretation appears to be that offered in Matthew 15:16. The "divine blessings" do not necessarily include worldly success.

Today, Winthrop's limited vision of the New World stands in sharp contrast with the broadly sweeping comments made by President George H.W. Bush in 1990 when he called for a "New World Order." The president's comments were driven by the notion that "because they are chosen by the people, democratic governments regard each other's regimes as legitimate and deserving of respect. Because, domestically, they use civilized non-violent means to solve disputes, democracies tend to prefer the same methods internationally."[65] Therefore, according to this line of reasoning, democracy's highest virtue is that it moderates both the domestic as well as the international political environment. This evaluation tends to produce an element of determinism in the American worldview. Accordingly, history, it seems, is moving inexorably toward greater democracy— and the more nations become democratically inclined, the greater the likelihood of peace in the international system.

However valid this theory may be, democracy was not the dominant regime type in the world when Wilson arrived in Paris in January 1919. Everywhere in Europe people had been tried, confused, and bereaved by a long and costly war; "they were stirred by Wilson's thrilling language in favor of a higher cause, of a great concert of right in which peace would be forever secure and the world itself at least free . . . and the world looked with awe and expectation to one man—the president of the United States."[66] Wilson's almost evangelistic vision to convince the world of the benefits of American democracy reverberated throughout the following century and continues to affect the minds of American policymakers today. His legacy is an American paradigm formed by a cluster of understandings about America's role in the world, the threats America faces, and the strategies that serve to fulfill that role and defeat those threats.[67] One contemporary scholar attributes this American perspective to the country's nineteenth-century westward continental expansion, "the idealistic imperialism of Theodore Roosevelt, and the haunting cadences of Abraham Lincoln."[68] Of course, Wilson's idealism did not produce a lasting peace in the wake of the 1919 Treaty of Versailles, and to put it somewhat irreverently, Americans have been attempting to "make the world safe for democracy" ever since.

Core Concepts of the Wilsonian Paradigm. Today's version of Wilson's idealistic paradigm has several closely interrelated components. First, it is based on the premise that democracies do not go to war against each other. This notion has almost attained the status of a mathematical law within the policy community. A

---

[65]Philip Bobbitt, *The Shield of Achilles* (New York: Alfred A. Knopf, 2003), 267.

[66]R. R. Palmer and Joel Colton, *A History of the Modern World*, 6th ed. (New York: Alfred A. Knopf, 1984), 687

[67]Bobbitt, 243.

[68]Bobbitt, 243-44.

close second is the concept that democratic governance is by far the best way to ensure that basic human rights are respected. It is assumed that democracy is almost synonymous with the guarantee of human rights. Third, free-market economics and democracy are mutually supportive, and may even be indispensable to each other's success.[69] Directly related to this is the idea that globalization seems to be inexorably spreading both democracy and free-market economics, and so it is perceived as a positive and stabilizing force in the international system. Fifth, the essential and basic foundation of these ideas is the institution of international law, which—it is believed—has universal credence because it is also believed that peoples and civilizations the world over believe in natural law. The universality of natural law receives classic expression in America's most basic documents. As the Declaration of Independence states, "We hold these truths to be self-evident, that all men are created equal, that they are endowed by their Creator with certain inalienable rights, that among these are life, liberty, and the pursuit of happiness." These rights, naturally given to all of human kind, are said to be incapable of being surrendered or transferred. They undergird American notions of humanity, civil rights, suffrage, and of defining the functions and purposes of government. Sixth, it is believed that because of the universal credibility of international law, multilateral organizations established within the bounds of international law also have fundamental credibility in the international system. Thus, the Wilsonian phrase "open covenants openly arrived at" would ultimately give birth to organizations like the International Court of Justice and the United Nations in order to regulate and administer relations between the member states of the international system.[70] It is therefore also assumed that international organizations like the United Nations have a profound authority and effect on international relations, and are able to moderate and control the behavior of states. Seventh, the Wilsonian paradigm upholds the system of analysis that views the nation-state as the primary actor within the international environment. State-centered analyses are the prevalent mode of understanding the international system; in fact, the focus of the paradigm is to uphold the sanctity of the state. Yet, as James Piscatori, a long-time scholar at Oxford University, argues, the state-entered or "top-down" view is distorting because it obscures the religious or cultural boundary markers that often resonate more deeply in societies with ancient histories.[71] Finally, perhaps less obvious is the notion that, as Bobbitt

---

[69]Bobbitt, 265.t

[70]Of course, Wilson's original League of Nations ironically did not fail because of a lack of international support, but because—among other factors—of the U.S. Senate's failure to ratify the treaty. To be fair, there was also some lack of international support, notably on the part of Germany, Japan, Italy, and the USSR.

[71]Dale Eickelman and James Piscatori, *Muslim Politics* (Princeton: Princeton University Press, 1996), 18.

points out, this paradigm "also downplays the fear of a hegemonic power or group of powers," *if* that power is exercised by a democratic state.[72] American hegemony is therefore perceived by some to be acceptable—since according to those who hold this view, America is ultimately the originator and sustainer of democratic government. In summary, the Wilsonian paradigm is profoundly universal in its application—the paradigm is seen to be not just beneficial to American society, but also essential for global progress. Fundamentally, it is believed that the essential democratic values, the focus on individual rights and freedoms, the undergirding mechanisms of international and natural law, the state-centered focus, and the belief in the efficacy of international organizations are values that have universal credibility.

Implications. While the aspirations of the Wilsonian paradigm are commendable, and an international system that upholds them is certainly desirable, the paradigm itself serves to critically blind many in the policy community to enduring realities. In the words of George Kennan, many of our foreign policy failures "stemmed from our general ignorance of the historical processes of our age and particularly from our lack of attention to the power realities in given situations."[73] Kennan continues his critique by squarely placing fault in America's legalistic-moralistic approach to international problems. In his words,

> this approach runs like a red skein through our foreign policy . . . It has in it something of the old emphasis on arbitration treaties, something of the Hague Conferences and schemes for universal disarmament, something of the more ambitious American concepts of the role of international law, something of the League of Nations and the United Nations, something of the Kellogg Pact, something of the idea of a universal "Article 51" pact, something of the belief in World Law and World Government.[74]

It is, as Kennan concludes, based on "the belief that it should be possible to suppress the chaotic and dangerous aspirations of governments in the international field by the acceptance of some system of legal rules and restraints."[75] Even more fundamentally, Kennan argued that "behind all of this, of course, lies the American assumption that the things for which other peoples in the world are apt to contend are for the most part neither creditable nor important and might

---

[72]Bobbitt addresses the fact that the United States is even prepared to look past nuclear proliferation if the proliferator is a democratic nation. The obvious example he brings up here is the state of Israel. Bobbitt, 268.

[73]George F. Kennan, *American Diplomacy*, expanded ed. (Chicago: University of Chicago Press, 1984), 88.

[74]Kennan, 95.

[75]Kennan, 95.

justly be expected to take second place behind the desirability of an orderly world, untroubled by international violence."[76]

This points to a significant blind spot in American strategic thought—not that American values are not worth pursuing in an international context. Indeed, American blood, treasure, and democratic values liberated millions from oppression and tyranny in the previous century. It is more nuanced than that. The blind spot resides in the fact that many policymakers assume that our democratic values are universally and automatically aspired to by *other*, especially non-Western cultures. It seems difficult for Americans to understand that our ideas, regardless of how worthy they have proven for Americans, may not have universal approbation—and especially not so in many non-Western cultures. It is arguably a strategic shortcoming—directly related to the predominant Wilsonian paradigm—that "Modern Americans have come to believe that the norms and values encapsulated in their form of government and their ways of conducting foreign relations are the birthrights and open options for men everywhere."[77] Adda Bozeman, the esteemed strategic thinker, thus succinctly diagnoses the American malady. There is "a pronounced tendency," she writes, "not to take ideas or concepts seriously as determinants of national identity but to treat them as mere functions of material forces."[78] In other words, Americans tend to believe that as long as material circumstances can be improved—primarily through economic aid, education, and/or political reform—people, regardless of their cultures and identities, will eventually come around to supporting democratic governments and international law. Yet this perspective completely ignores the uniqueness of the Western experience, vis-à-vis those of other, non-Western cultures. As Bozeman aptly points out, in the West, the foremost idea is individuation. Roman civil law and English common law

> converge on the commitment to identify the essence of law in counterpoint to other norm-engendering schemes such as nature, religion, or reliance on sheer force; to cast human associations, including those of the state and the church, in reliable legal molds; and to emancipate the individual from the group by defining his status not only as an autonomous person but also as a citizen of his state or city."[79]

In contrast to most of the non-Western world, the Wilsonian paradigm is squarely focused on individual rights, on the obligation of governments to pre-

---

[76]Kennan, 96.

[77]Adda B. Bozeman, *Strategic Intelligence and Statecraft* (Washington D.C.: Brassey's (US), 1992), 158.

[78]Bozeman, 159.

[79]Bozeman, 28.

serve those rights, and on the requirement of the system of international law to hold governments responsible if they do not. The American system of government is based on individuation. Since the individual is the main subject of society, the individual has both rights that are to be upheld by the state, as well as obligations to be fulfilled toward the state. The individual enters into a social contract with society and the state—and this contract, which enumerates both rights and responsibilities—is the core of constitutional democratic government. But what if other societies do not adhere to the primacy of individuation? What if their organizing principles are not individualistic, but communal or tribal or oriented toward the group, the family, or blood relationships?

The argument here is not that the Wilsonian paradigm has not produced tangible benefits for Americans domestically. Indeed, it has also arguably brought great good to millions of people abroad. But Bozeman exposes a critical vulnerability brought about by the Wilsonian paradigm—a gap, error, or miscalculation in American strategic thought. She offers the following summary of her concerns about Wilsonian idealism:

1. The nation as a whole has come to commit itself to a simplistic or reductionist version of the Declaration of Independence, which is to the effect that mankind is essentially undifferentiated and that the world society is therefore meant to be unified both morally and politically.
2. In this spirit Americans have gradually come to believe that the United States is a "lesson" and a guide for mankind and that it has a mandate to help democratize all others . . .
3. Next, modern American thought about relations between "the other" and "the self" is confounded by a neglectful disposition toward the human experience of the past.[80]

While the core principles of the Wilsonian paradigm are fundamental to the American experiment, they may not have universal credibility. We can and should argue on their behalf, especially within our own domestic context, but we should also understand that hard political and cultural realities conflict dramatically with the idealistic conceptualizations of the Wilsonian vision of the world. We must, as Bobbitt writes, put aside the vision of a world covenant of law, a picture that is so widely and tenaciously held by the American policymaking communities; "we must free ourselves from the assumption that international law is universal and that it must be the law of a society of nation-states"; and we must understand that Wilson's ideals have served to strategically blind us to the cultural, ethnic, and power realities of the world we live in.[81]

---

[80]Bozeman 190.
[81]Bobbitt, 477.

The Pedigree and the Loss of Strategic Insight

The three-fold Western intellectual pedigree discussed above forms the broad backdrop for the academic and policy community. Not only has it deterministically and substantively shaped our worldview; it has also constrained our analytical tool set. To put it bluntly, we are blinded to enduring strategic realities. Our cognitive processes are shaped and focused by an inherited myopia that would have been viewed as fundamental ignorance by our classical Greek predecessors. We are in peril, as Sun Tzu wrote, because we do not know ourselves.

First, because of our Enlightenment and post-Enlightenment philosophy, we are snared by rationalism and secularism. This is significant, but not because of the ongoing debate about the role of the Divine, the church, or religious expression in American society. Rather, it represents a critical rejection of an understanding and appreciation of "the religious" altogether—especially in the academic and analytical communities. Theology is often discarded out-of-hand as a variable or a tool of understanding. To the Western mind, the concept of religious passion seems incomprehensible. Bozeman understood this pathology, which she described as a "pronounced disinclination to acknowledge religions and other belief systems as constitutive elements of political order."[82] This is not a discussion about the modern relevance of personal religious experience. Rather it addresses, from an analytical and social science point of view, the "pronounced inability or unwillingness" of those disciplines "to come to terms with religions, philosophies, ideologies, and other bodies of belief that have decisively shaped the foreign mind sets but which continue to baffle Americans."[83] Simply put, the broad majority in our elite academic and policy communities do not "believe," and therefore find it difficult to understand or comprehend that anyone else might "believe."

The second element of our strategic myopia is more insidious. Our growing anti-Socratic mentality tends to stifle rigorous and open-minded debate. Academics no longer strive to expose the truth about alternative ideas—instead they praise the virtues of all of them. Because everything is deemed to be good and acceptable in our modern *polis*—except for what is thought to be "politically incorrect"—the merits of individual ideas are no longer exposed to public scrutiny in open debate. Instead, ideologically driven sentiment[84] or *doxa* is the norm. In effect, we are losing our cognitive edge, our ability to discern that which has value, the truth, or episteme. Thus, instead of attaining insight as a result of tough

---

[82]Bozeman, 166.
[83]Bozeman, 191.
[84]Aptly represented by both mainstream political parties.

public debate, we accept all religions, all cultures, all philosophies, and all ideas equally. The great tradition of the Lincoln-Douglas debates has been eclipsed by a comfortable relativism. The public *writ large* is poorly served by an academic, policy, and political elite that has lost its ability to engage in the Socratic method.

Finally, the last component of our strategic myopia, twentieth century Wilsonian idealism, compels us to uphold an irrational sense of predetermination with regard to world history. Not only do we assume that we are nearing the "end of history," but we also make the dangerous assumption that other cultures endorse our ideas about culture, the individual, and proper form of government. This is not an argument about the merits of our own American experiment, but rather points toward the error that assumes that our American experiment has universal credence. It causes our strategic culture to deny the significance and reality of other cultural phenomena. Instead, the prevalent American worldview is that societies are evolving and modernizing, and are inevitably becoming more democratic and enlightened by the irresistible forces of globalization. Again, Bozeman reveals the significance of this error:

> [N]o general intelligence schemes or particular intelligence agendas can be either constructed or deciphered unless one has come to terms with the political system and the cultural matrix in which the intelligence matter is enclosed . . . It is thus important to identify component elements of culture such as language, race, religion, shared historical experiences and ways of thinking, or attachment to a particular spot on earth.[85]

Strategic Consequences within the Intelligence Community

These strategic misperceptions have real and tangible effects on the Intelligence Community. The Community, steeped in the ethos described above, has come to favor quantitatively-driven methodologies as the predominant form of analysis. The quantitative approach, grounded in scientific rationalism, stands in contrast to qualitative methodologies, which tend to favor the classical historical, anthropological, and theological disciplines. "Where is the *knowledge* we have lost in *information?*" T.S. Eliot once asked.[86] The Intelligence Community has lost its strategic insight in the deluge of information generated by its collection-centric mentality. Henry Kissinger puts it this way: "Since the mass of information available tends to exceed the

---

[85] Bozeman, 2-3.
[86] T.S. Eliot cited in Kevin O'Connell and Robert R. Tomes, "Keeping the Information Edge," *Policy Review* (December 2003), URL: www.policyreview.org/dec03/oconnell, accessed 23 April 2004.

capacity to evaluate it, a gap has opened up between information and knowledge and, even beyond that, between knowledge and wisdom."[87]

The three-fold intellectual myopia weighs heavily on this massive data processing effort. First, the focus of our postmodern philosophy causes us to disregard religious variables and instead mine the data for systemic economic, political, or social underdevelopment. Second, the leveling effect of our anti-Socratic mentality denies us the ability to constructively sort through, vigorously debate, and attempt to make sense of the great quantity of data. Third, our Wilsonian imperative causes us to deny the basic validity of other, perhaps adversarial, cultural systems of thought. Strategically-oriented "why" questions have been replaced with technical and detail-oriented "who," "what," "where," and "how" questions. This is not to say that the latter questions are not essential to a comprehensive understanding of the challenges we face. Rather, strategic thinkers and their quest for insight have been replaced by experts in data processing and management who may have little or no contextual appreciation for the current epoch of strategic change. Indeed, as one observer has noted, "[T]he intelligence community's antiquated capabilities are devoted to exploitation of clandestinely acquired information that collectively sheds only a narrow light on the broad array of national security threats."[88] As data are analyzed, they are "cleansed" and "polished" for political purposes, yielding a sanitized product devoid of thought-provoking debate or alternatives, instead being laced with jargon and carefully phrased predictions. "Analysis moves painstakingly slowly through bureaucratic structures, and iconoclastic views that challenge conventional wisdom are very likely to have their edges substantially smoothed in the laborious review process . . . Even uncontroversial analysis suffers from pronounced dumbing-down effects as it passes up and through the chain of command."[89] This combines with the imperatives of the day-to-day data crunch to considerably degrade opportunities for deep analytical research and study.

This is not a new problem. In the 1940s and 1950s, in their debate about strategic intelligence, Wilmoore Kendall and Sherman Kent revealed the effects of the Western intellectual pedigree in times when technology was less of an enabler than it is today. It seems that Kendall and Kent agreed about certain "recognizable pathological aspects of existing intelligence arrangements,"[90] in particular the Intelligence Community's state of mind. First, "it is a state of mind which—is dangerously . . .

---

[87]Henry Kissinger, cited in O'Connell and Tomes.

[88]Richard L. Russell, "Intelligence Failures," *Policy Review* (February 2004), URL: www.policyreview.org/feb04/russell, accessed 23 April 2004.

[89]Russell.

[90]Sherman Kent, Strategic Intelligence (Princeton: Princeton University Press, 1949), review by Willmoore Kendall entitled "The Function of Intelligence," in *World Politics 1*, no. 4 (July 1949), 547, hereafter referred to as *World Politics*.

dominated by an essential wartime conception of the intelligence function."[91] Thus, intelligence seems to serve the narrow focus of "winning wars" rather than the broader focus of strategic insight—which, in Kendall's words, is the big job of carving out the destiny of the United States in the world as a whole. Second, "it is a state of mind dominated by an essentially bureaucratic conception of United States government, and of the intelligence problem . . . [and] of the relation between the 'producers' and 'consumers' of intelligence."[92] Kendall lamented that in this relationship, the producers failed to draw the requisite strategic pictures in the minds of the consumers, instead contending with the task of arranging, collating, and sorting through the data. Third, Kendall argued that

> it is a state of mind characterized by a crassly empirical conception of the research process in the social sciences . . . the performance of the intelligence function accordingly becomes a matter of somehow keeping one's head above water in a tidal wave of documents, whose factual content must be "processed"—i.e., in Mr. Kent's language, "analyzed," "evaluated," and exploited as raw material for "hypotheses."[93]

Once again, the focus is not on strategic insight, but on attempting to somehow process the data. Finally, in Kendall's opinion, it is also a state of mind characterized by an "uncritical optimism regarding the supply of skills upon which the effective performance of the intelligence function depends." Given that the Intelligence Community looks mostly toward the quantitatively oriented social sciences for these skills, Kendall expressed "grave misgivings" about "the ability of our sciences to supply the sort of knowledge which . . . our highly placed civilians and military men must have."[94]

It seems reasonable to conclude that because Kent's systematic and scientific approach carries the day in today's Intelligence Community, Kendall's misgivings about sterile, scientific objectivity also ring true. As David Brooks writes, today's intelligence reports reveal that scientism is in full bloom. "The tone is cold, formal, depersonalized and laden with jargon. You can sense how the technocratic process has factored out all those insights that may be the product of an individual's intuition and imagination, and emphasized instead the sort of data that can be processed by an organization."[95] In the end, this process yields strategic blind spots that are obscured by, in Brooks' words, a thin "veneer of scientism."

---

[91] *World Politics*, 548.

[92] *World Politics*, 549.

[93] *World Politics*, 550.

[94] *World Politics*, 552.

[95] David Brooks, "The C.I.A.: Method and Madness," *New York Times*, 2 February 2004, A27.

Historical Examples of Strategic Myopia. Our intellectual pedigree, our corresponding lack of insight, and our collection-centric intelligence mentality have combined in the past to obscure significant religious phenomena. Several recent examples come to mind: (1) the Iranian revolution; (2) the Soviet occupation of Afghanistan; (3) the Balkan wars of the 1990s; and (4) the war in Chechnya. Perhaps the most notable of these was the failure to provide strategic warning of the Iranian revolution. Dr. Sam Chetti[96] was formerly the chaplain at the University of Southern California (USC) and the University of California, Los Angeles (UCLA). He presently serves as the archbishop of the American Baptist Churches of greater Los Angeles, presiding over 150 churches, many of which have Pushtun, Arabic, and Farsi-speaking members. In the years preceeding the fall of the Shah in 1979, Dr. Chetti noticed how the Islamic students on campus were becoming increasingly enthralled by correspondence coming from an obscure cleric living in Paris. As the fervor spread, especially among Shiite students, he became interested in both the content of the letters, as well as their dissemination. Dr. Chetti noted how broadly the letters were being circulated among American Shiite Muslim students, not only in the Los Angeles area, but throughout the country. He realized that a feverish phenomenon was starting to build, and that Iranian Shiites were becoming collectively mobilized, not just in Iran, but throughout the entire world. Thus, it came as no surprise to him when that obscure cleric from Paris—the Ayatollah Khomeini—stepped onto the tarmac in Tehran one afternoon and announced that the Shah had been overthrown and that Iran was to become a theocracy. It was, in Chetti's words, a classic failure of the intelligence agencies to track the right indicators. In the run-up to the revolution, the focus of U.S. intelligence agencies was "the future"—assumed by the powers-that-were to consist of Iranians in business suits carrying attaché cases. Equal focus should have been given to bearded medieval characters sitting on prayer rugs—and, as it turns out, "the future" did indeed wear strange clothes.[97]

The religious Islamic impetus of the Afghan resistance to the 1979 Soviet invasion of Afghanistan also went largely unnoticed in the U.S. Intelligence Community, yet the seeds of 9/11 and the current Iraqi insurgency were sown in Afghanistan. Saudi Arabia's generous financial support to the spread of Wahhabism among Afghan refugees and the funding of religious schools throughout the Peshawar region of Pakistan infused a powerful Islamic vector into the struggle

---

[96]Dr. Sam Chetti, Archbishop of the American Baptist Churches of Greater Los Angeles, interview by the author, 20 January 2004. The following comments regarding the Iranian revolution are based on an extended conversation between Dr. Chetti and the author.

[97]This summary of the U.S. intelligence approach was distilled from a set of arguments outlined by Stanton Burnett in "Implications for the Foreign Policy Community," 287-301.

against the Soviets. Though estimates vary regarding the number of Arabs who joined the Afghan *jihad*, it is clear that many—up to twenty-five thousand—came from Saudi Arabia.[98] Indeed, one small piece of anecdotal evidence illustrates the level of Saudi commitment: Saudi Arabia's national airline gave a 75 percent discount for volunteers heading to fight in the *jihad* in Afghanistan.[99]

Again, in the wars in the Balkans, the Intelligence Community failed to comprehend the religious undercurrents reverberating throughout the region. While analysts seemed to focus on Serb atrocities against Bosnian Muslims, they dismissed the significance of the influx of Afghan war veterans to fight against the Serbs. In March 1992, about 4,000 Arab Islamist veterans of the Afghan war made their way to Bosnia.[100] Indeed, "Arab forces acquired a reputation as fierce fighters, known to have severed the heads of the 'Christian Serbs' and mutilated their enemies' bodies."[101] Though Serb atrocities were equally horrendous, intelligence analysts failed to grasp the religious fault lines in the Balkans and instead focused on human rights violations and atrocities. After 9/11, the Intelligence Community began to realize the depth of *jihadi* Muslim penetration in the Balkans, especially when a NATO raid found computer files containing photographs of terrorist targets and street maps of Washington, DC, with government buildings marked on them—all at the Sarajevo office of the Saudi High Commissioner for Aid to Bosnia.[102] Items found included photos of the World Trade Center, the Pentagon, the USS *Cole*, and the U.S. embassies in Kenya and Tanzania. The same lack of strategic, religious appreciation continued in the Intelligence Community's evaluation of the war in Chechnya, where *mujahideen* elements from Afghanistan, led by Wahhabi-educated insurgents, fomented a secessionist movement against the Russian Federation.[103] Chechen rebel leader Shamil Bassayev went so far as to proclaim a *jihad* to liberate not only Chechnya but neighboring Muslim-dominated states from Russian domination.[104]

---

[98]Dore Gold, *Hatred's Kingdom* (Washington D.C.: Regnery Publishing, Inc., 2003), 128-29.

[99]Gold, 128-29.

[100]Gilles Kepel, quoted in Gold, 143.

[101]Gold, 143-44.

[102]"Terrorist Targets, Washington Maps found in October Raid," *News Tribune Online Edition*, 21 February 2002. Please see URL: www.newstribune.com/articles/2002/02/21/export181125.txt, accessed 13 December 2004.

[103]Though Chechnya's struggle for independence goes back to the eighteenth century and long precedes the existence of Saudi Arabia and *mujahideen* from Afghanistan, the post-Soviet unrest throughout Chechnya is predominantly fueled by Islamic *jihadists*.

[104]"Terrorist Targets, Washington Maps found in October Raid,"138-39.

A Return to Strategic Insight

How does one overcome this strategic myopia and begin to follow Sun Tzu's original maxim? First, we need to begin to appreciate the impact of our three-fold intellectual pedigree—how it filters and focuses our worldview in some areas, and blinds us to strategic realities in others. Post-Enlightenment philosophies, a growing anti-Socratic mentality, and deterministic Wilsonian idealism serve as strategic blinders in our search for meaning in the world around us. As a result, we need to (1) rediscover the reality of religious identity; (2) reinvigorate public discourse with rigorous debate aimed at critically examining all alternative ideas in the pursuit of truth and knowledge; and (3) question whether foreign and anthropologically diverse cultures are truly receptive to the American experiment with democracy. Moreover, we need to give renewed attention to non-quantitative methodologies employed in the classical disciplines: history, anthropology, and theology. This is not to say that quantitative analyses are fruitless, but rather that a comprehensive and holistic approach is essential if one is to gain *strategic insight*. This will involve a quest for cultural intelligence, for what Ralph Peters has called "a granular understanding, a tactile feel for foreign cultures."[105] It is a *strategic insight* that can only result from a penetrating understanding of culture, people, and religion. Finally, we need to anticipate the political and social difficulties that will challenge this new approach. As Carl Builder has written, "History tells us that strategic thinking requires courage and perseverance: courage because it demands departures from mainstream thinking and perseverance because it takes time for institutional mainstreams to move and join the 'discovered' innovative courses of thought."[106]

> From Voltaire to Marx, every Enlightenment thinker thought that religion would disappear in the 20th century, because religion was fetishism and animistic superstition. Well, it's not true, because religion is a response, and sometimes a very coherent response, to the existential predicaments faced by all men in all times. Empires have crumbled; political systems have crumbled; economic systems have crumbled. The great historical religions have survived.[107]

---

[105]Frederic Smoler, "The Shah Always Falls: An Interview with Ralph Peters," *American Heritage 54*, no. 1 (February/March 2003), URL: http://www.americanheritage.com/xml/2003/1/2003_1_feat_0.xml, accessed 30 January 2004.

[106]Carl H. Builder, "Keeping the Strategic Flame," *Joint Force Quarterly 14* (Winter 1996-97), 84.

[107]Daniel Bell, *The Winding Passage* (Lanham, MD: Rowman & Littlefield, 1984). This quote is attributed to Dr. Daniel Bell, Professor Emeritus, Department of Sociology, Harvard University. According to telephonic confirmation by the author with Dr. Bell on 13 December 2004, it is from an essay entitled "The Return of the Sacred," which is excerpted in the book.

II. On Islam and Christendom

Comparisons & Imperatives

In the world there is only one party of God; all others are parties of Satan and rebellion.

There is only one way to reach God; all other ways do not lead to Him.

For human life, there is only one true system, and that is Islam; all other systems are *Jahiliyyah*.

There is only one law which ought to be followed, and that is the Shari'ah from God; what is other than this is mere caprice.

The truth is indivisible; anything different from it is error.

There is only one place on earth which can be called the home of Islam (*Dar-ul-Islam*), and it is that place where the Islamic state is established and the *Shari'ah* is the authority and God's limits are observed, and where all the Muslims administer the affairs of the state with mutual consolation. The rest of the world is the home of hostility (*Dar-ul-Harb*).[108]

—**Sayyid Qutb** in *Milestones*

Jesus summarized all his teaching for us in two great propositions which have provided Christendom with, as it were, its moral and spiritual axis. The first and great commandment, he said, was: *Thou shalt love the Lord thy God with all thy heart, and with all thy soul, and with all thy mind*, and the second, *like unto it: Thou shalt love thy neighbour as thyself*. On these two commandments, he insisted, hang all the law and the prophets. His manner of presenting them indicates their interdependence; unless we love God we cannot love our neighbour, and, correspondingly, unless we love our neighbour we cannot love God. Once again, there has to be a balance; Christianity is a system of such balanced obligations—to God and Caesar, to flesh and spirit, to God and our neighbour, and so on. Happy the man who strikes the balance justly; to its imbalance are due most of our miseries and misfortunes, individual as well as collective.[109]

—**Malcolm Muggeridge** in *Jesus: The Man who Lives*

The statements above are from two 20th-century thinkers and believers. In many ways, both summarize the essence of their respective faiths. Sayyid Qutb, an Egyptian scholar and modern-day interpreter of Islam, remains widely published

---

[108]Sayyid Qutb, *Milestones* (Delhi: Markazi Makraba Islami, 1996), 220-21.

[109]Malcolm Muggeridge, *Jesus: The Man who Lives* (New York: Harper & Row, 1975), 130-31.

and read throughout the Islamic world. Malcolm Muggeridge was a well-known British journalist and intellectual contemporary of G. K. Chesterton. That the perspectives of these two men are linked to rich theological histories is undeniable. That their respective ideas about religion have modern cultural and political imperatives seems clear. To show why those imperatives result in significantly different outcomes and that those outcomes have strategic consequences is now the aim of this work.

In order to appreciate the cultural and political imperatives of each religion, we must understand the crucial differences between the core belief structures of Islam and Christianity. We achieve this by first unpacking and rediscovering theology. The word theology stems from the Latin word *theologia* and has two primary meanings: (1) the study of religious faith, practice, and experience, and (2) the study of God and his relation to the world.[110] In the first and broader sense, theology can be defined as the systematic study of the theories that form the foundations of those faiths, practices, and experiences—called *theological doctrine*. In the second and narrower sense, theology is simply the study of God and his relation to the world.

The core *theological doctrines* of both Islam and Christendom can be seen to rest on four central premises: *anthropology, theology, soteriology*, and *eschatology*. First, in this case (as opposed to the broader classical meaning of the word), anthropology is defined as the study of man's essential nature within the physical universe or natural order. Fundamentally, this addresses how man's nature is constituted, whether man naturally inclines toward good or evil. Second, as mentioned in the narrow sense above, *theology* is the study of God and his divine relationship with mankind as well as with the physical universe. It addresses all aspects of God, including the essence of his being, his character, and his sovereignty in the unfolding of history, the present age, and the time to come. Third, *soteriology* involves the study of salvation. Both Islam and Christianity acknowledge the problem of evil in this world, and both see profound consequences of that evil. It is the study of *soteriology* that addresses how man can be absolved or rescued from the consequences of that evil. Finally, *eschatology* is defined as the study of the hereafter or after-life. This, quite simply, relates to each religion's perspective about our existence after a final divine judgment period that is believed to be inevitable due to the presence and influence of evil on the natural order as well as on mankind.

---

[110]*Webster's Ninth New Collegiate Dictionary*, 1986, under the term "theology."

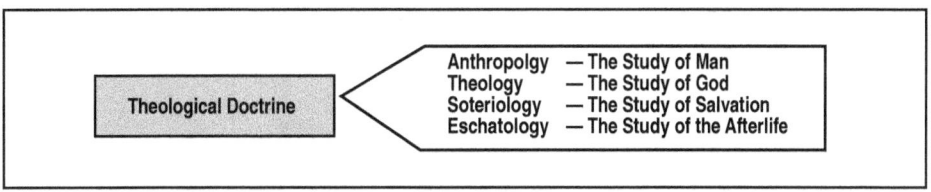

Figure 1: Premises of Theological Doctrine

(Source: Author)

Although a basic understanding of these theological doctrines is necessary, it is not sufficient in creating a satisfactory picture of the social and political imperatives of the two religions. To do this, one must also begin to comprehend the impact of the respective scriptures and canon as well as the influences of the founding prophets. In this regard, the *scriptures* and *canon* are the collective written and oral traditions that are accepted as authoritative and doctrinally applicable. In considering the prophets, one must look at the key messianic or divinely inspired leaders who had a founding role and whose interpretations and teachings about the scriptures have enduring value and legitimacy—specifically Mohammed and Jesus Christ. Once these three major areas are explored—theological doctrines, scriptures and canon, and founding prophets—then their political and historical imperatives may become clearer.

Different Core Beliefs Lead to Different Imperatives

Although there are many superficial similarities between Islam and Christianity—both, for example, have Abrahamic roots and both can be seen as monotheistic religions,[111] significant differences in their core belief systems have produced very different political and historical imperatives. The next few paragraphs outline these differences. This is presented only as an initial outline, after which the doctrines, scriptures, prophets, and political and historical imperatives of each religion are investigated in greater detail (for a summary, please see figure 2).

Islam. Islam is centered on the unity of Allah and the pivotal role of his divinely inspired messenger, Mohammed, who orally revealed the Koran (or Qur'an) to his followers. The Islamic canon consists chiefly of the Qur'an, but also of a large body of traditions about the words, actions, and deeds of the prophet (*hadith*) and the traditions of conduct and faith within the Islamic community (*sunnah*). Only the Qur'an, which is less an integrated narrative, and more a topical reference, remains unchanged and undisputed. The corpus of *hadith*s

---

[111]Though most Muslims see the idea of a Christian Trinitarian Godhead as heretical.

tends to be fractionalized—there are tens of thousands of *hadiths* of varying significance and credence.

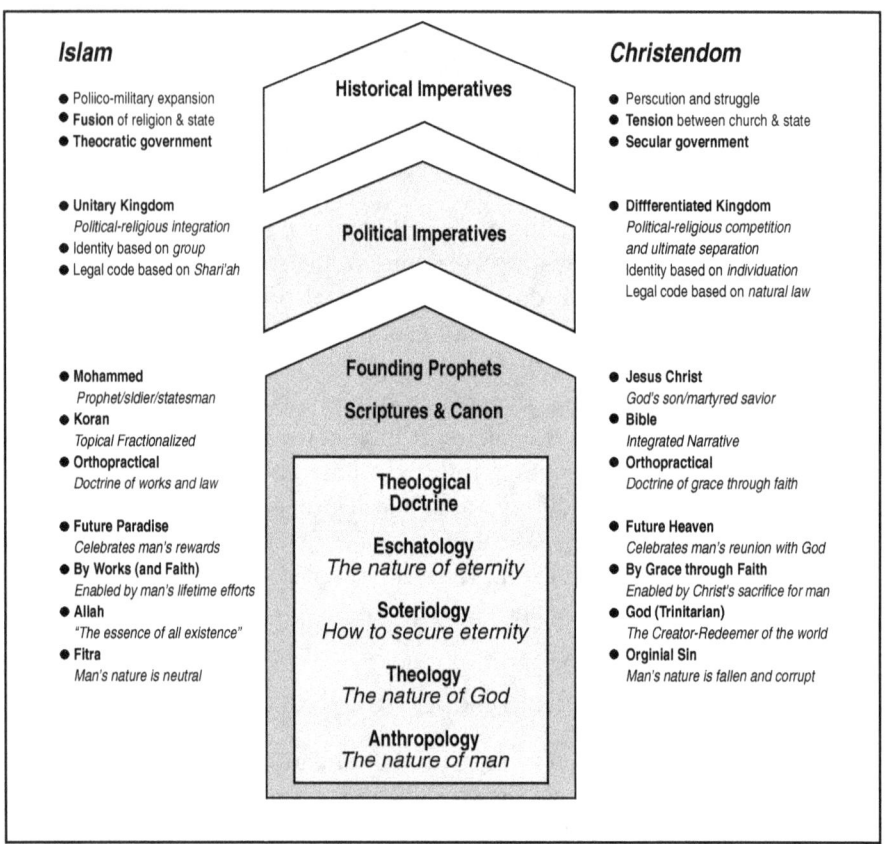

Figure 2. Core Doctrines and Historical/Political Imperatives
(Source: Author)

Mohammed was not just a deeply religious prophet who brought the holy revelation to his followers. He was also a visionary politician, who dramatically unified a fractious set of Arabian tribes under his guidance, and imbued them with a theocentric identity. He was a competent soldier-statesman who led his religiously motivated Muslim fighters to over 70 victories and provided the impetus for a dramatic and strategic military expansion of the fledgling Islamic caliphate. Islam, as an orthopractical belief, obliged all its followers to comply with a set of common ritualistic observances. This doctrine of works required a cultural and political infrastructure that would support these common observances. Over time, an integrated, group-oriented system of *shari'ah* law was developed. Within this society, religion and the state were tightly fused and propelled by a determination to bring the rightly guided truth to the rest of mankind. It was Islam's role to liberate the lost from their ignorance and to establish a sacred geography that permitted all followers to abide by its requirements. This religiously and politically unified space came to be known as the *Dar-ul-Islam* or the Islamic Caliphate. It was the kingdom of God *combined with* the kingdom of man.

Christendom. On the other hand, Christianity's foundations produced a very different set of imperatives. Christianity centers on the triune identity of the Godhead—God the Father, God the Son, and God the Holy Spirit. It is profoundly tied to the life of Jesus Christ, who as God incarnate, came to this world as a substitutive sacrifice for man's sin. Christianity was profoundly rooted in man's fallen anthropology, and therefore also saw it necessary to follow Jesus' mandate to bring the message of the gospels to the rest of the world. Yet in doing so, the aim was not to establish an earthly kingdom of Christians or the kingdom of God—it was understood that this world was only temporal, and that true believers waited with expectation for the future, heavenly kingdom of God.

Christianity's canon is the Bible, an integrated historical narrative that reveals comprehensively God's plan to rescue his people, both Jews and Gentiles, from their condemnation under sin. Jesus Christ was a servant prophet, the Son of God, who was brutally martyred on a cross, and then, as Christians believe, was resurrected and returned to heaven. Christian belief structures are orthodoxical, focusing on the key faiths and beliefs and ultimately relying on a doctrine of grace, and not of works. As such, Christians believed from the outset in the salvationary power of faith, made possible through God's redeeming grace—not the redeeming potential of a set of obligatory rituals and observances.

Christianity evolved under extreme persecution, and with an almost immediate antagonistic relationship with the Roman state. It was propelled by a vision of differentiated kingdoms—the imperfect kingdom of man, and the perfect and desirable kingdom of heaven. Christians were seen to exist in the kingdom of this world, while always ultimately looking forward to a perfect and future kingdom of heaven, to be revealed at the end of the secular world kingdom. Thus, Christianity was born with an inherent separation of church and state, and remained that way for its first 300 years. During the reign of Constantine, the divide began to fade as the Roman emperor attempted to integrate Christians in a bid to stabilize his empire. Constantine's reign was followed by centuries of struggle and conflict between church and state in Christendom. Ultimately, the two entities would again diverge to form the church, which was responsible for the stewardship of the believers, and the state, which administered the secular realm. Yet Western societies, their historical roots in Christianity, came to focus on so-called God-given, inalienable rights, and concomitantly, legal systems were developed to protect and define those individual rights. Historical imperatives led to persistent tensions between church and state, and a continuing perception that Christians are persecuted because they live their lives in the less-than-perfect kingdom of this world, while awaiting the future kingdom of God.

Theological Doctrines: *Anthropology*

One could argue that anthropology—the study of man's nature—is one of the most basic premises or building blocks of religious belief. The central question can be stated as follows: Is mankind's essential nature inclined toward evil and depravity, or does evil and depravity in his surrounding environment corrupt man? The answer to this question, in itself the subject of philosophical debate throughout history, underlies most other religious doctrines about man's interaction with the divine, the universe, and general society. Islam and Christianity answer it in fundamentally different ways.

Islam and the Concept of *fitra*. Traditional Islamic doctrine about man's essential nature espouses the concept of *fitra*. According to *fitra*, man is created by God with a balanced soul or a neutral state of mind—man is born with a neutral constitution and with the capacity for both good and evil. It is man's surroundings, primarily in the form of the family and of society, which tend to either promote good or encourage evil in man. One Islamic scholar writes that man is envisaged "not as a fallen being needing a miracle to save him, but as man, a theomorphic being endowed with an intelligence capable of conceiving of the Absolute and with a will capable of choosing what leads to the Absolute."[112] In other words, man is conceived as a neutral receptacle capable of relating to and choosing the divine Absolute—but also capable of being influenced by unbelief, sin, and depravity.

The image of an empty vessel comes to mind. The vessel, according to the Qur'an, was divinely created and endowed with the ability to choose what is good. The Qur'an indicates in Surah *Al Rum: So set thou thy face steadily and truly to the Faith (establish) Allah's handiwork according to the pattern on which he has made mankind: no change (let there be) in the work (wrought) by Allah: that is the standard Religion: but most among mankind understand not* (30:30).[113] As explained by one Muslim commentator, man was therefore created by Allah as "innocent, pure, true, free, inclined to right and virtue, and endowed with true understanding about his own position in the Universe and about Allah's

---

[112]Schuon, 13.

[113]*The Meaning of the Holy Qur'an*, trans. Abdullah Yusuf 'Ali, in *The World of Islam: Resources for Understanding* (Colorado Springs: Global Mapping International, 2000), CD-ROM. Hereafter referred to as *The Meaning of the Holy Qur'an*. Surah 30 is introduced and commented on by Al Mawdudi.

goodness, wisdom, and power." Yet, man is also "caught in the meshes of customs, superstitions, selfish desires, and false teaching" and this "may make him pugnacious, unclean, false, slavish, hankering after what is wrong or forbidden, and deflected from the love of his fellow-men and the pure worship of the One True God." The Qur'an thus presents man, in the words of the commentator, as "universally sinful in act, but this comes of his weakness, not from a sinful taint. Man is prone to sin, but not of sinful nature. He has lost Paradise, but he is not radically estranged from God." [114]

Crowded market in Rabat, Morocco.

Photo by author.

To summarize, traditional Qur'anic doctrine holds that "humans have been created with a sound nature and provided by God with a true religion that enables them to have fullness of life through close communion with God in this world and the next. Each human is a religiously grounded person, created and endowed with a *fitra*, a 'sound constitution' that acts as a kind of internal guidance system and way to God."[115] It is the responsibility, first of the parents and immediate family members, and then of the greater society, to provide the conditions for the proper fulfillment of this divinely emplaced knowledge. This has led one Muslim

---

[114]Commentary by Yusuf Ali in *The Meaning of the Holy Qur'an.*

[115]Frederick Denny, *Islam and the Muslim Community* (Prospect Heights, IL: Waveland, 1987), 41-2.

observer to conclude that "whatever becomes of man after birth is the result of external influence and intruding factors."[116] Islam teaches, as Isma'il R. Al-Faruqi explains, "that people are born innocent and remain so until each makes him or herself guilty by a guilty deed."[117]

As such, most Muslims tend to have an enlightened view of human nature. The well-respected Islamic scholar H.A.R. Gibb has written that in Islam, "There is nothing in humans that is essentially—that is fundamentally and irrevocably—evil. At their core, recall, humans are constituted according to the fitra."[118] This fitra is that unfulfilled empty vessel, with a divinely-inspired inclination toward Allah, yet also with the potential to be corrupted by evil. According to Dr. Dudley Woodberry, a Harvard-educated dean emeritus and professor of Islamic studies, most Islamic scholars have normally maintained that man is not a fallen being, but rather a fundamentally good and dignified human being.[119] This perspective offers an affirmative outlook on human nature—that is, given appropriate circumstances (the correct upbringing, education, social environment), mankind has a divinely provided ability to work toward achieving the will of Allah. Interestingly, much as Rousseau and his fellow revolutionaries believed in the pure virtues of human nature and that it was society that corrupts man's innate goodness, similarly, Islam seems to blame society and its organizing mechanisms for the corruption of the faithful. Politically speaking then, the focus on Islam has always been to purge society of its wayward influences and apply correctives so as to arrange society as a constructive religious milieu for mankind.

Christianity and Original Sin. Unlike Islam, however, Christianity takes a dim view of human nature. According to the Christian doctrine of original sin, Adam's historic choice fundamentally damned the rest of the human race to an irrevocable sinful condition, and the human species has ever since been born with a natural inclination toward sin. Man was not divinely created with this predisposition—indeed, Christian doctrine holds that God created man in his divine image; however, without exception, sin distorts that image. St. Paul made this doctrine plain in his letter to the Romans: *There is no one righteous, not even one; there is no one who understands, no one who seeks God. All have turned away, they have together become worthless; there is no one who does good, not even one* (Romans 3:10-12); and *There is no difference, for all have sinned and*

---

[116]Abdalati, quoted in Norman L. Geisler and Abdul Saleeb, *Answering Islam: The Crescent in Light of the Cross* (Grand Rapids: Baker Books, 2002), 45, hereafter referred to as *Answering Islam*.

[117]Al-Faruqi quoted in *Answering Islam*, 45.

[118]H. A. R. Gibb, *Mohammedanism* (London: Oxford University Press, 1970), 45.

[119]Dr. Dudley Woodberry, Dean Emeritus and Professor of Islamic Studies, School of International Studies, Fuller Theological Seminary, interview by the author, 19 January 2004.

fall short of the glory of God (Romans 3:23); and *sin entered the world through one man, and death through sin, and this way death came to all men, because all sinned* (Romans 5:12-13). Thus, while the Islamic view of human nature acknowledges no fallenness or depravity, but instead argues that man's fundamental problem relates to the weakness and forgetfulness that are inherent in human nature, Christianity sees man's essential nature in a state of rebellion against God.[120] Sin has caused man to rebel and resist God's righteousness, as first revealed by Adam's actions in the Garden of Eden, when he hid from his creator because of his newly gained knowledge and awareness of evil.

Thus, Christianity believes that the ills of this world came about as a result of the unchecked sinful inclinations of human nature. To put it bluntly, Christianity views man's nature as corrupted and prone toward evil. Politically speaking, secular society is not the corrupting mechanism (as is the Islamic view). Rather, since man himself is by nature corrupt, civil society and government are to serve as the restraining mechanism to curb the vagaries of fallen, sinful individuals. Therefore, Christianity bequeathed to Western political philosophy the notion that power concentrated in the hands of the few was to be avoided, because of the corrupt nature of individual man. Political power, in this sense, was best diffused and placed in the hands of the many, thereby avoiding the inevitable tyranny of the few. Based on this view of the depravity of man, power is best entrusted in the hands of a civil society rather than an individual ruler. Not that a society made up of sinful individuals would necessarily be a perfectly constituted society. In the American example, a solution was proposed to limit the effects of man's original sinful nature on the very mechanisms of organized government and civil society. The answer was a constitutionally grounded concept of limited government, and the principle of the separation of powers.[121]

Summary: The *Fitrah* in Islam—Original Sin in Christianity. In conclusion, Islam and Christianity make significantly different assertions about human nature. Islam believes that man is divinely constituted with a balanced and neutral inclination, and that this fitra incorporates in all of mankind the ability to choose to submit to Allah. It is therefore the burden of the immediate family and of society to enable the individual to live up to this unfulfilled potential. There is, as Michael Sells has written, "no doctrine of original sin in Islam, no doctrine of an innate sinfulness that makes every human inherently unworthy of salvation without the saving grace of the deity. Instead, the Qur'an affirms that humankind is in a state of forgetfulness, confusion, and loss and in need to remember."[122] Christianity, on the other hand, views the fallen nature of man with pessimism and apprehension. The

---

[120]Geisler and Saleeb, 124.

[121]See for example Thomas Sowell's comparison of the constrained versus unconstrained vision of the role of government in society in *Conflict of Visions.*

doctrine of original sin imbued Christianity with a healthy skepticism toward the concentration of political power because of man's corrupt state. Collective, civil society was viewed as a means, though not a perfect one, of mitigating the sinful effects of fallen human nature.

Theological Doctrines: *Theology*

If anthropology is one of the sources of religious doctrine, then theology—the study of God and his relationship with mankind as well as with the physical universe—constitutes an equally significant building block. The study of theology is the study of the divine being and addresses all aspects of God, including the essence of his being, his character, and his sovereignty in the unfolding of history, the present age, and the time to come. From the outset, it must be said that both Islam and Christianity are monotheistic religions—that is, both are centered around a single divine God-head, as opposed to, for example, the polytheistic Greek and Roman religions.[123] However, the character and nature of the two God-heads differ in many respects.

The God of Islam: Allah. Islam stresses belief in the oneness of God. The emphasis of the entire system of Islamic belief is underscored by the following creedal statement: *La ilaha illa Allah, Muhammad rasul Allah*— "there is no god but Allah and Mohammad is Allah's prophet."[124] This forthright, monotheistic focus is summarized by the ancient Muslim jurist al-Ghazali: "We believe that the world has a Maker, Who is One, Powerful, Knowing, Willing, Speaking, Hearing, and Seeing; Who has no one like Him."[125] The often repeated first Surah of the Qur'an, the Al Fatihah, captures the Muslim believer's approach toward Allah:

> *In the name of Allah, Most Gracious, Most Merciful.*
> *Praise be to Allah, The Cherisher and Sustainer of the Worlds;*
> *Most Gracious, Most Merciful;*
> *Master of the Day of Judgment.*
> *Thee do we worship, and Thine aid we seek.*
> *Show us the straight way,*
> *The way of those on whom Thou hast bestowed Thy Grace, those whose*
> *(portion) is not wrath, and who go not astray.*[126]

---

[122]Michael Sells, *Approaching the Qur'an: The Early Revelations*, trans. Michael Sells (Ashland, OR: White Cloud Press, 1999), 117.

[123]Whether or not Muslims consider Christianity a monotheistic religion is an important question, and will be addressed throughout this work.

[124]Geisler and Saleeb, 15.

[125]Ghazali quoted in F. E. Peters, *A Reader on Classical Islam* (Princeton: Princeton University Press, 1994), 77

The absolute oneness, indivisibility, and centrality of Allah is fundamental to the Muslim believer's understanding of the divine. As one Muslim writer has noted, "God is the essence of existence. His Arabic name is Allah. He is The First and The Last. He is unique and nothing resembles him in any respect. He is One and The One. He is self-sustained, does not need anything but everything needs Him."[127] The Islamic tendency to list ninety-nine names of God in order to ascribe due reverence to the name alone has a basis in the Qur'an itself. In the *Al Hashr* Surah (59:22-24), the Qur'an refers to Allah's most beautiful names:

> *Allah is He, than Whom there is no other god; who knows (all things) both secret and open; He, Most Gracious, Most Merciful. Allah is He, than Whom there is no other god; the Sovereign, the Holy One, the Source of Peace (and Perfection), the Guardian of Faith, the Preserver of Safety, the Exalted in Might, the Irresistible, the Supreme: Glory to Allah! (high is He) above the partners they attribute to Him. He is Allah, the Creator, the Evolver, the Bestower of Forms (or Colours). To Him belong the Most Beautiful Names; whatever is in the heavens and on earth, doth declare His Praises and Glory: and He is the Exalted in Might, the Wise.[128]*

This passion, commitment, and deep conviction that Muslims feel toward the supremacy of Allah is difficult to understand in today's Western world. Islam is, as one scholar describes it, a religion of absolute certitude—and this certitude is characterized most of all by the persuasive ardor that comes from the fact that at root it teaches the reality of the Absolute and the dependence of all things on the Absolute.[129] To understand how central a notion this is, consider what is most detested by Muslims. Muslims, at their very core, hate most "the rejection of Allah and of Islam because the supreme Unity and its absoluteness and transcendence appear to [them] dazzlingly evident and majestic . . ."[130] Muslims learn about the most perfect and authoritarian revelation of God in and through the Qur'an.

The Triune God of Christianity. In Christianity, God is revealed through the Bible, which speaks of His sovereignty, majesty, and absolutely righteous nature. Perhaps best described as eternal, transcendent, without sin, and loving, the God of the Old and New Testament is revealed most profoundly in the Christian faith through the person of Jesus Christ. As Norman Anderson, the preeminent scholar

---

[126]*The Meaning of the Holy Qur'an.*

[127]Muhammad Abdul Rauf, Islam: *Creed and Worship* (Washington D.C.: The Islamic Center, 1974), 2-3.

[128]*The Meaning of the Holy Qur'an.*

[129]Schuon, 18.

[130]Schuon, 21.

of Oriental Law, wrote, to Christians "God's supreme revelation of himself is in a person, the Lord Jesus Christ, rather than in a book, however inspired—although it is an inspired and much revered book that the coming of that person was foreshadowed and predicted in the Hebrew scriptures; that his life, teaching, death and resurrection are recorded in the Gospels; and that authoritative teaching about the significance of what he said and did are to be found in the remainder of the New Testament."[131]

The God of Christianity is uniquely Trinitarian: God is a trinity of persons consisting of God the Father, Son, and Holy Spirit. The trinity is strictly a monotheistic concept; this is a hallmark of Biblical doctrine. Nevertheless, this was never meant to undermine the fact that Christians, no less than Muslims and Jews, believe in one, and only one, God. The doctrine of the trinity is meant as an explanation of the trinity—not a subversion of it. Christians have historically shared Muslim's aversion to both idolatry and polytheism. The triune Godhead was revealed during the baptism of Jesus Christ, when after John baptized Jesus, the Gospel of Matthew reveals the following:

> As soon as Jesus was baptized, he went up out of the water. At that moment heaven was opened, and he saw the Spirit of God descending like a dove and lighting on him. And a voice from heaven said, "This is my Son, whom I love; with him I am well pleased." Matthew 3:16-17.

God the father spoke his blessing upon God the son as the Holy Spirit descended upon Jesus Christ.

Summary: The Absolute Unity of Allah—the Unmerited Love of God. While Islam is intensely focused on the absolute unity and supremacy of Allah, one of the most enduring Christian doctrines about God is the divine display of unmerited love toward the creation. Given that mankind, through Adam's original sin, had fatally distanced itself from God, Christianity reveals God's love through his plan for redemption. This love is made available to all of mankind. The Gospel of John reports in John 3:16 that *"God so loved the world that he gave his one and only Son, that whoever believes in him shall not perish, but have eternal life."* This is the very core of Christianity, and the twin doctrines of love for the Lord and love for one's neighbor descend directly from this doctrine, which implicitly states that God loved man first—before mankind loved him.

---

[131]Norman Anderson, *Islam in the Modern World* (Leicester: Apollos Press, 1990), 208.

Al-Azhar Mosque, Cairo.

Photo by author.

While Islam is deeply concerned with man's obligation to submit to the will of Allah, Christianity balances God's demand for divine justice with his all-encompassing love for mankind. Anderson writes that "it would be wrong to suggest that there is no concept of love of God in Islam," and notes that "indeed, a number of verses in the Qur'an declare that Allah 'loves' those who in any measure deserve it."[132] Yet Allah's love for mankind seems to be conditionally based on man's works in service to Him— *"If ye do love Allah, follow me: Allah will love you and forgive you your sins; for Allah is Oft-Forgiving, Most Merciful. Obey*

---

[132]Anderson, 215.

Allah and His Messenger: but if they turn back, Allah loveth not those who reject Faith (Surah 3:30-32)." As Anderson concludes, there are no verses in the Qur'an which declare that

> Allah loves the unbelieving and the unrepentant, or seeks to woo the unfaithful back to himself . . . we do not find 'Loving' or 'Lover' among the seven divine 'attributes' or 'qualities'—which al-Ghazali lists as 'Living, Knowing, Powerful, a Willer, a Hearer, a Seer and a Speaker. In Islam, the relationship between God and man (except for some Sufis) is always that of a Master (*rabb*) and slave (*abd*).[133]

This stands in contrast to the image of the righteous God of Christianity, who in loving forbearance sent his son to die as an atoning sacrifice for man's sinful rebellion—in order to reconcile man to God. As the Bible explains it, *"This is love: not that we loved God, but that he loved us and sent his Son as an atoning sacrifice for our sins (1 John 4:10)."* Who is the recipient of the divine love of Christianity? *"This is good, and pleases God our Savior, who wants all men to be saved and to come to a knowledge of the truth (1 Timothy 2:4),"* and *"He is patient with you, not wanting anyone to perish, but everyone to come to repentance (2 Peter 3:9)."*

Finally, Islam's intense monotheistic passion is also revealed by what Muslims consider to be the greatest of all sins. Ignaz Goldziher, scholar of Islamic theology and law, explains that for the monotheism of the Qur'an, the greatest of all sins is *shirk*—the association of other gods with the only god, Allah—and that for shirk, there is no forgiveness.[134] In Surah Al Nisa'(4:16), the Qur'an explains that *"Allah forgiveth not (the sin of) joining other gods with him; but he forgiveth whom he pleaseth other sins than this: one who joins other gods with Allah, hath strayed far, far away (from the right)."*[135] Again, in Surah Luqman (31:13), the Qur'an indicates that associating others with the deity of Allah is the highest of errors: *"Behold, Luqman said to his son by way of instruction: O my son join not in worship (others) with Allah: for false worship is indeed the highest wrong doing."*[136] Muslims tend to believe that Christians commit the sin of shirk by espousing the Trinitarian Godhead. This becomes especially clear when discussion centers on the incarnation of Jesus Christ. Though anecdotal, the following comment provides insight regarding the deep skepticism with which many Mus-

---

[133]Anderson, 215.

[134]Ignaz Goldziher, *Introduction to Islamic Theology and Law.* Trans. Andreas and Ruth Hamori (Princeton: Princeton University Press, 1981), 42.

[135] *The Meaning of the Holy Qur'an.*

[136]*The Meaning of the Holy Qur'an.*

lims view Christian Trinitarian beliefs. During a lengthy theological conversation with the author, an esteemed Shiite cleric in Azerbaijan revealed that it is inconceivable how Jesus Christ could be God incarnate. After all, the cleric reasoned, that would mean that God would have engaged in bodily functions such as urinating and defecating—which would, in this Muslim cleric's opinion, be inconceivably un-divine.[137] Ultimately, it is reasonable to assume that most practicing Muslims tend to view Christian Trinitarianism as a polytheistic doctrine, but the degree to which they condemn it as *shirk* is difficult to determine. However, that the Qur'an addresses the subject directly and casts doubt on Christ's crucifixion is discussed in subsequent sections of this work.

In summary, Islam may be described as a doctrine of unity—the all-encompassing, all-prevailing, all-powerful, absolute pristine monotheism of Allah. On the other hand, Christianity may be described as a doctrine of union—the union of man to God by way of God's love manifested in his son's sacrificial atonement. Islam operates on the principle of divine Unity—and proceeds through a unitary faith that demands logical consistency with the Absolute, by requiring a Muslim's complete submission to the certitude of that Unity and of that Absolute.[138] "Christianity operates through the love of God—a love which responds to the divine love for man, God being Himself Love."[139] In this sense, the unity and certitude of Islam evoke a predeterminism with respect to the will and presence of Allah; on the other hand, in Christianity, the concept of union evokes a deeply individual response to the immensity of divine love.

Theological Doctrines: *Soteriology*

Both anthropology and theology, as discussed above, are basic elements of theological doctrine. They are, in effect, principal assumptions that outline the foundation of religious belief. Upon this foundation are layered the building blocks that define the shapes and structure of religious belief. One of those key building blocks is the concept of soteriology—the study of salvation, addressing how man can be absolved or rescued from the consequences of evil in the world.

Soteriology in Islam. The concept of salvation implies, most basically, that there is a need for salvation. The intensity of that need is dependent upon the nature of the predicament that one believes oneself to be in. If, as in Islam, the faithful hold that their natural state, as evidenced by the notion of *fitra*, is neutral, then the need for a life-changing rescue or transformation (as in Christianity)

---

[137]Interview by the author with *Akhund* Tilman (Islamic scholar of high rank) in Baku, Azerbaijan, 3 April 2004.

[138]Schuon, 118-19.

[139]Schuon, 118.

becomes less critical. While Islam does not discount evil in the world, it also does not attribute that evil to man's fallen nature. As seen in Islam's anthropology, man is stained by evil as a consequence of moments of weakness, a lack of resolve, and the negative influences of culture in the form of the immediate family and the greater society. The challenge in Islam is to overcome these negative influences and to conform to man's natural constitution, or *fitra*, which will naturally lead individuals to God. This process must occur meritoriously. In other words, Islam is an orthopractical doctrine in that it provides, with Allah's guidance, a set of rules that enable the faithful to earn their salvation by their own merit. Islam is therefore predominantly a religion of rules, practices, and observances.

That is not to say that Islam does not require Muslims to display faith. One Muslim theologian, Muhammad Abul Quasem, writes that "the Qur'an teaches that the means to salvation in the Hereafter on the human side are belief or faith (*iman*) and action (*amal*): salvation cannot be achieved without these two means."[140] The faith that Quasem is talking about consists of two parts: the Islamic *shahada* (belief in the oneness of Allah and in the prophet Mohammad), and belief in life after death. The Qur'an underscores the requirement for faith in Surah Al Ma'idah (5:9): "*To those who believe and do deeds of righteousness hath Allah promised forgiveness and a great reward.*"[141] Nevertheless, the overwhelming focus in Islam is not on a system of beliefs, but rather on a system of works. The articles of faith, while inviolable, seem rather simple compared to the orthopractical elements of Islamic soteriology.

Indeed, numerous *hadiths*—or traditions—record that it is the deeds of believers that earn merit in the sight of Allah. For example, in one *hadith* Mohammad is recorded as stating that Allah said, "My servant does not draw near to Me with anything more loved by Me than the religious duties I have imposed upon him, and My servant continues to draw near to Me with supererogatory works so that I shall love him."[142] The obligatory religious duties are in many ways the most visible elements of Islam: (1) the shahada, or confession of faith, (2) the *salat*, or ritual prayer, performed five times daily; (3) the saum, or fast performed during the month of Ramadan; (4) the *zakat*, or tithe and alms giving; and (5) the *hajj*, or pilgrimage to Mecca. Sometimes among Sunnis, and always among Shiites, *jihad* is added as a religious duty—in the context of both an internal struggle, as well as an external military struggle in defense of the ummah, or

---

[140]Muhammad Abul Quasem, *Salvation of the Soul and Islamic Devotions* (London: Kegan Paul International, 1983), 29.

[141]*The Meaning of the Holy Qur'an.*

[142]A popular *hadith* cited in Norman Anderson, *God's Law and God's Love: An Essay in Comparative Religion* (London: Collins, 1980), 100.

community of believers.[143] The supererogatory works mentioned in the *hadith* above are those duties that extend beyond the traditional obligatory ones—in other words, acts that go above and beyond the call of duty.

Frithjof Schuon, in *Understanding Islam*, conveys exceptionally well the depth of emotion and feeling that Muslims attach to these obligatory rituals:

> [T]he *shahadah* indicates in the final analysis . . . discernment between the Real and the unreal and then, in the second part, the attaching of the world to God in respect both of its origin and of its end, for to look on things separately from God is already unbelief . . . The *prayer* integrates man into the rhythm of universal adoration and—through the ritual orientation of the prayer towards the Kaaba—into its centripetal order . . . The *fast* cuts man off from the continual and devouring flux of carnal life, introducing into our flesh a kind of death and purification; the *alms* vanquish egoism and avarice and actualize the solidarity of all creatures, for alms are a fasting of the soul, even as the fast proper is an almsgiving of the body. The *pilgrimage* is a pre-figuration of the inward journey towards the kaaba of the heart and purifies the community, just as the circulation of the blood, passing through the heart, purifies the body; finally, the *holy war* is . . . an external and collective manifestation of discernment between truth and error; it is like a centrifugal and negative complement of the pilgrimage—complement, not contrary, because it remains attached to the center and is positive through its religious content.[144]

In a sense, the fulfillment of these ritualistic obligations aligns the will of the faithful with the will of Allah. These obligations contextualize the *tawhid*, the doctrine of the central unity of Allah. As a set of physical observances, they provide visceral evidence of man's submission to Allah. Enshrined in Islamic jurisprudence, they form the foundation of the concept of *shariah*, a system of rules and laws designed to regulate the society of the faithful. The *shariah* and the religious obligations are the vehicles that allow the faithful to meritoriously achieve their purification and salvation. Thus, as one observer notes, "Muslims have the obligation to create a social world in which they can implement *sharia*, the social world in which it is possible to do good works, a social world that is all-encompassing, regulating most aspects of their lives."[145] While the tawhid sets the stage and

---

[143]The concept of *jihad* will be discussed in greater detail in the coming pages.

[144]Schuon, 39.

[145]Mark Gould, "*Eschatology and Soteriology: Religious Commitment and Its Consequences in Islam and Christianity*" (Department of Sociology, Haverford College), draft paper submitted for publication, August 2003, 18.

teaches Muslims what should be believed, it is the obligations and *shariah* that provide the orthopractical guide regarding how to behave.[146]

In summary, Islamic scholars emphasize that belief alone is not enough. Man must practically and correctly perform all the duties required of him by the Islamic faith. This is why almost all Islamic religious manuals go into meticulous detail about the correct way that each of the ritualistic obligations must be performed.[147] The modern-day Egyptian Islamic scholar Sayyid Qutb summarizes this well:

> One of the characteristic marks of this faith is the fact that it is essentially a unity. It is at once worship and work, religious law and exhortation. . . . [T]he essential spirit of this religion is found in this—that practical work is religious work, for religion is inextricably bound up with life and can never exist in the isolation of idealism in some world of the conscious alone.[148]

Christian Soteriology. The point of departure between Christianity and Islam is the anthropology of man. Christianity's dim view of human nature asserts that mankind has hopelessly fallen prey to its sinful nature. This stands in strong contrast to the Islamic concept of *fitra*. As seen previously, in Christianity, man's depravity is profound, to the point where Christian doctrine asserts that nothing that man can do is capable of saving him from condemnation. Instead, Christian soteriology relies purely on divine grace. John Newton captured the essence of this doctrine when he penned these famous lines: "Amazing grace—how sweet the sound—that saved a wretch like me." In effect, sin acts as the great equalizer of humanity, making each person responsible for his wrongdoing and incapable of meritoriously gaining his salvation by works. In the Christian perspective, there is no race, ethnicity, nationality, or creed that escapes this condemnation—all are equally and irrevocably fallen. Salvation is presented as a gift to mankind, given by a merciful and loving God who wishes to reconcile his creation to himself. Thus, St. Paul writes in the New Testament: "*For it is by grace you have been saved, through faith—and this not from yourself, it is the gift of God—not by works, so that no one can boast. For we are God's workmanship, created in Christ Jesus to do good works, which God prepared in advance for us to do* (Ephesians 2: 8-10)." Christians, according to the Bible, cannot even take credit for their own faith. Rather, that faith is also a divine gift, thereby ensuring that no believer can credit that faith as meritorious for salvation.

---

[146]Norman Anderson, *Islam in the Modern World*, 43.

[147]Geisler and Saleeb, 126-27.

[148]Sayyid Qutb, *Social Justice in Islam*, trans. John B. Hardie (Oneonta, NY: Islamic Publications International, 2000), 27-29.

The Christian doctrine of grace emerged during the Reformation, when Luther struggled to understand why the traditional means offered by the church—the sacraments, prayer, and attendance at Mass—gave him no respite from spiritual fears. In reading and pondering the Pauline epistles, Luther gained a new realization and sense of peace as a result of the doctrine of grace. Man, he asserted, was justified by faith alone—*sola gratia*. In other words, "what 'justifies' a man is not what the church knew as 'works' (prayer, alms, the sacraments, holy living) but 'faith alone,' an inward bent of spirit given to each soul directly by God." Good works, Luther thought, "were the consequence and external evidence of this inner grace, but in no way its cause. A man did not 'earn' grace by doing good; he did the good because he possessed the grace of God."[149] Thus, Luther would write in his monumental *On Christian Liberty*:

> Good works do not make a good man, but a good man does good works. Bad works do not make a bad man, but a bad man does bad works. Thus it is always necessary that the substance or person should be good before any good works can be done, and that good works should follow and proceed from a good person. As Christ says: "A good tree cannot bring forth evil fruit, neither can a corrupt tree bring forth good fruit."[150]

The Christian doctrine of grace stipulates that salvation is obtained by grace through faith. Grace, in that God the father freely and lovingly offered his son as an atoning sacrifice for the sins of mankind. Faith, in that God (not ritualistic observances embedded in a theocentric social structure) is the enabler, convicting individual believers of sin, and making them personally aware of their need to accept His free gift of salvation. Good works come into play, Luther proclaimed, because they are evidence of a change in the individual after the individual believer comprehends a personal need for salvation. They are a sign to others of spiritual conviction and change, but they are not meritorious for salvation.

Summary: Islamic Orthopraxy—Christian Orthodoxy. Soteriology perhaps represents the most significant doctrinal difference between Islam and Christianity. Islam's orthopractical imperatives lead to a system of ritualistic obligations that compel the faithful along a never-ending quest for salvation. Muslims live under persistent uncertainty about the successful completion of this quest; ultimately, their afterworldly lives hang in the balance. In the end, good works will be balanced against evil deeds. As is written in the Qur'an, "*Then those*

---

[149]Palmer and Coulton, 75.

[150]Martin Luther, "Sola Fide, Sola Scriptura," in *Western Heritage: A Reader*, 1st rev. ed., ed. History Department, Hillsdale College (Acton, MA: Tapestry Press, 2000), 463.

whose balance (of good deeds) is heavy, they will attain salvation: But those whose balance is light, will be those who have lost their souls; in Hell will they abide. The Fire will burn their faces, and they will therein grin, with their lips displaced (Surah *Al Mu'minun*, 23: 102-104)."[151] The Qur'an speaks highly of those who meritoriously earn their salvation from Allah: "*And there is the type of man who gives his life to earn the pleasure of Allah; and Allah is full of kindness to (his) devotees (Surah Al Baqarah, 2:207).*"[152] A Muslim can never have eternal assurance, because the weighing of deeds does not occur until the end. As Al-Faruqi wrote, "Islam denies that a human can attain religious felicity on the basis of faith alone . . . only the works and deeds constitute justification in God's eyes. . . *Religious justification is thus the Muslims' great eternal hope, never their complacent certainty, nor for even a fleeting moment* [emphasis in the original]."[153] Al-Ghazali praises the example of one Muslim, a certain Alqamah, who was once asked if he was a believer. He replied: "I do hope so. If it be the will of God."[154]

The impetus to work harder, given this lack of assurance, should not be discounted in Islam. The focus is on tipping the balance in one's favor, and the ritualistic obligations, along with the entire dogma of Islamic religious thought, provide mechanisms to do so. It was Ibn Taymiyya, the 14th century Islamic scholar, who argued that for Islamic soteriology, man's focus was to understand Allah's will and become ever more obedient to his commands.[155] As W. Montgomery Watt eloquently states, "Islam does not normally think of the rights of man because it is more conscious of the commands of God."[156] The emphasis on deeds, practical works, and meritorious achievements is unmistakable. Ultimately, one cannot but be struck by the fact that for the Muslim, there may be expectation of salvation, but not, as Dr. Woodberry puts it, certainty of salvation. "Put more starkly," Anderson writes, "the salient impression one gets from Islamic theology as a whole is that of the sovereign Lord for whose mercy one may certainly hope, but of which one can never be assured."[157] For this reason, Muslims focus on obligatory and supererogatory works to assuage their doubt—to gain merit by obeying the commands of God, accepting of the dogmas of Islam, and diligently performing its prescribed duties of prayer, fasting, almsgiving, pilgrimage, and jihad.[158]

---

[151]*The Meaning of the Holy Qur'an.*

[152]*The Meaning of the Holy Qur'an.*

[153]Al-Faruqi quoted in Geisler and Saleeb, 128.

[154]Al-Faruqi quoted in Geisler and Saleeb, 128.

[155]Geisler and Saleeb, 49.

[156]W. Montgomery Watt, *Islamic Political Thought* (Edinburgh: Edinburgh University Press, 1999), 121.

[157]Anderson, *God's Law and God's Love*, 100.

[158]Anderson, *Islam in the Modern World*, 217.

Conversely, Christian soteriology starts with assurance. Given that "*God so loved the world that he gave his only begotten Son that whosoever will believe shall have eternal life*" (John 3:16), believing Christians understand that the doctrines of grace assure their eternity. This places their works in a non-meritorious light. Persistent works reveal a saved soul, rather than promoting its salvation. It is, of course, correct, as one scholar writes, that "various forms of Christianity, including Roman Catholicism, emphasize works as an instrument of salvation, as an instrument to God's grace . . . Even so, in Islam the expectation is that God's justice will entail salvation for those who fulfill their obligations. In Christianity, the capacity to fulfill God's obligations is compromised by original sin; faith in God, even when complemented by works, is the crucial variable evoking God's mercy."[159]

The Christian focus on "grace through faith" tends to produce less of an imperative to rigorously structure society for the accomplishment of ritualistic obligations. This is because the doctrine of grace absolves Christians from the requirement to meritoriously earn salvation. Instead, Christians—having obtained assurance through their soteriology—are challenged by a very different, dual imperative. First, through a process called sanctification, Christians seek to allow God's grace to gradually transform the believer's self-focused sinful nature into a nature that more reflects God's love and God's righteousness. The end result of Christian soteriology is for the individual believer to know God and to conform more closely to His character. Second, Christians are encouraged to live up to the challenge of Christ's commission to witness to non-believers throughout the world about the free gift of God's grace; in other words, to evangelize the lost and spread the message of the gospel. It is noteworthy that these two imperatives alone engender no political, social, or cultural structuring requirements—save the right to religious self-expression.

Theological Doctrines: *Eschatology*

The final component of theological doctrine is eschatology, the study of the hereafter or after-life. Both Islam and Christianity concern themselves with a final divine judgment that is believed to be inevitable due to the presence and influence of evil in the natural order as well as in mankind. Both religions place the unfaithful or unbelievers in hell or purgatory. Both religions also assert that there will be a final place for the faithful or the redeemed—for Islam this is paradise, and for Christianity it is heaven.[160] The pathways to that final place, as described above, are very different. The Islamic faithful hope to go to paradise

---

[159]Gould, 17.

[160]The concepts of Christian heaven and Islamic paradise are explored more fully later in this chapter.

after having their ritualistic works balanced favorably against their sinful deeds. Redeemed Christians claim their admission to heaven by faith through God's grace. In Islam and Christianity, the visions of—and man's purpose in—paradise and heaven are also very different.

The scales of justice depicted on ruins in Baku region, Azerbaijan.
Photo by author.

The Islamic Day of Judgment and Vision of Paradise. The Qur'an addresses the day of divine judgment in the following way:

> (It is) a Day whereon men will be like moths scattered about,
> And the mountains will be like carded wool.
> Then he whose balance (of good deeds) will be (found) heavy,
> Will be in a Life of good pleasure and satisfaction.
> But he whose balance (of good deeds) will be (found) light,
> Will have his home in a (bottomless) Pit (Surah Al Qari'ah, 101: 4-9).[161]

The focus of divine judgment is on the most discriminate weighing of man's deeds. The Qur'an specifies in Surah 99 that an atom's weight of good or evil could make a difference in the final accounting. Al Mawdudi, in his commentary on the Qur'an, writes about this passage: "it has been said that men on that Day, rising

---

[161]*The Meaning of the Holy Qur'an.*

from their graves, will come out in their varied groups from all corners of the earth, to be shown their deeds and works, and their presentation of the deeds will be so complete and detailed that not an atom's weight of any good or evil act will be left unnoticed or hidden."[162] Professor Mark Gould, a Harvard-educated sociologist and head of the Department of Sociology at Haverford College, notes that there is a strong structure of religious commitment embedded in this type of eschatology.[163] The individual believer's powerful desire to be preferred by Allah on the final judgment day can engender significant passions to secure future success in this endeavor. Indeed, as Gould writes, it can facilitate a commitment to extraordinary actions, especially to those that could short-circuit Allah's weighing of activities on the scales of justice at the Last Judgment.[164] In some cases, it facilitates supererogatory displays beyond the normal, more traditional religious obligations. Thus, for example, with an act of *jihad*, if a believer survives, he accumulates credits for following God's commands, and if he dies a martyr, he gains access to paradise.

***Jihad* as a Supererogatory Mechanism**. The concept of *jihad* can generally be divided into an internal, personal exertion against one's evil desires (sometimes characterized as the greater *jihad*), and an external, military struggle against threats to the Islamic community *writ large* (sometimes characterized as the lesser *jihad*). Al-Ghazali, speaking on the former, wrote that "every one who gives himself wholly to God in the war against his own desires (*nafs*) is a martyr when he meets death going forward without turning his back. So the holy warrior is he who makes war against his own desires, as it has been explained by the Apostle of God. And the 'greater war' is the war against one's own desires, as the Companions said: We have returned from the lesser war unto the greater one, meaning thereby the war against their own desires."[165] It is within this context that Gould explains the influence of the more ascetically-oriented Sufism on the concept of *jihad*. "As all the works prescribed by the canonical law reached their real value when they were considered as symbols of spiritual ideas," Gould writes, "so the true martyr in this system became he that partook of warfare not against the infidels but against his own sensual nature, in order to reach a more spiritual stage."[166] From this perspective, the primary purpose of *jihad* is a struggle against personal sin and impurity. This battle against one's nafs appears to be an important element of modern Sufi philosophy. It seems worth noting, however, that based on numerous discussions with Sufis and with both Shia and

---

[162] Al Mawdudi's commentary on the Surah 99 in *The Meaning of the Holy Qur'an*.

[163] Gould, 16-17.

[164] Gould, 13, 16-17, 27.

[165] Al-Ghazali quoted in A. J. Wensinck, *Semietische Studien Uit De Nalatenschap* (Leiden: A.W. Sijthoff, 1941), 96.

[166] See Gould, explanations in the lengthy footnote 13, 11.

Sunni clerics, this particular interpretation of *jihad* is not universally accepted by Muslims, and tends to be limited to some Shia and mainly to the more ascetically-oriented Sufis.

Indeed, the more visceral and supererogatory concept of *jihad* is the one propagated by the prophet Mohammed, numerous *hadiths*, the Qur'an itself, as well as by many Islamic jurists and scholars, including the renowned 14th century jurist Ibn Taymiyya. This concept of jihad is, Taymiyya tells us, "the *jihad* against the unbelievers (*kuffar*), the enemies of God and his Messenger."[167] The struggle, according to the Qur'an, must continue until there is no more persecution and all mankind's religion belongs to Allah: "*And fight them until there is no more tumult or oppression, and there prevail justice and Faith in Allah altogether and everywhere* (Surah 8:39)."[168] Taymiyya underscores this by asserting that "all lawful warfare is essentially jihad"—which is ultimately the quest to make the true religion (understood to be Islam) universal and to recognize that God's word is uppermost: "*But the word of Allah is exalted to the heights: for Allah is Exalted in might* (Surah 9:40)."

According to Taymiyya, jihad "is the best voluntary [religious] act that man can perform. All scholars agree that it is better than the *hajj* (greater pilgrimage) and the *umra* (lesser pilgrimage), than voluntary *salat* [alms giving] and voluntary fasting, as the Koran and Sunna indicate."[169] The prophet Mohammad himself is quoted as saying: "The head of the affair is Islam, its central pillar is the *salat* and its summit is the *jihad*."[170] The following statement is also widely attributed to the prophet: "In Paradise there are a hundred grades with intervals as wide as the distance between the sky and the earth. All these God has prepared for those who take part in *jihad*."[171] The *hadiths* of Al-Bukhari[172] state that the prophet said: "Him whose feet have become dusty in the way of God [jihad] will God save from hellfire." The *hadiths* of Muslim[173] attribute the following to the prophet: "A day and a night spent in *ribat*[174] are better than one month spent in fasting and vigils. If he dies [in the fulfillment of this task], he will receive the

---

[167]Ibn Taymiyya, "The Religious and Moral Doctrine of Jihad," in Rudolph Peters, *Jihad in Classical and Modern Islam* (Princeton: Markus Wiener Publishers, 1996), 44.

[168]*The Meaning of the Holy Qur'an.*

[169]Taymiyya, 47.

[170]The Prophet Mohammed quoted in Taymiyya, 47.

[171]The Prophet Mohammed quoted in Taymiyya, 47.

[172]The Al-Bukhari are one of the six canonical, authoritative traditions and perhaps also the most widely-distributed one, quoted in Taymiyya, 47.

[173]The Muslim are also one of the six canonical, authoritative traditions, quoted in Taymiyya, 47.

[174]*Ribat* is a verbal noun meaning remaining at the frontiers of Islam with the intention of defending Islamic territory against the enemies. See Rudolph Peters, 178.

recompense of his deeds and subsistence, and he will be protected from the Angel of the Grave."

There are significant eschatological benefits connected to the concept of *jihad*. Allah promises forgiveness of sins and admission into paradise as recompense for the struggle in the way of God: "*That ye believe in Allah and His Messenger, and that ye strive (your utmost) in the Cause of Allah, with your property and your persons: that will be best for you, if ye but knew! He will forgive you your sins, and admit you to Gardens beneath which Rivers flow, and to beautiful Mansions in Gardens of Eternity: that is indeed the supreme Achievement (Surah Al Saff, 61: 11-12).*"[175] According to the Qur'an, Allah shows preference toward those who perform *jihad*:

> *Not equal are those Believers who sit (at home) and receive no hurt, and those who strive and fight in the cause of Allah with their goods and their persons. Allah hath granted a grade higher to those who strive and fight with their goods and persons than to those who sit (at home). Unto all (in Faith) hath Allah promised good: but those who strive and fight hath he distinguished above those who sit (at home) by a special reward, Ranks specially bestowed by him and forgiveness and mercy. (Surah Al Nisa', 4: 95-96)*[176]

In a doctrine where life in the hereafter is gained meritoriously and one's deeds are balanced in divine judgment, the benefits described above are of tremendous consequence.

Taymiyya offers three broad reasons why *jihad* is unequalled by other subjects as far as the reward and merit of human deeds is concerned:

1. The [first] reason is that the benefit of jihad is general, extending not only to the person who participates in it but also to others, both in a religious and a temporal sense.
2. [Secondly,] *jihad* implies all kinds of worship, both in its inner and outer forms. More than any other act it implies love and devotion to God . . . *Any individual or community that participates in it, finds itself between two blissful outcomes: either victory and triumph or martyrdom and Paradise.*
3. [Thirdly,] all creatures must live and die. *Now, it is in jihad that one can live and die in ultimate happiness, both in this world and in the Hereafter.* [emphasis added][177]

---

[175]*The Meaning of the Holy Qur'an.*
[176]*The Meaning of the Holy Qur'an.*
[177]Taymiyya, 48-49.

In this context, *jihad* is not just a supererogatory mechanism to gain access to paradise. It is also an act of worship, love, and devotion to God that benefits not only the individual performing the act, but also the greater community of believers. To summarize, the majority of classical and modern Islamic commentaries on *jihad* seem to endow it with important supererogatory promises. This complements the primary focus of the entire Islamic orthopractical system, in which every believer is striving to meritoriously gain access to paradise.

The Islamic concept of Paradise. Muslims look forward to a hereafter filled with pleasure and sensual gratification, regardless of whether they gain access via a life of meritorious religious obligations, or an act or acts of supererogatory *jihad*. It seems reasonable to assert that based on the evidence presented in the *hadiths* and the Qur'an, the focus of Islamic paradise is the gratification of the individual believer. Paradise is presented as a reward for man's earthly efforts: "*Allah created the heavens and the earth for just ends, and in order that each soul may find the recompense of what it has earned, and none of them be wronged* (Surah *Al Jathiyah* 45: 22)."[178] Accordingly, sinners will also receive their just rewards: "*And thou wilt see the sinners that day bound together in fetters; Their garments of liquid pitch, and their faces covered with fire; That Allah may requite each soul according to its deserts; and verily Allah is swift in calling to account* (Surah *Ibrahim* 14: 49-51)."[179]

Those who are admitted into paradise can look forward to times of blissful existence, underscored by pleasures provided by Allah, on whose account they will be content, peaceful, and secure:

> *But the sincere (and devoted) servants of Allah,*
> *For them is a Sustenance determined,*
> *Fruits (Delights); and they (shall enjoy) honour and dignity,*
> *In Gardens of Felicity,*
> *Facing each other on Thrones (of dignity):*
> *Round will be passed to them a Cup from a clear flowing fountain,*
> *Crystal white, of a taste delicious to those who drink (thereof),*
> *Free from headiness; nor will they suffer intoxication therefrom.*
> *And besides them will be chaste women, restraining their glances, with*
> *big eyes (of wonder and beauty).* (Surah *Al Saffat* 37:40-48)[180]

---

[178]*The Meaning of the Holy Qur'an.*
[179]*The Meaning of the Holy Qur'an.*
[180]*The Meaning of the Holy Qur'an.*

Much has been made in Western writing about the apparent sexual overtones of the end of this passage. However, the chaste women described here have a function that may be more accurately characterized as virtuous adulation rather than physical gratification. As the commentator explains: "They are chaste, not bold with their glances: but their eyes are big with wonder and beauty, prefiguring grace, innocence, and a refined capacity of appreciation and admiration."[181] Nonetheless, the focus of this part of the passage remains the gratification of the individual's sense of honor and virtue. In addition, the faithful will also be freely bestowed with fruit and meat, and anything that they desire, all to be served by devoted, youthful, and handsome man servants.[182] The Islamic afterlife is thus characterized as an ideal life in a paradise conceived around human concepts of peace, relaxation, honor, and sensual pleasure.

Christian Eschatology and the Concept of Heaven. That Christian doctrine foresees a final judgment, and that in that judgment there will be a separation of the faithful from the unrepentant lost—of wheat from the chaff—is a familar concept, even among non-believers. The righteousness and sinless nature of God demands a final accounting of mankind's sinful nature. How true Christian believers gain access to heaven was described previously. The eternality of that final judgment is emphasized throughout the Bible. As Jesus himself states: *"Then they will go away to eternal punishment, but the righteous to eternal life* (Matthew 25:46)." The Apostle Paul chronicles how Christians will be taken up into heaven: *"We will not all sleep, but we will all be changed—in a flash, in the twinkling of an eye, at the last trumpet. For the trumpet will sound, the dead will be raised imperishable, and we will be changed* (1 Corinthians 15:51-52)."

In Christianity, hell is a place where non-believers are consigned for eternal punishment. "In this place they will be totally deprived of the divine favor, will experience an endless disturbance of life, will suffer positive pains in body and soul, and will be subject to pangs of conscience, anguish, and despair."[183] Hell is a place where the intensity of the physical torments will only be supplanted by the deep and sustained agony of the soul due to its eternal and irreversible separation from God. Yet for Christians the eschatological future is not a paradise—in the sense that it is for Muslims. The focus in heaven is not on man; it is neither a place for sensual gratification nor a place where man is to be accorded honor and praise. Instead, the focus of the redeemed in heaven is the honor and glory of

---

[181]Commentary by Yusuf Ali in *The Meaning of the Holy Qur'an.*

[182]See Surah Al Tur (52:22-24).

[183]Louis Berkhof, *Summary of Christian Doctrine* (Grand Rapids, MI: William B. Eerdmans, 2000), 195.

God. As shown in the Revelation, the heavenly center of attention is the creator and master of the universe, and the adulation accorded him is never-ending:

Whenever the living creatures give glory, honor and thanks to him who sits on the throne and who lives for ever and ever, the twenty-four elders fall down before him who sits on the throne, and worship him who lives for ever and ever. They lay their crowns before the throne and say: You are worthy, our Lord and God, to receive glory and honor and power, for you created all things, and by your will they were created and have their being (Revelation 4: 9-11).

Christian church and Muslim Mosque together in northern Jordan.
Photo by author.

Christianity holds that as long as believers live in the secular, fallen world, their ultimate purpose in creation cannot be achieved—namely the full enjoyment and worship of God. Heaven is the place where that purpose will be fulfilled. On earth, man's intellectual, emotional, and spiritual limitations serve as impediments to that goal. In heaven, Christians will be made perfectly blessed in the full enjoyment of God for all eternity. Thus, as one scholar has written, "in heaven believers can await eternal life—but not merely endless life, but life in all its fullness, without the imperfections and disturbances of the present. This fullness of life is enjoyed in communion with God, which is really the essence of eternal life."[184] Heaven represents the climax of Christian doctrine—where man, through original sin, has fallen away from the creator God; God, because of his love for mankind, offered his son Jesus Christ as an atoning sacrifice for man's sin; man, in accepting God's gift of grace through faith, individually acknowledges guilt in sin and the need for salvation; God, at the end of this present world, effects reconciliation between himself

---

[184]Berkhof, 196.

and the redeemed—those who accept the gift of salvation. The Revelation summarizes these doctrines in the following way:

> *I saw the Holy City, the new Jerusalem, coming down out of heaven from God, prepared as a bride beautifully dressed for her husband. And I heard a loud voice from the throne saying, "Now the dwelling of God is with men, and he will live with them. They will be his people, and God himself will be with them and be their God. He will wipe every tear from their eyes. There will be no more death or mourning or crying or pain, for the old order of things has passed away* (Revelation 21:2-4)."

Summary: Islamic Paradise—Christian Heaven. As in the case of the other theological doctrines, an analysis of eschatology reveals that while Islam and Christianity have superficial similarities, they are markedly different in their core ideas. "In Islam, God's messengers, and most especially his last and final messenger, Muhammad, have told believers how they must act to be saved. God has requested nothing that believers cannot do. If they follow God's commandments (as enunciated in the Qur'an and the *Sunna*, the tradition), on the Day of Judgment God will judge them fairly, weighing the good against the bad.[185]

The preponderance of orthopractical Islam has focused on developing the ritualistic obligations, laws, and societal guidelines that serve as means to meritoriously gaining access to paradise. Because of the persistent lack of assurance in this quest, a structure of supererogatory religious commitment also developed. As Gould explains, this motivation stems from the eschatological premises of the religion, from the certainty that God has laid out a straight path, and that, if that path is followed, Muslims will, at the Last Judgment, be deemed worthy of everlasting life in paradise. Significantly, the promise of an immediate entrée into paradise for the martyrs of *jihad* is encouraged by the persistent lack of assurance. In Gould's words, "they may not know whether God has predetermined them to die or to gain victory in *jihad*, but they know that in the first instance their reward is immediate, while in the second instance, they have enhanced their chances of being rewarded at the Day of Judgment."[186] A paradise that promises honor, adoration, and physical pleasures awaits them.

On the other hand, Christians are incapable of earning heaven. They are doomed by sin, and their situation would be hopeless without God's grace. Christians believe that it is to the glory of God that his love shows a divine and salvationary grace that saves the undeserving sinner. Christian salvation is

---

[185]Gould, 6.
[186]Gould, 27.

non-meritorious—and because it is divine in origin, there is no doubt or lack of assurance and there is no weighing of deeds in the final judgment. The price has been paid, and the redeemed have been purchased by the blood of Jesus Christ. Christians anticipate a life in heaven that will bring a long-awaited reunion with a sovereign and loving God.

Scriptures and Canon

Having discussed the key premises of theological doctrine, we now move to compare and contrast the holy writings of the two religions. This requires a focus on the collective written and oral traditions that are accepted by believers as both authoritative and as doctrinally applicable. In Islam, this amounts to the Qur'an, as well as the collected *hadiths* and juristical writings. In Christianity, the canon is the Bible.

The Dogma of Islam. Islam promulgates a broad array of official and doctrinal writings. Of course, the Qur'an is accepted as the *ipsissima verba* of God—but the Qur'an does not stand alone as authoritative in Islamic theology and jurisprudence. The *hadiths* (or traditions), while equally inspired and based on the life of the prophet, are not inspired in the same form; and the "whole vast structure of Muslim law and theology, developed by generations of jurists and commentators" acts as a binding mechanism on the mind and conscience of true believers.[187]

Undoubtedly, the Qur'an is the foundation of Islam. It represents the final revelation of God. It is final in the sense that it came after the Torah was revealed to the Jews and the Gospels of the New Testament were given to the Christians. Muslims believe that only the Qur'an is God's final revelation about his perfect religion—Islam. The revelation is believed to have come from the archangel Gabriel to the prophet over a period of 23 years. Mohammad did not write down his revelations, but passed them on in the oral tradition. This adds to the mystique of the Qur'an, for Muslims believe in what one scholar has called the *i'jaz* or *mu'jizah* of the Qur'an—its matchlessness and incomparability.[188] Muslims hold that "the Qur'an cannot be rivaled in form or in worth. This superlative eloquence is regarded as the crowning evidence of its divine origin, the more so because it is found on the lips of a Prophet who disowned all poetic competence and was understood to be ummi, or 'illiterate.'"[189] The hadiths of Al-Bukhari relate that those who surrounded Mohammad during his life as the prophet wrote down his revelations on pieces of paper, stones, palm-leaves, and bits of leather.[190] Eventu-

---

[187]Anderson, *Islam in the Modern World*, 39.

[188]Kenneth Cragg and R. Marston Speight, *The House of Islam*, 3d ed. (Belmont, CA: Wadsworth Publishing, 1988), 32.

[189]Cragg and Speight, 32.

[190]Geisler and Saleeb, 92.

ally, about a year after the prophet died, the various revelations were assembled and redacted into the format that is now recognized as the Qur'an.

To a Muslim, the Qur'an has its own special mystique, derived from the language of the revelation, Arabic, as well as its style of prose. To understand its full scope, one must look beyond its important doctrinal content and get a sense of what Muslims see as its divine magic and miraculous power. That is, a sense of "metaphysical and eschatological wisdom, of mystical psychology and theurgic [magical] power [that] lie hidden under a veil of breathless utterances often clashing in shock, of crystalline and fiery images, but also of passages majestic in rhythm, woven of every fiber of the human condition."[191] The language of the Qur'an is considered the sacred language of the revelation and of the religion. As such, Arabic is accorded special status because Allah chose it above all others to make his revelation known. It must be said that translations of the Qur'an from its original Arabic are generally not considered canonically legitimate by doctrinaire Muslims, and certainly are looked upon as rhythmically and ritually inferior by Muslims at large.[192]

Muslim students learning how to chant the Qur'an at Al-Azhar Mosque, Cairo.
Photo by author.

Structurally, the Qur'an is divided into 114 surahs, which can be viewed as being like chapters in the Christian Bible. Collectively about as long as the New

---

[191]Schuon, 48.
[192]Schuon, 49.

Testament, the Qur'an is not arranged in any particular chronological order, and does not read like an integrated, historical narrative. It seems to be laid out by chapter length, generally from longest to shortest, and can roughly be divided into the Medina and Mecca surahs. The roughly ninety Meccan surahs were revealed when the prophet was struggling with the pagan religion around him from A.D. 609-622. They are broad and metaphysical, with themes of impending judgment, warnings toward unbelief, and poetic and fervent descriptions of the divine. The subsequently revealed Medina surahs (A.D. 622-632) came after Mohammed and his followers emigrated to Medina. They tend to focus on the societal and political structure of the *umma* (the community of the believers), on rules for everyday living, and on the proper establishment of religious rituals and observances.

The prevailing opinion among scholars is that most translations fail to preserve the unity and linguistic cohesiveness of the original Arabic. But beyond this language barrier, the literary structure of the Qur'an also seems to pose unique challenges. As Ignaz Goldziher comments, "there is one thing even prejudice cannot deny. The people entrusted . . . with the redaction of the unordered parts of the book occasionally went about their work in a very clumsy fashion. With the exception of the earliest Meccan surahs, which the Prophet had used before his emigration to Medina as liturgical texts, and which consist of self-contained pieces so brief as to make them less vulnerable to editorial confusion, the parts of the holy book, and particularly certain Medinese surahs, often display a disorder and lack of coherence that caused considerable difficulty and toil to later commentators who had to regard the established order as basic and sacrosanct."[193] On the other hand, Yusuf K. Ibish, a Muslim scholar and professor, writes that

> I have not yet come across a western man who understands what the Qur'an is . . . There are western orientalists who have devoted their life to the study of the Qur'an, its text, the analysis of its words, discovering that this word is Abyssinian, that word Greek by origin. . . . But all this is immaterial. The Qur'an was divinely inspired, then it was compiled, and what we have now is the expression of God's Will among men.[194]

Some of the difficulty in understanding the Qur'an may stem from the change in Mohammad's role from Mecca to Medina. Though Mohammad's impact is more fully explored in the following section, suffice it to say that while in Medina, Mohammad was a preacher, passionately driven to change people's focus from what he viewed as dark and pagan practices toward the one

---

[193]See lengthy footnote on p. 28-29 in Goldziher.
[194]Ibish quoted in Chris Waddy, *The Muslim Mind* (London: Longman, 1976), 14.

true religion. By the time Mohammad reached Medina, he served primarily as a political and military leader—in effect a prince, now concerned with ordering and directing the affairs of his followers, and protecting them from both internal and external threats.

That the Qur'an is the basis for Islam is indisputable. However, it is equally relevant that Islam's canon of sacred and doctrinal writing extends well beyond the Qur'an. Goldziher wisely observed that "it would be a great error if, in a comprehensive characterization of Islam, we considered the Qur'an our most important source, and an even greater error if we based our opinion of Islam exclusively on the holy book of the Muslim community. The book covers at most the first two decades of the evolution of Islam. . . . No other written book in the world is likely to have had such a share of admiration," and yet, as Goldziher concludes, "we must not overlook that the Qur'an by itself will not at all suffice for an understanding of Islam as an historical phenomenon."[195] Before briefly engaging these extra-qur'anic elements of Islam, we must consider the three mechanisms with which Islamic scholars and jurists have expanded and argued their doctrines within and beyond the Qur'an: *nasikh* (abrogation), *ijma* (agreement), and *qiyas* (analogy).

The principle of abrogation is related to the Islamic concept of progressive revelation. This concept means that Islam is the perfected revelation of divine truth, as evolved from the earlier manifestations of monotheism. Judaism and Christianity are both seen by Muslims to be descendents of the religion of Abraham, though both contained errors and flaws. Islam, while of the same origin, is the final, flawless, progressive and divine revelation of that tradition. This doctrine of nasikh, or progressive revelation/abrogation, is imbedded in the Qur'an. In Surah Al Baqarah (2:106), the Qur'an states the following: "*None of Our revelations do We abrogate or cause to be forgotten, but We substitute something better or similar: knowest thou not that Allah hath power over all things?*" What is meant by this passage? As one commentator explains, "if we take it in a general sense, it means that God's Message from age to age is always the same, but that its form may differ according to the needs and exigencies of the time. That form was different as given to Moses and then to Jesus and then to Muhammad."[196] Thus and within the context of progressive revelation, abrogation implies that there is both continuity and change—continuity in the sense that God's revelation is consistent across time, but also change in the sense that the divine will is revealed differently in different circumstances.

---

[195]Goldziher, 28-29.
[196]Commentary by Yusuf Ali in *The Meaning of the Holy Qur'an.*

There are several examples that demonstrate this concept. The initial practice of facing toward Jerusalem during ritualistic prayer (Surah 2:143) was abrogated by the change in Surah 2:144 to now turn toward Mecca: *"Turn then thy face in the direction of the Sacred Mosque: wherever ye are, turn your faces in that direction."* The importance of ritualistic prayer did not diminish, but the direction that the faithful were to face was changed. In another example, the faithful were initially directed to fast during the ten days of Ashura—based on a Jewish tradition. Later, fasting during Ashura was abrogated by new guidance: *"Ramadan is the (month) in which was sent down the Quran as a guide to mankind, also clear (Signs) for guidance and judgment (between right and wrong). So every one of you who is present (at his home) during that month should spend it in fasting* (Surah 2:185)." Again, the necessity of the fast continued, while the method and timing of fulfilling it was changed. A third example of abrogation applies to polytheists and how conflicts with Jews and pagan unbelievers caused a change in the revelation. If contact with polytheists could not be avoided, and if the Muslim faithful were increasingly subjected to challenges by other so-called polytheistic religions, then the way the polytheists were supposed to be treated evolved over time. Initially, when Mohammad was still in Mecca, the faithful were ordered to turn away from the ignorant ones and from the unbelievers and to ignore them or avoid them altogether (see for example, Surah 25:63, 43:88-89, 7:199). However, after the migration to Medina, with Mohammad as the leader of an increasing and influential community of believers, in close proximity to the pagans, a new revelation came down from Allah:

> *Fight in the cause of Allah those who fight you, but do not transgress limits; for Allah loveth not transgressors. And slay them wherever ye catch them, and turn them out from where they have turned you out; for tumult and oppression are worse than slaughter; but fight them not at the Sacred Mosque, unless they (first) fight you there; but if they fight you, slay them. Such is the reward of those who suppress faith* (Surah 2:190-91).

Thus, the principle of avoiding pagan ignorance was confronted with the reality of an expanding community of believers that no longer was able to avoid contact with nonbelievers. The order to "turn away from the ignorant" was abrogated or superseded by the new "order of the sword."

The second of the three interpretive mechanisms is the principle of *ijma*, which means agreement or consensus. *Ijma*, according to Goldziher, is "the key to a grasp of the historical evolution of Islam in its political, theological, and legal aspects." It is based on the following often quoted statement of the prophet: "My community will never agree on error."[197] It encapsulates

---

[197]Goldziher, 50.

Mohammad's three-fold promise to the faithful: "Allah has granted you protection from three things: your Prophet lays no curse upon you, lest you utterly perish; the party of falsehood among you will never triumph over the party of truth; you will never agree on false doctrine."[198] The principle of *ijma* is the concept within Islam closest to the ecclesiastical sanction of the Catholic Church, or to a denominational resolution in Protestantism. *Ijma* had the power, though not overwhelmingly so, to smooth out differences among the various schools of jurisprudence and to promote the general and broader development of doctrine after Mohammad died in A.D. 632. While it is an important concept and in some ways resembles ecclesiastical sanction in Christianity, its authority was more nebulous and not as authoritatively defined. Notwithstanding, it served as a mechanism whereby that which was accepted by the entire Islamic community as "true and correct" was therefore assumed to be "true and correct." Goldziher concludes that "only the continued effectiveness of this principle, throughout the history of Islam, explains that certain religious phenomena gained the stamp of orthodoxy because they gained general acceptance, although in theory they should have been censured as being contrary to Islam."[199]

The third and final mechanism is *qiyas*, or analogy. Islamic scholars used the principle of *qiyas* to ground new developments in doctrine and jurisprudence in the foundation of the Qur'an and the earlier traditions. The doors of revelation closed when Mohammad died. Individual opinion about what was right and wrong was arguably an unacceptable basis for further development of doctrine and law. Therefore, scholars began to insist on the analogical extension of well-known or recognized texts in order to justify new situations that could legitimately be held to be covered by the same principles that the original texts enunciated.[200] Qiyas provided a way to avoid the appearance of subjectivity because it allowed scholars to develop logical extensions of previous doctrine—in the absence of an ecclesiastical body or council to sanction their work. In that sense, both ijma and qiyas provided legitimacy in the extra-qur'anic development of doctrine and law.

A discussion of the Islamic canon would not be complete without addressing the *hadiths* (or traditions) of Islam. The *hadiths*, of which there are literally thousands, base their legitimacy on their connection to the life of the prophet. After a time of oral transmission, they were mainly included in six recognized books, all of which derive their authority and authenticity from something that Mohammad

---

[198]Goldziher, 50.
[199]Goldziher, 51.
[200]Anderson, *Islam in the Modern World*, 48.

himself did, said or permitted to be said or done.[201] In other words, according to Anderson, "the normative element in the traditions is the *sunna* or practice of the Prophet which they alleged to establish . . . but the authority of the vast majority [of *hadiths*] rests on the belief that all the Prophet of Islam did, said, or permitted was divinely inspired in content, although in the *hadith* (in contradistinction to the Qur'an) this inspiration does not extend to the actual wording."[202] Perhaps the most famous collections are the Muslim and Al-Bukhari *hadiths*. The Al-Bukhari collection is said to have been condensed from an initial collection of over 600,000 down to 3,000—which shows how many of the initial traditions were deemed to be spurious.[203] Modern-day scholars continue to debate the accuracy of the hadiths. One accepted way of determining authenticity is to look for a historically verifiable chain of narration in addition to the basic details or substance of the specific tradition.

The Qur'an and the *hadiths* (which incorporate the sunna) form the foundation of the Islamic canon. That canon, through the mechanisms of nasikh (abrogation), ijma (agreement), and qiyas (analogy), has been expanded to formulate the doctrines of the major schools of Islamic jurisprudence and Islamic law, or shariah. Together, these elements form a comprehensive code of life covering every aspect and phase of human existence. Muslims believe that this canon promulgates the most reliable rules relating to social life, commerce and economics, marriage and inheritance, penal laws, and international conduct.[204] Ultimately, the entire Islamic code of conduct traces its origins back to the revelation provided by the prophet in the Qur'an, as well as to the day-to-day life and practices of the prophet, as revealed in the hadiths. It was the 14th-century Islamic scholar Ibn Taymiyya who wrote:

> The guidance and true religion which is in the shari'a brought by Mohammad is more perfect than what was in the two previous religious laws. . . . In the Torah, the Gospel [the New Testament] and the books of the prophets [the Old Testament] there are no useful forms of knowledge or upright deeds which are not found in the Qur'an, or else there is found that which is better. In the Qur'an there is found guidance and true religion in beneficial knowledge and upright deeds which are not in the other two books.[205]

---

[201] Anderson, *God's Law and God's Love*, 77.
[202] Anderson, 77.
[203] Anderson, 46.
[204] Geisler and Saleeb, 103.
[205] Ibn Taymiyya quoted in Geisler and Saleeb, 104.

The Christian Canon: The Bible. Christians believe that the entire Bible is the inspired word of God. They believe that the Holy Spirit acted upon the writers "in harmony with the laws of their own inner being, using them just as they were, with their character and temperament, their gifts and talents, their education and culture, their vocabulary and style."[206] The Holy Spirit guided the writers by illuminating their minds, aiding their memory, prompting them to write, repressing the influence of sin on their writings, and guiding them in the expression of their thoughts even to the choice of their words.[207] Christians assert that "this divine inspiration extends equally and fully to all parts of the writings—historical, poetical, doctrinal, and prophetical—as [it] appeared in the original manuscripts."[208]

Structurally, the Bible is presented as an integrated historical narrative that encompasses God's designs and purposes for man, man's fall from grace, and the fulfillment of God's covenant to restore man to himself. It begins with the creation of the world and ends with an eschatological treatise on the end of the world. Though the original Biblical texts were written in Hebrew, Aramaic, and Greek, most Christian scholars hold that the divine impetus in the original texts transcends the barriers of modern translations. In other words, there is no language preference—indeed, the Bible has been translated into more languages and dialects than any other book in the history of mankind.

Unlike the Qur'an, the Bible has been the subject of a great deal of academic criticism. Especially in the late 19th century, secular scholars developed so-called "higher" criticisms of the Bible in an effort to incorporate archeological discoveries and to reconstruct a naturalistic, historical account of ancient religious times.[209] David Strauss published *Das Leben Jesu* (the Life of Jesus) in 1835, asserting that Jesus' miracles were in fact modern mythology; Ferdinand Baur used Hegel's dialectic to suggest that the cohesion of the New Testament could never have emerged from the anti-thetical pictures of Christ and his work; in 1863 the famous French historian Ernest Renan, in *La Vie de Jesus* (The Life of Jesus) painted Jesus Christ as a simple-minded Galilean fisherman without divine power or intent; and there were numerous other criticisms that emerged from the post-Enlightenment academic milieu in Western universities.[210] These writings were, if nothing else, evidence of the increasing separation between the scientific rationalism of the secular realm, and the metaphysical claims of the religious realm.

---

[206]Berkhof, 20.

[207]Berkhof, 20.

[208]C. Donald Cole, *Basic Christian Faith* (Westchester, IL: Crossway Books), 1985.

[209]Palmer and Colton, 597.

[210]For further discussion on this topic, see Noll, 255-58.

Finally, the Bible stands as a unique source of doctrine in Christianity. Certainly among Protestants, but even among more traditionally minded Eastern Orthodox and Roman Catholics, there are no extra-Biblical texts that carry the same weight as, for example, the *hadiths* in Islam. While there were tensions between the extra-Biblical canonical texts of Roman Catholicism and the claim of the Reformation to proceed sola scriptura, these differences within Christianity do not have the same relevance and importance as do the broader dogmas of Islam. Ultimately, both Roman Catholics and Protestants come to base their key doctrines on the Biblical texts of the Old and New Testaments.[211]

Summary: The Collective Writings of Islam—the Book of Christianity. In conclusion, as with the key theological doctrines, at first glance, there are several similarities between the dogma of Islam and the Christian canon. Both religions assert the infallibility of their respective holy books. Both claim that the texts are divinely inspired. Both view alterations of the original scriptures as heretical. But there are significant differences: (1) while the Qur'an remains a relatively untouched, mystical document, the Bible has been the subject of vigorous secular analysis and criticism; (2) while the authenticity of the Qur'an is based exclusively upon the orally transmitted tradition of one divinely-inspired, illiterate individual, the Bible was chronicled by numerous writers who witnessed many of the events that they wrote about; (3) whereas the Qur'an forms the basis of a much larger doctrinal and juristical canon in Islam, the Bible stands by itself as the sole repository of Christian truth.

The Founding Prophets: Mohammad and Jesus Christ

Thus far we have addressed the key theological doctrines and the canons of both Islam and Christianity. Yet an overview of these religions would be dramatically incomplete without an understanding of the profound impact of Mohammad and Jesus Christ. Their lifestyles, interpretations, and teachings about the scriptures left indelible marks on the nature of their respective religions. Both Islam and Christianity owe their core ethos to the lives and characters of their prophets. Their legacies powerfully endure to this day.

Mohammad: Prophet and Prince of Islam. Apart from Allah and the sacred text of the Qur'an, the prophet Mohammad occupies the most exalted position in Islam. The Qur'an itself praises the model life of the prophet: "*Ye have indeed in the Messenger of Allah a beautiful pattern (of conduct) for any one whose hope is*

---

[211]The Eastern Orthodox, Roman Catholics, and Protestants have different ways of handling traditions. All three strains of Christianity would say that the Bible is the certain revelation from God. None of them, not even Protestantism, would discount the importance of tradition, though they have different ways of assessing the value and relevance of any given tradition.

in Allah and the Final Day, and who engages much in the praise of Allah (Surah *Al Ahzab*, 33:21)." The prophet is a source of guidance and inspiration for Muslims, and his life and personal habits, down to the discriminating detail, are held up as a model for all to follow. It is said that one ancient Muslim refrained from eating watermelon for most of his life because he could not ascertain whether the prophet spit the seeds out or swallowed them. One of the best-known Muslim scholars of all time, Al-Ghazali, wrote about the prophet in the following way:

> Know that the key to happiness is to follow the sunna [Mohammad's actions] and to imitate the Messenger of God in all his coming and going, his movement and rest, in his way of eating, his attitude, his sleep and his talk. . . . God has said: "What the messenger has brought—accept it, and what he has prohibited—refrain from it!" (59:7). That means, you have to sit while putting on trousers, and to stand when winding a turban, and to begin with the right foot when putting on shoes.[212]

This scrupulous attitude toward imitating the detailed behavior of Mohammad is not just an historical phenomenon, but continues to this day. As Annemarie Schimmel, a scholar of Islam at Harvard University, observes: "It is this ideal of the *imitatio Muhammadi* that has provided Muslims from Morocco to Indonesia with such uniformity of action: Wherever one may be, one knows how to behave when entering a house, which formulas of greeting to employ, what to avoid in good company, how to eat, and how to travel. For centuries Muslim children have been brought up in these ways."[213] As the Qur'an ultimately is focused on the divinity of Allah, so the thousands of *hadiths*, compiled in six official collections, pay tribute to the life of the beloved prophet. Kamal ud Din ad Damiri, in a popular Muslim classic, gives the following description of the prophet:

> Mohammed is the most favored of mankind, the most honored of all apostles...He is the best of prophets, and his nation is the best of nations...and his creed is the noblest of all creeds. He performed manifest miracles, and possessed great qualities. He was perfect in intellect, and was of noble origin. He had an absolutely graceful form, a complete generosity, perfect bravery, excessive humility, useful knowledge...perfect fear of God and sublime piety. He was the most eloquent and the most perfect of mankind in every variety of perfection.[214]

---

[212]Al-Ghazali quoted in Geisler and Saleeb, 83-84.

[213]Annemarie Schimmel, *And Muhammad Is His Messenger* (Chapel Hill: The University of North Carolina Press, 1985), 55.

[214]Kamal ud Din ad Damiri quoted in Geissler and Saleeb, 86-87.

The Cordovan theologian Abu Muhammad Ali ibn Hazm considered it an ethical requirement to intimately follow the example of the prophet: "If someone aspires to felicity in the next world and wisdom in this, to righteousness in his conduct, he should follow the example of the Prophet Muhammad and copy in practice, as much as possible, the Prophet's character and conduct. May God aid us with His favor that we might follow this example."[215] Muslims show a deep sense of respect and love for the prophet. Indeed, "Love of the prophet constitutes a fundamental element in Islamic spirituality," according to Frithjof Schuon, a contemporary Islamic scholar. Though Muslims stop just short of worshipping Mohammad, there is, in a sense, a compelling metaphysical quality attached to this phenomenon. Schuon explains that the virtues displayed by the prophet are seen to be those that are crucial to individual Muslims achieving that ultimate and elusive divine assurance (of entry into paradise).[216] It is therefore not without due justification that D. G. Hogarth remarks: "Serious or trivial, his daily behavior has instituted a Canon which millions observe to this day with conscious mimicry. No one regarded by any section of the human race as Perfect Man has been imitated so minutely."[217]

To understand the impact of the prophet of Islam, one has to realize that Mohammad was both the prophet and prince of Islam. He began his journey in Mecca, where he was troubled by the influence of paganism and of non-Arabic tribal religions. The beginning of his prophetic career was therefore spent on trying to peacefully reform and change his immediate environment. He was driven by somber and apocalyptic images as he resigned himself to long suffering, preaching in patience, and persevering with a handful of faithful companions. All the while, he endured the scorn and abuse of the dominant Meccan traders and business class. The turning point came in A.D. 622 with what Muslims now call the *hijra*, when Mohammad decided to leave Mecca and emigrate with his small band of followers to Medina. It was in Medina that he consolidated his followers and became a statesman.

In his expanded role, he served as a prophet-prince—taking on the roles of politician and military leader. His religious revelations became increasingly pragmatic and served the needs and contingencies of the situation he was dealing with. They addressed day-to-day issues of governance, details about familial and social organization, and rules of combat and warfare. It was in Medina that Islam became an institution and a fighting organization.[218] The hijra is therefore prop-

---

[215]Abu Muhammad Ali ibn Hazm quoted in Goldziher, 21.
[216]Schuon, 95.
[217]D.G. Hogarth quoted in Anderson, *Islam in the Modern World*, 10.
[218]Goldziher, 9.

erly understood not only for its practical consequences, but also for its symbolic ones—it represents a key turning point in the struggle and evolution of Islam. While in Mecca, Mohammad "saw himself as a prophet summoned to take his place alongside the Biblical prophets and, as they had done, to warn his fellow men and rescue them from perdition."[219] But he failed to realize his vision in Mecca. In Medina, he continued to pursue his religious goals, though with a different strategy. "He now demanded recognition as the renewer of Abraham's religion, as its restorer from distortion and decay . . . the adherents of the older religions had distorted their and suppressed passages in which prophets and evangelists had predicted his future coming."[220] Mohammad now viewed the other Abrahamic religions as competitors instead of brothers. "Polemics against Jews and Christians occupy a large part of the Medinese revelations. If in earlier passages the Qur'an acknowledges that monasteries, churches, and synagogues are true places of worship (22:40), the later passages attack Muhammad's original teachers, the Christian *ruhban* (monks) and the Jewish *ahbar* (scholars of scripture)."[221] In Mecca, Mohammad had been rejected as a prophet, but now in Medina he rapidly became the compelling and unifying force behind a new and militant theocracy.

To avoid jumping to what Kenneth Cragg has called "the hackneyed and oversimplified conclusion that Islam was spread by the sword," we must consider that Islam did not grow in a vacuum. Instead, in Medina Mohammad now labored to unify a set of fractious and quarrelsome tribes, using his theocratic vision as a unifying mechanism to create a new identity—the Islamic *ummah*. Religion served to define the new identity in a way that no economic or political structure had been able to satisfy previously. It was also convenient, in a Machiavellian sense, to be surrounded by competitors and threats. This allowed Mohammad to empower his followers with a new sense of security heretofore unknown by the quarreling tribes. In a series of raids known as *razzias*, he slowly consolidated his base in Medina, using these expeditions to begin to focus the attention of his followers to outside threats—and away from internal conflict. Islam served a dual purpose: Internally it regulated the daily affairs of its adherents, creating an ordered society of believers; externally, it focused the energies on the unbelievers and enemies of Allah, and gave added impetus to the warrior ethos by providing a supererogatory mechanism of gaining access to paradise.

The Battle of Badr, often referred to by Muslims to this day, was the first stunning success for the Muslims after years of struggle in Mecca and Medina. In A.D.

---

[219]Goldziher, 10.
[220]Goldziher, 10.
[221]Goldziher, 10.

624, Mohammad and his followers, with a force of about only 300 men, set out against a large Meccan caravan of 1,000 camels and almost 1,000 men. In the initial exchanges of the battle, Mohammad exhorted his men by offering heavenly paradise to those who were slain. Ibn Ishaq records that "the Apostle went forth to the people and incited them saying, 'By God in whose hand is the soul of Muhammad, no man will be slain this day fighting against them with steadfast courage advancing not retreating but God will cause him to enter Paradise.'"[222] Mohammad continued to solidify his regional hold on Medina. A year after the Battle of Badr, 700 faithful fought at Uhud against 3,000 Meccans; two years later at the Battle of Trench, 3,000 Muslims were pitted against 10,000 Meccans.[223]

Yet while these battles show how Islam was transforming and expanding under the leadership of the prophet, economic competition from Mecca was not the main threat to Mohammad at this time. Instead, it was religious competition from the Jewish clan of Qurayza. The Battle of Badr, and later the Battle of Uhud, according to scholars, were both followed by expulsions of two Jewish clans, the Qaynuqa and the al-Nadir.[224] Now it was time to deal with the Qurayza, who directly competed with the Muslims for primacy in Medina. After several minor military skirmishes, the Qurayza surrendered unconditionally to Mohammad and his followers. Mohammad chose to personally decapitate the men, divide the property among his followers, and sell the women and children into slavery. Ibn Ishaq records the execution in the following way:

> Then the Apostle went out to the market of Medina (which is still the market today) and dug trenches in it. Then he sent for them and struck off their heads in those trenches as they were brought out to him in batches . . . There were 600 or 700 in all, though some put the figure as high as 800 or 900. As they were being taken out in batches to the Apostle they asked Ka'b what he thought would be done to them. He replied: 'Will you never understand? Don't you see that the summoner never stops and those who are taken away do not return? By Allah it is death!' This went on until the Apostle made an end of them.[225]

Having firmly consolidated his hold on Medina, the prophet now turned toward Mecca. Historians tells us that a large army of Muslim faithful assembled to lay siege on Mecca in early 630 A.D.; on January 11th, Mohammad divided his forces into four columns and entered the city from four directions,

---

[222]Inamdar, 153.
[223]Inamdar, 218.
[224]Inamdar, 165.
[225]Ibn Ishaq quoted in Inamdar, 166.

surrounded by 400 heavily armed horsemen and 10,000 foot soldiers.[226] He arrived with the military might of a conqueror, driven by the political vision of a united Arabia, and sanctioned as the prophet of God's final revelation and purest religion. The same year, Mohammad led 30,000 men, of which 10,000 were mounted cavalry, on a Syrian campaign to challenge the Byzantine Empire to the north. Mohammad looked to challenge the Byzantine empire—in one *hadith*, the prophet is quoted as saying: "You will certainly conquer Constantinople. Excellent will be the amir and the army who take possession of it."[227] In what may be a spurious tradition, he is also reputed to have predicted that the imminent fall of Constantinople would be followed by that of Rome.[228] Mohammad had reached his zenith as a military leader—he dressed for battle wrapping a turban around his helmet, donned a breastplate under which he wore a coat of mail, belted himself with a leather sword-belt, and slung his shield across his back.[229] But Mohammad's most potent weapon was not physically donned before battle. This was the weapon of "assurance of paradise"— wielded by Mohammad in his role as prophet and priest of Islam. For as one scholar explains,

> Muhammad offered a totally different form of immortality in war for an entire group of armed warriors. Death did not really exist for them; they had absolutely nothing to lose. Instead they could gain victory on earth or look forward to paradise where pleasures and happiness abounded. Life and death were both transcended. War was a celestial game in the magic realm between heaven and earth.[230]

From a religious perspective, Mohammad commanded the faithful in an attempt to bring the "rightly-guided" divine message to an ever-increasing geographical area. From a decidedly secular perspective, Mohammad is to be studied for his dogged tenacity, visionary leadership, and compelling personality and charisma. He has been described as one of the most successful politicians of all time. After forming a "government in exile" in Medina, he steadfastly pursued his goal to overthrow paganism and replace the regime in Mecca with Islam and the new Islamic order.[231] Thus, as F.E. Peters has written, "Muhammad was not simply God's envoy; he was also, for much of his later life, judge, spiritual guide, and

---

[226]Inamdar, 177.

[227]Mohammad quoted in Bernard Lewis, *The Political Language of Islam* (Chicago: The University of Chicago press, 1988), 75.

[228]Mohammad quoted in Lewis, *The Political Language of Islam*, 75.

[229]Inamdar, 218-19.

[230]Inamdar, 222.

[231]Goldziher, 91.

military and political leader, first of a community, then of a city-state, and finally of a burgeoning empire."[232] He remains to this day the *uswa hasana* of Islam—the most excellent role model.[233]

Jesus Christ: Man as God Incarnate. The very foundation of Christian belief rests inextricably on the nature and ministry of Jesus Christ. According to Christians, Christ walked this earth both as a man, and as God's holy son. This incarnation of Christ is profoundly important to Christians. Christianity would cease to exist as a faith without it, simply because its soteriology holds that the divine Christ fulfilled God's plan for redemption by dying on the cross as a sacrifice for man's sin. Without Christ's divinity, without his sacrificial death, and without his resurrection, Christianity would become a version of generic Abrahamic monotheism. Thus the centrality of the doctrine of Christ rests on five principles: (1) that he was God's son; (2) that he was born a man to the virgin Mary; (3) that he lived a sinless life on this earth; (4) that he was crucified and died on the cross; and (5) that three days later God the father raised him from the dead and that after a short period of time spent with followers, he returned to heaven. The New Testament summarizes these doctrines:

> *He committed no sin, and no deceit was found in his mouth . . . God made him who had no sin to be sin for us, so that in him we might become the righteousness of God . . . He was chosen before the creation of the world . . . For Christ's love compels us, because we are convinced that one died for all . . . Through him you believe in God, who raised him from the dead and glorified him, and so your faith and hope are in God.*[234]

Jesus Christ's earthly ministry is best characterized by a haunting transcendence that spoke to his divine nature. His service and humility were an inspiration to his followers. His acts of mercy and love were a persistent and nagging nemesis to his opponents. His focus did not involve political or military ends, but rather involved transmitting a message to those who listened to him. The message was that the requirements of divine justice—itself the result of divine righteousness juxtaposed against human sinfulness—were to be satisfied by the impending death and resurrection of its bearer. Therefore, the ultimate focus of his earthly existence was, according to Christians, the fulfillment of the will of his father—to sacrificially die on the cross. Jesus made it clear that there was a difference between the secular kingdom of this earth and the spiritual kingdom of heaven. In

---

[232]Peters, 99.

[233]Goldziher, 92.

[234]Please see 1 Peter 2:22, 1 Peter 1:20, 2 Corinthians 5:21, 2 Corinthians 5:14, and 1 Peter 1:21.

answering the Roman governor Pilate's assertion that Jesus was a king, he answered: *"You are right in saying that I am a king. In fact, for this reason I was born, and for this I came into the world, to testify to the truth* (John 18:37)." But he unmistakably separated the two kingdoms: *"My kingdom is not of this world. If it were, my servants would fight to prevent my arrest by the Jews. But now my kingdom is from another place* (John 19:36)."

In addressing the conflicted nature of the two kingdoms, Malcolm Muggeridge writes that

> Jesus continually stressed the fallacy of looking to this world and its rulers for help and guidance in fulfilling God's purposes; and though in the subsequent centuries his ostensible followers have often enough on his behalf gone after the support of the rich and the mighty, of millionaires and demagogues and kings and revolutionaries . . . the profound distrust of power which Jesus inculcated has lived on in the hearts of those who have loved him most and served him best.[235]

Jesus was not concerned with consolidating political power or accumulating military might. His love and passion to fulfill the will of his father were demonstrated in acts of service to those who surrounded him. An example of this attitude is when Jesus washed the feet of his disciples during their last meal together. As Muggeridge eloquently observes,

> they call him Master, and rightly so, but in washing their feet the Master deliberately abases himself in order to demonstrate that greatness lies, not in self-assertion, but in self-abnegation . . . In washing the disciples' feet Jesus demonstrated once and for all that the Son of Man was the servant of men; that whatsoever was arrogant, assertive, dogmatic or demagogic belonged to the gospel of power, not to his gospel of love; that humility is not just virtuous but the very condition of all virtue . . .[236]

Summary: Warrior Prophet and Servant King. In no other manner are the differences between Muslims and Christians more sharply contrasted than in the difference between the characters and legacies of their prophets. Perhaps the contrast is best symbolized by the way Mohammad entered Mecca and Jesus entered Jerusalem. Mohammad rode into Mecca on a warhorse, surrounded by 400 mounted men and 10,000 foot soldiers. Those who greeted him were absorbed into his movement; those who resisted him were vanquished, killed, or enslaved.

---

[235]Muggeridge, 143.
[236]Muggeridge, 150-51.

Mohammad conquered Mecca, and took control as its new religious, political, and military leader. Today, in the Topkapi Palace in Istanbul, Turkey, Mohammad's purported sword is proudly on display—for the Arabian prophet, it symbolized "striving in the way of God."[237]

Jesus entered Jerusalem on a donkey, accompanied by his 12 disciples. He was welcomed and greeted by people waving palm fronds—a traditional sign of peace. Jesus wept over Jerusalem because the Jews mistook him for an earthly, secular king who was to free them from the yoke of Rome, whereas Jesus came to establish a much different, heavenly kingdom. Jesus came by invitation and not by force; for him "striving in the way of God" could never take on a military form. One of Jesus' disciples, the Apostle Peter, learned this lesson even during Jesus' apprehension by the Roman authorities. When Peter saw Jesus being taken away by the Roman legionaries and temple guards, he drew his sword and attacked one of the Jewish high priest's servants, cutting off his ear. Jesus, stopping Peter's aggression, healed the wound, and told him to put away his sword: "*Put your sword back in its place,*" Jesus said to Peter, "*for all who draw the sword will die by the sword* (Matthew 26:52)." Shortly thereafter, Jesus was arrested, tortured, and crucified. This was the example of the prophet whom Christians hold was both God and man. Muggeridge writes that "to fulfill the purpose of the Incarnation Jesus had to be both Man and God; only so could God make Himself known to men, and men truly relate themselves to God. On the Cross Jesus died as Man, but only to rise from the dead as God. This was the Resurrection . . . God Incarnate was Jesus, and Jesus Resurrected was God."[238]

It is therefore significant that Islam explicitly denies all the key doctrines about Jesus Christ: his divinity, his crucifixion, and his resurrection. In addressing the deity of Christ, the Qur'an asserts: *The Jews call Uzair a son of Allah, and the Christians call Christ the son of Allah. That is a saying from their mouth; (in this) they but imitate what the Unbelievers of old used to say. Allah's curse be on them: how they are deluded away from the truth* (Surah *Al Tawbah*, 9:30).[239] The Qur'an repeatedly attacks Christ's divinity: *In blasphemy indeed are those that say that Allah is Christ the son of Mary* (Surah *Al Ma'idah*, 5:17); Christ, the son of Mary, was no more than a Messenger; many were the Messengers that passed

---

[237]Woodberry interview.

[238]Muggeridge, 189.

[239]*The Meaning of the Holy Qur'an.* It is perhaps not without significance that immediately preceding this passage in the Qur'an is found the following: *Fight those who believe not in Allah nor the Last Day, nor hold that forbidden which hath been forbidden by Allah and His Messenger, nor acknowledge the Religion of truth, from among the People of the Book, until they pay the Jizyah with willing submission, and feel themselves subdued* (9:29).

away before him (Surah *Al Ma'idah.* 5:75).[240] As Yusuf Ali explains in his commentary on these surahs, "all power belongs to Allah, and not to any man. No creature can be God."

Islam also denies the crucifixion and resurrection of Jesus Christ. *That they said (in boast), "We killed Christ Jesus the son of Mary, the Messenger of Allah." But they killed him not, nor crucified him, but so it was made to appear to them, and those who differ therein are full of doubts, with no (certain) knowledge, but only conjecture to follow, for of a surety they killed him not. Nay, Allah raised him up unto Himself; and Allah is Exalted in Power, Wise.* (Surah Al Nisa' 4:157-158).[241] Here the Qur'anic commentator delivers the classic Muslim interpretation of these surahs.

> The Orthodox Christian Churches make it a cardinal point of their doctrine that his life was taken on the Cross, that he died and was buried, that on the third day he rose in the body with his wounds intact, and walked about and conversed, and ate with his disciples, and was afterwards taken up bodily to heaven. This is necessary for the theological doctrine of blood sacrifice and vicarious atonement for sins, which is rejected by Islam. The Qur'anic teaching is that Christ was not crucified nor killed by the Jews, notwithstanding certain apparent circumstances which produced that illusion in the minds of some of his enemies: that disputations, doubts, and conjectures on such matters are vain; and that he was taken up to Allah.[242]

Many Muslims believe what is purported by the Gospel of St. Barnabas, which supports the theory of substitution on the cross. In other words, *if* Jesus was indeed God's son, *then* God would never have permitted him to suffer such a brutal death. Therefore, God *would* have spirited Jesus away just before the crucifixion and would have substituted a human body for his holy body.[243]

---

[240]*The Meaning of the Holy Qur'an.*

[241]*The Meaning of the Holy Qur'an.*

[242]Commentary by Yusuf Ali in *The Meaning of the Holy Qur'an.*

[243]The Gospel of St. Barnabas is widely held by Muslims as a more authoritative accounting of the life of Jesus Christ than the four Biblical gospels (Matthew, Mark, Luke, and John). It asserts that Jesus Christ did not die on the cross, but that Judas Iscariot was substituted for Jesus. The Gospel of St. Barnabas has been exhaustively studied and rejected by Biblical scholars as a late-medieval era fabrication or forgery. Scholars contend that while there is no original language manuscript evidence that supports the Gospel of St. Barnabas, the New Testament books of the Bible have been verified by nearly 5,700 Greek manuscripts. For further detail, please see Geisler and Saleeb, 303-308, or David Sox, *The Gospel of Barnabas* (London: George Allen & Unwin, 1984).

Finally, in concert with denying Christ's deity, crucifixion, and resurrection, Islam also rejects the doctrine of the trinity. *O People of the Book! Commit no excesses in your religion: nor say of Allah aught but the truth. Christ Jesus the son of Mary was (no more than) a Messenger of Allah, and His Word, which He bestowed on Mary and a Spirit proceeding from Him: so believe in Allah and His Messengers. Say not "Trinity": desist: it will be better for you: for Allah is one God: glory be to him: (far exalted is He) above having a son. To him belong all things in the heavens and on earth. And enough is Allah as a Disposer of affairs* (Surah *Al Nisa'*, 4:171).[244] Again, it is perhaps best to listen to the words of the Muslim commentator:

> Just as a foolish servant may go wrong by excess of zeal for his master, so in religion people's excesses may lead them to blasphemy or a spirit the very opposite of religion. The Jewish excesses in the direction of formalism, racialism, exclusiveness, and rejection of Christ Jesus have been denounced in many places. Here the Christian attitude is condemned, which raises Jesus to an equality with Allah; in some cases venerates Mary almost to idolatry; attributes a physical son to Allah; and invents the doctrine of the Trinity, opposed to all reason. Let our Muslims also beware lest they fall into excesses either in doctrine or in formalism. The doctrines of Trinity, equality with Allah, and sonship, are repudiated as blasphemies. Allah is independent of all needs and has no need of a son to manage His affairs.[245]

In conclusion, the two prophets established legacies that endured in the lives of their successors. Muhammad's religious zeal, political leadership, and call to arms resonated among his companions and followers. In the words of one scholar, his use of force radically altered the actual shape of the phenomenon he created—the initial smaller raids, or *razzias*, became more aggressive as the *ummah* transformed them into religious missions directed by revelations, first against the unjust Meccans, then later against an ever-expanding periphery of unbelievers.[246] His passion and encouragement toward supereregatory zeal—his tempting offers of a heavenly paradise—transformed the odds of war by offering an attractive new form of immortality.[247] "If you love God, follow me, and God will love you and forgive your sins,"[248] exhorted the warrior prophet, and bequeathed an expansive legacy to the newly unified tribes of Arabia. On the

---

[244]*The Meaning of the Holy Qur'an.*

[245]Commentary by Yusuf Ali in *The Meaning of the Holy Qur'an.*

[246]Inamdar, 217.

[247]Inamdar, 222.

[248]Goldziher, 24.

other hand, Christ's legacy was one that rejected the politico-military route and instead focused the zeal of his followers on the internal transformation of the soul. *"No one can see the kingdom of God,"* he taught, *"unless he is born again"* (John 3:3). His followers remained a suffering minority for the next three centuries. Most of his closest disciples and followers were persecuted, tortured, and martyred by the Roman state.

Conclusions: Divergent Political & Historical Imperatives

It would seem reasonable to conclude that the respective doctrines, scriptures, and prophets lent divergent political and historical imperatives to each of these two religions. In the case of Islam, political and religious integration, group-driven identity mechanisms, and the primacy of religious jurisprudence led to a united kingdom. This fusion of religion and state supported an inherent preference for theocratic forms of government. The close intertwining of religion and state, combined with the predeterminism ingrained in Islam by the prophet—Islam was to be the final and rightly guided religion for mankind—led to a broad vision of politico-military expansion. In a sense, this was religious imperialism, an attempt to expand the kingdom of Allah, not just transcendentally, but through vigorous political and military ardor. It required the establishment of a sacred geography with the requisite political and societal structures that would enable Muslims to fulfill their orthopractical obligations.

In the case of Christianity, early doctrines firmly established a differentiated kingdom—a secular realm and a divine realm, a sinful world and a redeemed world. These were the essential elements of the founder's message. The first 300 years brought great persecution and struggle to the faithful. Not until the emperor Constantine inaugurated a radical reversal did Christianity gain ascendancy in the Roman state. The conflicted nature of the differentiated kingdom would take over a millennium to resolve, and only in the turbulent times of the Reformation would the tensions between church and state be resolved in Western societies, gradually yielding differentiated and sanctioned authorities.

This brief synopsis greatly simplifies complex religious, social, and political events. Nonetheless, the outcomes of the two different paths are strategically significant. Having thus far discussed the doctrinal foundations, the following paragraphs aim to show how these two divergent doctrines have yielded profoundly different political and historical imperatives that continue to affect the world today. The aim here is not to write an authoritative historical account—though some history is necessary and relevant—but rather to gain a strategic understanding of the imperatives discussed above.

Islam's Political & Historical Imperatives. The prophet Mohammad died in 632 A.D. What happened in the next 100 years remains, to this day, militarily, politically, and religiously impressive. In the words of the classical historian Victor Davis Hanson, "in that century between 632 and 732, a small and rather impotent Arab people arose to conquer the Sassanid Persian Empire, wrest the entire Middle East and much of Asia Minor from the Byzantines, and establish a theocratic rule across North Africa. In the past the Romans had built a wall to protect their province of Syria from the warring tribes of Arabia . . . Yet by the mid-eighth century, the suddenly ascendant kingdom of the Arabs controlled three continents and an area larger than the Roman Empire itself."[249] Most historians agree that the collapse of *pax Romana*, propelled by the Persian Sassanids and the Visigoths and Ostragoths, provided an exploitable strategic vacuum. In the first 100 years of post-Mohammedan existence, Islam surged into that vacuum and established an enduring presence. This dramatic expansion left an indelible impression on the psychology and ethos of Islam. The following description offers a strategic sense of that impact:

> The breakneck spread of Islam was astounding. By 634, a mere two years after Muhammad's death, Muslim armies were well engaged in the conquest of Persia. Syria fell in 636; Jerusalem was captured in 638. Alexandria was stormed in 641, opening the entire Visigothic realm to the west. Forty years later Muslims were at the gates of Constantinople itself, and from 673 to 677 nearly succeeded in capturing the city. By 681 the Arabs neared the Atlantic, formalizing Islam's incorporation of the old kingdoms of the Berbers. Carthage was taken for good in 698 and their last queen, Kahina, captured, her head sent to the caliph in Damascus. Only seventeen miles now separated Islam from Europe proper. By 715 the Visigoths had been conquered in Spain, and periodic forays into southern France were commonplace. In 718 Arabs had crossed the Pryrenees in large numbers and occupied Narbonne, killing all the adult male inhabitants and selling the women and children into slavery. By 720 they were freely raiding in Aquitane.[250]

The immediate and dramatic political and military success of Mohammad's legacy is significant for several reasons. First, in the eyes of his adherents, it lent compelling legitimacy to the prophet's religious revelations and to his social and political beliefs. How could Allah—and the doctrine of divine unity (*tawhid*) as revealed by the prophet—not be behind the stunning advancement of Islam in so

---

[249]Victor Davis Hanson, *Carnage and Culture: Landmark Battles in the Rise of Western Civilization* (New York: Doubleday, 2001), 146.

[250]Hanson, *Carnage and Culture*, 146.

short a period of time? The armies of Allah were imbued with the peculiar nature of their newfound religion, which offered a powerful "connection between war and faith, creating a divine culture that might reward with paradise the slaying of an infidel . . . killing and pillaging were now in the proper context, acts of piety."[251]

Second, the rapid expansion made permanent the fusion of political and religious realms in Islamic culture. The unitary kingdom, established and radically effective during Islam's period of ascendancy, was thereby firmly embedded and legitimized within Islamic psychology. The state was not seen, as in the beginnings of Christianity, as an instrument of persecution. As Bernard Lewis writes, in Islam "political authority was not a human evil . . . it was a divine good. The body politic and the sovereign power within it [were] ordained by God himself, to promote faith and to maintain and extend the law . . . for the Muslim, God's main concern was to help [and] in particular to help them achieve victory and paramountcy in this world."[252]

Roman ruins at Jarash in northern Jordan: As *Pax Romana* collapsed, Islam filled the void.
Photo by author.

Third, it created a sense of anticipation and historical determinism with respect to the future of Islam. Islam, as the final and perfect revelation of Allah,

---

[251] Hanson, *Carnage and Culture*, 147.
[252] Lewis, *The Political Language of Islam*, 25.

was destined for all of mankind. As Hanson puts it, the advance of "Muslims into the Persian, Byzantine, and European realms was considered a natural—or fated—act. The world was no longer bound by national borders or ethnic spheres, but was properly the sole domain of Muhammad—if only his followers were courageous enough to fulfill the prophet's visions."[253] In this sense, "Islam was not a static or reflective religion, but a dynamic creed that saw conquest and conversion as prerequisites for world harmony."[254]

Fourth, as the sacred geography expanded, Islamic soteriology demanded that appropriate political and social institutions be established to enable the faithful to meet their orthopractical requirements. Islam's all-encompassing holy law, *shariah*, fulfilled this role. It embraced the entire range of human activity and behavior, and as Lewis notes, was therefore also naturally concerned with the conduct of government.[255] "Since the law, in the Muslim conception, is divine and immutable, that part of it concerned with government shares these attributes," and the Muslim jurist therefore "sees the state as a divine instrument—as a necessary and inherent part of God's providential dispensation for mankind."[256] Ultimately, in Islam the principal function of that government, then as now, is to enable the individual believer to lead a good life and meet the requirements of the religion. Finally, Islam's rapid military ascendancy, combined with its political and social imperatives, formed a dramatic challenge to the constellation of Christian peoples on the European continent. At times, it provided sufficient impetus to unite the conflicted, medieval European powers in defense against a common adversary.

One of the first, and perhaps most significant examples, occurred on 11 October 732, when Charles Martel and his Frankish army of heavy infantry men stopped the Muslim advance into the heart of Frankish Europe in what today is known as the Battle of Poitiers. In many respects, Poitiers represents a turning point in the dramatic expansion of Islam; numerous historians have commented on its significance. Hanson characterized it as the high tide of the Muslim advance into Europe.[257] The well-known European historian Leopold von Ranke, in *The History of the Reformation*, described it as "one of the most important epochs in the history of the world, the commencement of the eighth century when on the one side Mohammedanism threatened to overspread Italy and Gaul."[258] Hans Delbruck, the German historian of military affairs, wrote

---

[253]Hanson, *Carnage and Culture*, 147.
[254]Hanson, *Carnage and Culture*, 147.
[255]Lewis, *The Political Language of Islam*, 28.
[256]Lewis, *The Political Language of Islam*, 28.
[257]Hanson, *Carnage and Culture*, 166.
[258]Leopold von Ranke quoted in Hanson, *Carnage and Culture*, 166.

that there was "no more important battle in world history."[259] The Battle of Poitiers effectively ended Islam's initial expansion, setting the stage for a European reaction. Seen in this light, the reaction that came in the form of the Crusades was a European response to Islam's military and religious challenge. "By 1096 a fragmented western Europe was strong enough to send thousands of soldiers across the sea to the Middle East. In a series of three Crusades between 1096 and 1189, Europeans occupied Jerusalem and carved out Western enclaves in the heart of Islam."[260] Placed in the proper historical context, the Crusades were a reaction to ascendant Islamic imperialism. One scholar notes that "in the eleventh century, the forces of Christendom began to regain some of their lands in major victories against Islam. . . . the Crusaders ruled parts of Palestine and Syria for over two centuries, but their overall impact on these lands was slight, and they were finally evicted in crushing defeats."[261] That the Crusaders shed blood in the name of Christendom is not contested here. In fact, European soldiers not only slaughtered Muslims, but equally attacked heretics and pagans. Instead, the focus is on the cause-and-effect relationship between the rapidly expanding Muslim geographic space and the peoples and religions that it came in contact with as a result of that expansion.

The conflict would endure, as the Mediterranean basin became a contested region fought over by what Halford J. Mackinder has called the peoples of the Latin Peninsula (Western European Christendom) and the Islamic invaders surging out from the heartlands of Arabia.[262] Mackinder, a strategic geographer, argued that the peoples of the Latin Peninsula, hardened by a winter of centuries called the Dark Ages, were besieged in their homeland by the Mohammedans.[263] Indeed, Christendom was defeated in the Crusades and was obliged to endure the Islamic siege for centuries. Only with the relative weakening of Islam during the sixteenth and seventeenth centuries did the danger to Christendom begin to wane, though the struggle continued to play itself out throughout the Mediterranean sphere. Islam's religious imperative continued to motivate attempts to expand the sacred geography. "From the fourteenth to the seventeenth century Muslims were engaged, once again, in a Holy War against Christians. This time the leaders of Islam were Turks, newly militant and powerful. Under the Ottomans they captured Constantinople in 1453 and surged into Europe."[264] At the siege of Constantinople, Edward Gibbon

---

[259]Hans Delbruck quoted in Hanson, *Carnage and Culture*, 166.

[260]Hanson, *Carnage and Culture*, 168.

[261]Inamdar, xi.

[262]Halford J. Mackinder, *Democratic Ideals and Reality*, ed. Anthony J. Pearce (Westport, CT: Greenwood Press, 1962), 45.

[263]Mackinder, 48.

[264]Inamdar, xii.

records that Mahomet, the Islamic commander, exhorted his troops with promises of Paradise. "In this holy warfare, the Moslems were exhorted to purify their minds with prayer, their bodies with seven ablutions; and to abstain from food till the close of the ensuing day. A crowd of dervishes visited the tents, to instill the desire of martyrdom, and the assurance of spending an immortal youth amidst the rivers and gardens of paradise and in the embraces of black-eyed virgins."[265] At the Battle of Lepanto in 1571, Ottoman naval forces were repulsed by a Christian alliance tenuously cobbled together because of defensive necessity. Hanson tells us that "the Ottomans had fashioned a brilliant military empire based on the courage of nomadic warriors, the purchase of European firearms and military expertise, and the great schisms in Christendom between Catholics, Orthodox, and Protestants."[266] Yet, he also observes that the market economics required to drive military advancement never fully developed in the Muslim world because they were antithetical to the Qur'an, which made no distinctions between political, cultural, economic, and religious life.[267]

The Mohammedan imperative seemed to lose its potency as the Renaissance gave way to the Reformation, the Enlightenment, industrialization, and European modernity in Mackinder's Latin Peninsula. After centuries of challenges from Islam, Europeans initiated their own period of imperialistic expansion. Napoleon Bonaparte landed on the shores of Alexandria in 1798 and brought colonialism to the Islamic world. The Ottoman Empire suffered steady decline throughout the 19th century—pressured by internal corruption and division, as well as by Western political, technological, and military ascendancy. The proverbial "sick man of Europe" was completely vanquished in the aftermath of World War I. In 1924, soon after the end of hostilities, the newly secularized Turkish government dissolved the last symbol of Islamic expansion—the Islamic Caliphate.

Islam's historical politico-military expansion has been seen by many Muslims to be an inevitable occurrence. In his writings, the Egyptian Muslim scholar Sayyid Qutb described the Islamic imperative in detail. In *Islam and Universal Peace*, Qutb wrote that "the only use of force throughout the long history of Islam was in order to give people freedom of choice and eliminate the injustices of oppressors who tried to usurp God's divine right to rule and deny Muslims the right to preach their religion."[268] Thus, as Qutb argued, "the aim of the Islamic wars was to keep 'the word of God' supreme on earth by insuring the sovereignty

---

[265]Edward Gibbon, *The History of the Decline and Fall of the Roman Empire*, Vol. 6 (Norwalk, CT: The Easton Press, 1974), 2347.

[266]Hanson, *Carnage and Culture*, 269.

[267]Hanson, *Carnage and Culture*, 269.

[268]Sayyid Qutb, *Islam and Universal Peace* (Indianapolis: American Trust Publications, 1977), 14.

of those who believed in the oneness of God, to allow people the freedom to promote the Islamic welfare and to establish justice and peace in all societies."[269]

Many Islamic scholars, along with Qutb, argue that Islam advocates peace and freedom of choice. Yet the Islamic concepts of peace and choice seem somewhat paradoxical. The freedom of choice is really not free, but rather a compulsion to submit to the divine unity and Allah's rightly-guided religion—or, at best to be treated as a second-class minority, at worst to be pursued as an unbeliever or infidel. Qutb apparently appeals to Islam's universal aspirations of peace when he writes that "this religion is not merely a declaration of the freedom of the Arabs, nor is its message confined to the Arabs. It addresses itself to the whole of mankind, and its sphere of work is the whole earth."[270] But it is Kant, the German philosopher, who poignantly addresses the paradoxical nature of Islam's concepts of peace and choice. In his ironic essay entitled On Perpetual Peace, Kant suggests that ". . . it is the desire of every state, or of its ruler, to attain to a condition of perpetual peace . . . by subjecting the whole world, as far as possible, to its sway."[271]

The paradox is summarized in Qutb's own words:[272]

1. The general Islamic outlook confirms the unity of all humanity, of religion and of believers. It considers Islam as the final religion [while confirming the previous monotheistic religions as its predecessors].
2. Accordingly, Muslims have a responsibility toward humanity. They are to achieve peace on earth, within themselves, at home, and in society. It is a peace based on recognizing God's oneness and omnipotence, on instituting justice, equality and liberty; and on achieving social equilibrium and cooperation.
3. Islam is not an arbitrary religion, nor has it ever ordered Muslims to force others to adopt it even though it is the final and complete revelation from God.
4. [But] Muslims are commanded to eliminate any oppressive force that would suppress the propagation of Islam and to establish the sovereignty of God on earth and to repel aggression against it.
5. Following the Islamic criterion, peace cannot be established by abstaining from war when there is oppression, corruption, despotism and denial of God's supremacy.
6. The struggle to establish the sovereignty of God on earth is called

---

[269]Qutb, *Islam and Universal Peace*, 15.

[270]Sayyid Qutb, *Milestones*, 106.

[271]Kant quoted in Martin Wight., *Power Politics*, eds. Hedley Bull and Carsten Holbraad (London: Leicester University Press, 1978), 144.

[272]The following is a compilation from Qutb, *Islam and Universal Peace*, 73-74.

jihad. Jihad is achieved by giving men the chance to emancipate themselves from their oppressors and to restore their human rights granted by God to all of mankind.

7. It was inevitable that Muslims would declare *jihad*. They had to save humanity—individuals and societies—from prevailing injustices. They had to fight in order to establish peace.

8. Islam ordains that men persevere in their efforts to establish the Word of God on earth. Islam does not tolerate oppression, whether it is an individual who imposes himself on others, or a class that exploits other classes, or a state that exploits other states.

9. When dealing with its enemies Islam takes one of three courses: They may adopt the religion, or they may pay a tribute to the Islamic state (the tribute is a token that hostilities have ceased and the enemy will not obstruct the religion), or they may fight (if the enemy rejects the religion and also refuses to pay tribute, Muslims must declare war on those who obdurately stand between men and Islam's righteous and peaceful principles).

Thus, freedom of choice means that either one chooses to become a Muslim, or one is left with two alternatives: to pay the religious tax, or resist and fight. In order to underscore their arguments and prime them with Islam's historical imperatives, Qutb and other Muslim scholars make continual references to the Qur'an as well as the role model and hadiths of the prophet Mohammad.

Yet, many Muslim scholars claim these imperatives do not mean that others are compelled to convert to their religion. They refer to the Qur'an, which indicates in Surah *Al Baqarah* (2:256): *Let there be no compulsion in religion: truth stands out clear from error: whoever rejects evil and believes in Allah hath grasped the most trustworthy handhold, never breaks. And Allah heareth and knoweth all things.*[273] Yusuf Ali writes in his commentary on this verse of the Qur'an that "compulsion is incompatible with religion, because 1) religion depends upon faith and will, and these would be meaningless if induced by force; 2) truth and error have been so clearly shown up by the mercy of God that there should be no doubt in the minds of any persons of goodwill as to the fundamentals of faith; and 3) God's protection is continuous and His plan is always to lead us from the depths of darkness into the clearest light."[274] So what became of those who were absorbed by the expansion of Islam, yet who also felt unconvinced by its religious doctrine?

---

[273]*The Meaning of the Holy Qur'an.*
[274]Commentary by Yusuf Ali in *The Meaning of the Holy Qur'an.*

Just as Qutb's concept of Islamic choice is paradoxical, so the phrase "no compulsion in religion" is not synonymous with the concept of religious liberty or religious self-expression. The so-called "peoples of the book"—Christians and Jews, as members of the two non-Muslim, Abrahamic, monotheistic faiths—acquired a special status within Islam. These tolerated minorities were called *dhimmis*. Under the conditions of *dhimmitude*, Christians and Jews were largely permitted to maintain their faiths, though under strict conditions. As Kenneth Cragg explains, "they were tolerated because they were religions mentioned in the Qur'an, and although they were duty bound to acknowledge the final truth of Islam, this was not to be compelled upon them."[275] However, *dhimmis* were to follow the Qur'anic requirement to "pay the *Jizyah* [religious tax] with willing submission, and feel themselves subdued."[276] They were not allowed to propagate their faith, to worship in public (to ring bells, have solemn funerals, or engage in outside processions), to build new places of worship, to be functionaries of the state, to be witnesses in legal proceedings, to take daughters of Muslims to be their wives, to be guardians of underage Muslims, to receive inheritances from Muslims, to bear arms, or to ride on horseback. As Cragg writes, *dhimmis* "enjoyed a freedom only to persist, not a freedom to baptize or to receive. It was thus a toleration ensuring freedom to remain but not freedom to 'become,' except in one direction, namely to Islam." [277] Qutb's freedom to choose really meant that either one became a Muslim, or one was treated as a second-class citizen. As other scholars have noted, the *dhimma* arrangement only worked when the *dhimmis* themselves surrendered their rights to Islamic political supremacy.

Islamic historical and political imperatives demanded that society throughout Islam's sacred geography be organized according to the principles of Islamic theology and law. The peoples of the book that did not convert to Islam were to be permitted to exist under the restrictive and watchful eyes of the greater Islamic *ummah*. Islam brought this paradoxical "freedom" to its newly conquered realm. The "freedom" and "lack of compulsion" was therefore not true religious liberty or the right of religious self-expression. Islamic theocracy could never recognize another religion because Islam viewed itself as the ultimate and final divine revelation, and this lent it an historical imperative that endures to this day. Jews and Christians were sometimes allowed to exist at the enlightened mercies of their Islamic hosts. But it was only Islam that was viewed by Muslims as the ultimate and perfected culture and civilization for mankind—a culture that permanently fuses church and state to a divine and predeterministic historical imperative.

---

[275]Cragg and Speight, 82.
[276]*The Meaning of the Holy Qur'an.*
[277]Cragg and Speight, 82.

Most Muslims see the unification of political and religious realms as essential to their societal welfare; the notion of a religious polity is embedded in Islam's sacred and cultural history. Islamic scholars from Al Ghazali to Ibn Taymiyya to Ibn Hanbal to Sayyid Qutb stand behind this tradition. Qutb, representing this heritage, wrote that Islam "had to join together the world and the faith by its exhortations and laws. So [it] chose to unite earth and heaven in a single system, present both in the heart of the individual and the actuality of society, recognizing no separation of practical exertion from religious impulse."[278] This sacred geography, Islam's unified kingdom, is seen by Muslims to be the most evolved civilization of mankind. As Qutb concluded, "only Islamic values and morals, Islamic teachings and safeguards, are worthy of mankind, and from this unchanging and true measure of human progress, Islam is the real civilization and Islamic society is truly civilized."[279]

Christendom's Political and Historical Imperatives. The Christian imperative was clearly defined by Christ himself: *"Give to Caesar what is Caesar's, and to God what is God's"* (Matthew 22:21). Christian anthropology acknowledged man's innate sinfulness, which inherently prevented the establishment of an earthly kingdom of God. Early Christians looked to the future kingdom of heaven and relied on the doctrines of grace as the means of securing eternal assurance. Christians were to obey the secular government to the extent that it did not usurp the divine realm.[280] St. Augustine wrote that the city of God—the community of Christian faith—"neither annuls nor abolishes" the secular institutions of the society "provided no obstacles are put in the way of the form of devotion that teaches the one supreme and true God is to be worshipped."[281] However, the Roman Empire, the cult of the Caesars, and Rome's pagan religion would challenge Christians for 300 years. Unlike Mohammed's companions, the disciples of Christ suffered, often under severe duress, and ultimately paid for their faith with their lives. It is said that St. Peter was not just crucified, but was martyred upside down. The ethos of early Christianity was therefore not one of victorious politico-military expansion, but was formed by waves of persecution at the hands of the Roman state.

In 325 A.D. the Christian church entered a new era, however. After a summons from Emperor Constantine himself, church leaders assembled at the Council of

---

[278] Qutb, *Social Justice in Islam*, 26.

[279] Qutb, Milestones, 186.

[280] Please see Romans 13:1-7 for a more detailed elaboration of the rights and limitations of civil government.

[281] St. Augustine quoted in Robert Louis Wilken, *The Spirit of Early Christian Thought* (New Haven: Yale University Press, 2003), 203.

Nicaea to adjudicate the meaning of Jesus Christ's divinity.[282] Constantine exploited the council, and Christianity as a whole, for its potential for unity within his weakening Roman empire. The council of Nicaea, which emphatically affirmed both Jesus Christ's divine essence and his incarnation, created political linkages between the state and the church. As Noll succinctly writes, with the eventual conversion of Emperor Constantine, the reality of the church as a pilgrim community of outsiders gradually gave way.[283] "In this sense, Nicaea bequeathed a dual legacy of sharpened fidelity to the great and saving truths of revelation, and also of increasing intermingling of church and world."[284]

In the wake of Constantine's reign, Christendom was, for over a millennium, characterized by the twin pillars of monasticism and the papacy until the Protestant Reformation fundamentally ruptured the relationship between church and state. This "medieval synthesis," as one scholar describes it, between the sacred and the secular spheres of life, was inaugurated by the cooperation between the emperor Charlemagne and Pope Leo III. The combination of church and state espoused an "integrated view of life in which everything—politics, social order, religious practice, economic relationships, and more—was based on the Christian faith as communicated by the Roman Catholic Church and protected by the actions of secular rulers."[285] The symbolic importance of Charlemagne and Leo III, the pope providing the crown to the most powerful ruler in Europe, is that it recognized a new comprehensive empire to replace the one destroyed by the collapse of Rome and the persistent challenge of Muslim armies encroaching on Christendom's peripheries.[286] Though the coming centuries would reveal what scholars know today as the great schism between the Eastern Orthodox church and the western Roman Catholic church, the die was cast for the relationship between the secular kingdom and the holy kingdom. It was a fractious, yet persistent, union that would only substantially be challenged when Luther ushered in the Reformation.

By the beginning of the sixteenth century, most Christians were beginning to agree that the church was in need of reform. The focus of Catholic doctrines, in combination with the evident corruption within the church, revealed to men like Luther a lack of correct Christian doctrines and a rejection of Christ's soteriology of grace. In his appeals, Luther called for reform in the church, alleging that the Romanists had insulated themselves from the very scriptures themselves, and that

---

[282]Noll, 48.
[283]Noll, 62.
[284]Noll, 63.
[285]Noll, 122.
[286]Noll, 124.

they mistakenly held that only the Pope could interpret the scriptures. He demanded a return to the scriptures, and the core message of salvation sola gratia, sola fide—salvation by grace alone through faith alone. He based his assertions on sola Scriptura—solely on the Holy Scriptures. At the Diet of Worms, where he was summoned to recant his challenge, Luther famously declared:

> Since then your serene majesty and your lordships seek a simple answer, I will give it in this manner, neither horned nor toothed: Unless I am convinced by the testimony of the Scriptures or by clear reason (for I do not trust either in the pope or in councils alone, since it is well known that they have often erred and contradicted themselves), I am bound by the Scriptures I have quoted and my conscience is captive to the Word of God. I cannot and I will not retract anything, since it is neither safe nor right to go against conscience.[287]

Luther's 1520 revolt against the church rocked the institutionalized relationship between the Catholic Church and the Holy Roman Emperor, ultimately ushering in a period of religious upheaval and warfare that would only conclude with the 1648 Peace of Westphalia. This turbulent century, ensnared in religious warfare—in particular the infamous Thirty Years' War—contained the seeds for the final dissolution of the "medieval synthesis" and the emergence of the modern nation-state.

In the temporary 1555 Peace of Augsburg, each state within the fracturing Holy Roman Empire received the liberty to choose to be either Lutheran or Catholic—*cuius regio eius religio* (whose the region, his the religion).[288] Individual religious freedom was not permitted; one's religion was determined by one's state. However, that individual rulers and states could choose their own religion revealed a significant fracture in the political power of the Roman church. The Peace of Augsburg therefore denied the heretofore universal order of the *Respublica Christiana*, and replaced that order with a society of princely states that were granted religious self-determination.[289] By the mid 16th century, John Calvin began to articulate a further refinement in the relationship between the divine and political realms. In his *Institutes of the Christian Religion*, Calvin argued that "man is under two kinds of government—one spiritual, by which the conscience is formed to piety and the service of God; the other political, by which a man is instructed in the duties of humanity and civility, which are to be observed in an intercourse

---

[287]Luther quoted in Noll, 154.
[288]Palmer and Colton, 78-9.
[289]Bobbit, 488.

with mankind."[290] Further expounding on the duties of each realm, Calvin wrote that the "spiritual jurisdiction pertains to the life of the soul," and the "temporal jurisdiction pertains not only to the provision of food and clothing, but to the enactment of laws to regulate a man's life among his neighbors by the rules of holiness, integrity, and sobriety." Calvin specifically noted that "the former has for its seat the interior of the mind and may be termed a spiritual kingdom"; the latter "only directs external conduct" and may be called "a political one."[291] Calvin was concerned that Christians abide by the laws of lawful governments (render unto Caesar what is Caesar's), so he wrote: "For man contains, as it were, two worlds, capable of being governed by various rulers and various laws. This distinction will prevent what the Gospel inculcates concerning spiritual liberty from being misapplied to political regulations, as though Christians were less subject to the external government of human laws because their consciences have been set at liberty before God." He saw divine providence in the creation of government—he argued that God uses just government to regulate the affairs of mankind. Finally, Calvin also recognized that the depravity of man required that government not be isolated in the hands of the few. "The vice or imperfection of men," he wrote, "renders it safer and more tolerable for the government to be in the hands of many, that they may afford each other mutual assistance and admonition, and that if any one arrogate to himself more than is his right, the many may act as censors and masters to restrain his ambition."[292] Thus, Calvin's writings, coming in the midst of the turbulent Reformation, argued for separately sanctioned roles for church and state, encouraged Christians to follow the laws of just governments, and recognized the necessity for the diffusion and separation of power within the temporal realm.

The Reformation is significant to Western political development because its soteriology fundamentally and permanently altered the relationship between church and state. Salvation was seen by the Reformers to be *sola fide, solo gratia*, and *sola Scriptura*, and most importantly, solely between the individual and God. As Max Scheler notes, the Reformation "destroy[ed] the very basis of the idea that the Church is the institution of salvation."[293] Both the pre-reform grip of the church on the faithful, as well as the political sanction of the church on the princely realms, were abolished. At first glance, this would seem, as one scholar argues, an invitation to moral and

---

[290]John Calvin, "The Institutes of the Christian Religion," in *Western Heritage: A Reader*, 1st ed. rev., ed. History Department, Hillsdale College (Acton, MA: Tapestry Press, 2000), 473.

[291]Calvin, "The Institutes of the Christian Religion," in *Western Heritage*, 473.

[292]Calvin, "The Institutes of the Christian Religion," in *Western Heritage*, 476.

[293]Scheler, 92.

social anarchy.[294] But the "priesthood of every man," in combination with the highest ideals of Christian love, formed the basis for a new appeal to conscience—not based on the performance of the sacraments or ritualistic prayers, but rather a transforming understanding of the liberating concept of divine grace.

Coming at the end of the wars of religion, the Peace of Westphalia again redefined the prevailing order. Beyond implicitly recognizing the legitimacy of territorial states, the treaty inaugurated further religious freedoms by (1) officially recognizing Calvinism, and (2) by moving beyond the Augsburg principle of *cuius regio eius religio*. Westphalia granted to individual states superiority in all ecclesial and political matters; but more importantly, it granted the right to individual citizens to choose their own religion, the right to public worship, and protection, subsequent to a five-year grace period, from expulsion by a prince of differing religion.[295] Thus were the principles of the separation of church and state, as well as religious liberty and the right to religious self-expression, embedded in the Peace of Westphalia.

It was the Puritans who left England to register their most ardent expression of religious freedom by starting a new life in the new world. Their voyage was a prelude to a new form of contractual, constitutional government that would enshrine the original Christian imperatives in modern American democracy. Christianity's anthropology, its distrust of human nature, would be revealed in the American attempt to limit and diffuse the powers of government. Calvin's "two-powers" view that both church and state are directly ordained by God, with neither subordinate to the other and neither entitled to control the other, is enshrined in the American political ethos. The heritage of this ethos can be found not only in Jesus Christ's directive to render appropriately to Caesar and to God, but also in writings such as St. Augustine's *The City of God*: "As citizens of the heavenly city, Christians knew that the yearnings of the human heart could be satisfied only in God and the hope for peace would be realized only in fellowship with God."[296] Yet, as Augustine also argued, in this temporal life, "Christians were full citizens of the communities in which they lived. Like other citizens, they cherished law, stability, [and] concord."[297] And while, as one scholar notes, the American system drew from many sources, including the secular Enlightenment, the Calvinist solution of the two-powers view of church and state was a prominent feature in the minds of the American founders. According to Douglas Kelly, a contemporary

---

[294]Lee Harris, *Civilization and its Enemies* (New York, NY: Free Press, 2004), 185.
[295]Bobbit, 506.
[296]Wilken, 202.
[297]Wilken, 202.

scholar of theology, it was the historical and political Christian imperatives and their underlying doctrines which featured prominently in the consent of the governed, in constitutional limitations of all civil power and all institutions, in the checks and balances of power in the political and legal structure, in the liberty of conscience, and in the inalienable right to resist tyranny.[298] In conclusion, as Kelly argues, by the late eighteenth century, Christian doctrinal imperatives "had exercised pervasive influence on civil polities throughout much of the Western world." Indeed, one could argue, as Kelly does, that the practical implications of Christian doctrine and its views on personal liberty and the social contract "came to play a major part in modern governmental arrangements because its theological assumptions about God's transcendent law, man's fallen state, and God's redemptive purposes for humanity were in general accord with a healthy and balanced functioning of society."[299]

---

[298]Douglas Kelly, *The Emergence of Liberty in the Modern World* (Phillipsburg, NJ: P&R Publishing, 1992), 141.

[299]Kelly, 142.

III. In the Mind of the Faithful

Identity — Trauma — Ressentiment
and Transnational Islamic Revival

There is something in the religious culture of Islam which inspired, in even the humblest peasant or peddler, a dignity and courtesy toward others never exceeded and rarely equaled in other civilizations. And yet, in moments of upheaval and disruption, when the deeper passions are stirred, this dignity and courtesy toward others can give way to an explosive mixture of rage and hatred which impels even the government of an ancient and civilized country—even the spokesman of a great spiritual and ethical religion—to espouse kidnapping and assassination, and try to find, in the life of their Prophet, approval and indeed precedent for such actions.

Bernard Lewis in The Roots of Muslim Rage[300]

Today's Islamic world seems riddled by a schizophrenia that confounds most Western observers. Celebrations in the Arab street after the attacks of 9/11 are juxtaposed against solemn official statements by Arab governments in support of the so-called war on terror. Virulent outbreaks of blood lust, as when the mutilated bodies of four American contractors were publicly hung for viewing on a bridge span in Fallujah (Iraq), are contrasted with the ecumenical religious service attended jointly by both Muslims and Christians in a Christian cathedral in Rabat, Morocco, in the wake of the Madrid train bombings in March 2004. Or, as a Muslim shopkeeper in Spain recently observed: "Saddam Hussein is a son of a bitch, a tyrant, but that's not a reason to drop that arsenal on Iraq."[301] In order to delve into this mind of the faithful, we need to come to terms with an identity phenomenon that strongly resides within the broad and transnational Islamic milieu. In doing so, Dale Eickelman, professor of anthropology at Dartmouth College, rightly states that "buzzwords such as 'fundamentalism,' and catchy phrases such as Samuel Huntington's 'West versus the Rest' or Daniel Lerner's 'Mecca or mechanization,' are of little use . . . they obscure or even distort the immense spiritual and intellectual ferment that is taking place today among the world's nearly one billion Muslims . . ."[302] Instead of reducing the analysis into

---

[300]Bernard Lewis, "The Roots of Muslim Rage," *The Atlantic Monthly* (September 1990), URL: www.theatlantic.com/issues/90sep/rage.htm, accessed 20 January 2004.

[301]"Madrid Suspect Was on Police Radar," *The Wall Street Journal Europe*, 19-21 March 2004, A5.

[302]Dale F. Eickelman, "The Coming Transformation of the Muslim World," the *Templeton Lecture on Religion and World Affairs*, Foreign Policy Research Institute, August 1999, URL: www.fpri.org/fpriwire/0709.199908.eickelman.muslimtransform.html. Accessed 6 April 2004.

made-for-television sound bites, true insight into the mind of the faithful requires that we come to terms with the fact that the Muslim world writ large has, in modern times, been profoundly traumatized.

The trauma comes primarily from four main influences: (1) the impact of European colonialism, (2) the pressures of modern secularism, (3) the blunt reality of military and scientific impotency vis-à-vis the West, and (4) the distorting influences of modern Arab successes. These four factors are perceived as hostile vectors eroding the core and foundation of the Muslim identity. The image of a religion or culture under assault—or of Islam besieged by Western culture, saturated as it is by secularism—is a pervasive theme throughout the Muslim world. As a result, Muslims have responded with a renewed emphasis on the images and convictions of their core identity. This manifests itself in the form of a widespread Islamic revival, or in the words of R. Hrair Dekmejian, a "recent quest for a return to the Islamic ethos." This return appears to be, in the words of the same scholar, "a natural response to the successive pathological experiences which have buffeted Islamic societies in contemporary times."[303]

Yet this renewal or revival also has given birth to a contrarian reaction which focuses itself against outside influences. The reaction often manifests itself in outbursts of frustration and a yearning for revenge, as seen, for example, in the spontaneous celebrations in response to the attacks of 9/11. This smoldering hostility makes for a fertile recruitment medium for those who wish to translate those collective emotions into military action. The phenomenon is best captured by Max Scheler's concept of ressentiment, which will be explored in the following pages. The diagram opposite is constructed to depict the pressures of an identity under siege combined with a desire for revenge. The Arabic scripted symbology on the inside of the picture is *Shahada* (the Muslim statement of faith), and the four arrows depict the four main pressures listed above. The backdrop—a group of youthful Muslim protestors—represents the collective frustration of the Muslim faithful. Ressentiment in some cases translates into passionate and suicidal military energy.

---

[303]H. Hrair Dekmejian quoted in John Obert Voll, *Islam: Continuity and Change in the Modern World*, 2d ed. (Syracuse, N.Y.: Syracuse University Press, 1994), 379.

Ressentiment and the Sources of Muslim Trauma
(Source: Author)

Identity as a Phenomenon

Before exploring the four sources of Islamic trauma, the concept of ressentiment, and the resulting transnational Islamic revival, it seems worthwhile to
pause and reflect on the complex ethos of Muslim identity. Islam is an
inheritance—in the same sense that Americans inherit their cultural identity.
This identity extends even to those Muslims who do not actually practice the
Islamic religion.[304] This is what one observer has called "practical Islam."
According to Dr. Mohammad Tozi, "practical Islam" is a way of life that is
passed on from generation to generation, a social phenomenon that defines

---

[304]A similar phenomenon or trend can be observed in the United States. Though many Americans call themselves "Christians," many are actually referring—knowingly or unknowingly—to a
set of cultural values or feelings or inheritances, rather than to a deeper faith and doctrinal understanding of the Christian religion.

one's values and that is part of one's thoughts and habits. As Tozi, a self-ascribed non-practicing Muslim, described it, "it is an inherited religious behavior—when I hear the call for prayer, it has cultural meaning for me—when I hear or do or say something, I naturally say *inshallah* (if Allah wills it), because this is how I think, even though I am not a religious person."[305] Tozi explained that while he does not practice Islam, this is his cultural identity, what is in his words a "transcendant, global value system that links me to other Muslims and their identity."

Dr. Mustafa Zekri, Professor of Anthropology and Religion at the University of Rabat, explains that to many Muslims, "Islam is a religion that comes as an inheritance. The practices are carried out as part of one's culture," and even if there are those who do not see a profound personal meaning in Islam, "there are rituals which one must follow, sets of forbidden things which are to be avoided, and texts which are to be treated respectfully, even though few know and study them in depth."[306] Mohammad Gessus, a well-known political pundit and strategist in Morocco—and also a non-practicing Muslim—warmly described the Islamic identity as "an historical and sociological phenomenon, something quite complex and diversified with a fourteen-hundred-year heritage—a religion, a culture, a way of life, and a brotherhood of faith." According to Gessus, "Islam is a total way of life, a way of eating, a way of social interaction, of dressing, of speaking, indeed a comprehensive and deeply ingrained inheritance that is difficult to shed. This extends right down to hearing someone's name—in the Muslim world, one's name is part of the uniqueness and the distinction."[307]

Dr. Daoud Casewit is the Executive Secretary of the Moroccan-American Commission for Educational and Cultural Exchange. He is an American convert to Islam, and used to go by Stephen Casewit—now Daoud Casewit. For Dr. Casewit, Islam's identity and the *ummah* (or the community of believers) is "a beautiful concept, a mythical community that has never been realized, an ideal but not a reality. The most tangible image of this community occurs during the hajj—especially when we pray; we pray in Arabic."[308]

---

[305]Dr. Mohammad Tozi, University of Casablanca, Morocco, interview by the author, 16 March 04.

[306]Dr. Mustafa Zekri, Professor of Anthropology and Religion, University of Rabat, Morocco, interview with the author, 18 March 04.

[307]Mohammad Gessus, Rabat, Morocco, interview with the author, 18 March 04.

[308]Dr. Daoud Casewit, Executive Secretary, Moroccan-American Commission for Educational and Cultural Exchange, Rabat, Morocco, interview with the author, 17 March 04.

Shiite religious leader in Baku, Azerbaijan.
Photo by author.

To a great extent, the common Islamic heritage prevails regardless of nationality, local contexts, or sectarian division (Sunni, Shia, and Sufi). As Dr. Abdallah Schleifer, a practicing Muslim and distinguished lecturer at the American University in Cairo comments, "I can be parachuted into a village in Indonesia and lead the daily prayer."[309] Islam thus provides a unifying and comforting identity to its believers; in it, people can find the answers to all their questions. According to a Shiite *akhund* (Islamic scholar) in Baku, Azerbaijan, "Islam is the only religion for Allah and the highest, most senior religion of all the world because it answers where people are from, where they are going, and what their duty and purpose is in the world."[310] Its comprehensive nature is said to reflect the unity of Allah. Vasim Mamedaliev, the

---

[309]Dr. Abdallah Schleifer, Distinguished Lecturer and Director of the Adham Center for Journalism, American University in Cairo, interview with the author, 22 March 04.

[310]*Akhund* Tilman, Shiite Islamic scholar, Baku, Azerbaijan, interview with the author, 3 Apr 04.

Chairman of the Religious Council of the Caucasus Muslim region, stresses the fact that "the Islamic community is a community of believers irrespective of nationality."[311] Mamedaliev is a Shiite who chairs the committee that represents the faithful from Turkey, Pakistan, Iran, Ukraine, and Azerbaijan. He is also the Chairman of the Department of Arabic Philology and the Dean of the Theological Faculty at the University of Baku in Azerbaijan. "Ultimately," he says, "all Muslims agree on the core beliefs about Allah, the Qur'an, and the prophet. Islam is a religion of unity—we all gather in Mecca—we are a brotherhood of peace and friendship."[312]

The Arabic word *ummah*—the community of believers—broadly comprehends the comments and thoughts shared by the individuals above. Words such as community, brotherhood, and identity begin to convey its meaning, yet they fall short of revealing the emotive depths of the phenomenon. There is a deep sense of history that is associated with the word ummah. The consciousness of this history may be regarded as what sociologist Herbert Spencer called "representative feelings—the organic results that a segment of mankind has gathered through the course of the centuries, that become condensed into an inherited instinct and constitute an object of heredity in the individual."[313] This heredity and sense of divine historical providence is conveyed to Muslims in the Qur'an. The Qur'an speaks to the special place that Allah reserved for the *ummah: Ye are the best of peoples, evolved for mankind, enjoining what is right, forbidding what is wrong, and believing in Allah. If only the People of the Book [Jews and Christians] had faith; it would be best for them. Among them are some who have faith, but most of them are perverted transgressors* (Surah Al 'Imran, 3:110).[314]

Others have commented on the unique characteristics of Muslim identity. Sayyid Qutb wrote that "A Muslim has no country except that part of the earth where the *Shariah* of God is established and human relationships are based on the foundation of relationship with God; a Muslim has no nationality except his belief, which makes him a member of the Muslim community in Dar-ul-Islam; a Muslim has no relatives except those who share the belief in God, and thus a bond is established between him and other believers through their relationship with God."[315] Dr. Tarek Mitri, a religious scholar at the World Council of Churches in Geneva, Switzerland, summarizes the meaning of the *ummah* in the following way: "In Islam, there is great force and strength that

---

[311]Vasim Mamedaliev, Chairman of the Department of Arabic Philology and Dean of the Theological Faculty, University of Baku, Azerbaijan, interview with the author, 23 March 04.

[312]Mamedaliev, interview with the author.

[313]Herbert Spencer quoted in Goldziher, 231.

[314]*The Meaning of the Holy Qur'an.*

[315]Sayyid Qutb, *Milestones*, 222-23.

stems from this feeling of belonging to a transnational and trans-historical identity—the *ummah*—it is at the same time both a church with kindred spirits and the fellowship of association, but also a political notion embodying patriotism and nationalism."[316]

It was the prophet Muhammad who first defined the *ummah*. Indeed, "the first Islamic community founded by the Prophet Muhammad constitutes for Muslims the perfect expression of social existence."[317] Muslims perceive that history with a special sense of nostalgia, viewing the first collective expression of the *ummah* with admiration and respect. For Muslims, it is the prophet Mohammad, the original *ummah*, and the revelations from Allah in the Qur'an that link a distant past to a glorious future, and offer perhaps a small glimpse of paradise on earth.[318] The chemistry of the original *ummah* was tribal—that of the Bedouin kinship group—an identity defined by its collective spirit and not, as predominantly in Western societies, the rights or responsibilities of the individual. The lack of clearly delineated geographical boundaries, the nomadic nature of Bedouin culture, and the physical features of the Hijaz region of the Arabian Peninsula imparted an enduring legacy to the nature of the ummah. The challenges posed by the Arabian desert and the lack of natural boundaries were overcome by tribal affiliation and strong group identity. Writing in the last century, T.E. Lawrence noted that the ummah lost its geographical sense because of its nomadic heritage.[319] This blurring of boundaries within the legacy of the *ummah* has been carried forward to the present day. Modern scholars speak of the "deterritorialization" of identity, ethnicity, and religious activism.[320] As James Piscatory, the eminent scholar of Islamic identity at Oxford, has written, "location and space have undergone such transformation that it is possible to argue that . . . geography is clearly not merely a physical construct; spatial relations may preeminently be a state of mind."[321]

---

[316]Dr. Tarek Mitri, Professor of Interreligious Relations and Dialogue, World Council of Churches, Geneva, Switzerland, interview with the author, 17 February 04.

[317]R. Hrair Dekmejian, *Islam in Revolution: Fundamentalism in the Arab World*, 2d ed. (Syracuse, N.J.: Syracuse University Press, 1995), 11.

[318]Inamdar, 228.

[319]T. E. Lawrence, *Seven Pillars of Wisdom* (New York: Anchor Books, 1991), 45.

[320]Eickelman and Piscatori, 136.

[321]Eickelman and Piscatori, 136-37.

Children playing soccer in the alleyways of Old Rabat, Morocco.
Photo by author.

The concept of sacred geography comes to mind—unconstrained by modern political boundaries, but fused together by the transnational religious identity of Islam. Susanne Rudolph, a scholar at the University of Chicago, describes this space as a "sacred territory" where "transnational activity [is] guided by imaginary maps whose boundaries do not approximate the spaces on political maps."[322] Islam's transnational sacred geography is concretized by ancient religious and tribal customs such as pilgrimage, trade, markets, and marriage networks.[323] Muslims are encouraged to complete the *hajj* at least once during their

---

[322]Rudolph and Eickelman, 12.
[323]Rudolph and Eickelman, 15.

lives. The annual pilgrimage to Mecca brings the *ummah* from throughout the world together for collective worship and prayer. On a daily basis, the faithful turn toward Mecca five times during ritual prayer. Mecca is the spiritual center of Islam's sacred space. It represents a powerful emotive wellspring—the epicenter of the collective identity and unity of all the faithful. But modernity has also affected the *ummah*. Today, modern communications techniques act as links across the religious space. The Internet, satellite television, DVDs, and cheaply reproduced audio and videocassettes make available a global information sphere that ties the community together. To some extent, it seems ironic that products of modernity have provided the *ummah* with heretofore unprecedented opportunities for visualization and communication. While this sacred geography does not replace standard political boundaries or territorial nation states, Rudolph argues that we can imagine it as a "transparent plastic overlay" or an "alternative meaning system superimposed upon the meaning system of political maps."[324] This has relevancy for both practicing and non-practicing Muslims throughout the Islamic world. It represents an inherited (or, in some cases, acquired) identity that binds Muslims together, especially during times of crisis, when it offers a means of psychological and cultural defense. Today, more than ever, that identity is experiencing the stresses of modernity. In the words of one thoughtful scholar, it is a crisis of spirit, of identity, of culture, and of legitimacy.[325]

Trauma and the Muslim Identity

Colonialism. The first external challenge to Muslim identity came in the form of European colonialism. On 1 July 1798 Napoleon Bonaparte landed 4,300 troops on the beaches of Alexandria, Egypt, and took control of the city after dawn the following day. As Karen Armstrong has written, "Napoleon brought with him a corps of scholars, a library of modern European literature, a scientific laboratory, and a printing press with Arabic type. The new scientific, secularist culture of the West had invaded the Muslim world, and it would never be the same again."[326] Colonialism was a shock to Muslim identity for several reasons. First, it challenged Islam's long-term historical imperatives. Islam was seen by Muslims as an ever-expanding missionary religion, bringing the ultimate unity of Allah and the rightly guided justice of Islamic society and law to the rest of the world. Historically, the Crusaders had been repelled and it was Islamic armies that continued to attempt to expand their influence in the Mediterranean and throughout Central Asia and the Caucasus. The Mongols, once a greater threat to Islam than the Crusaders, had been repelled, co-opted, or integrated into Islam.

---

[324]Rudolph and Eickelman, 12.

[325]Dekmejian, *Islam in Revolution,* 7.

[326]Karen Armstrong, *The Battle for God* (London: Harper Collins Publishers, 2000), 58.

But a crumbling Ottoman Empire proved incapable of defeating European powers. With the Ottoman Empire contracting and increasingly under siege, the French would eventually lay claim to much of the Maghreb region of North Africa, the British to the Levant, and Britain, France, and to a smaller extent Germany, to sub-Saharan Africa. By 1914 Morocco, Algeria, and Tunisia were under French control, and Egypt, Sudan and parts of the Arabian Peninsula were administered by the British government and British interests.

The second reason why European colonialism was a profound shock to the Muslim identity is that traditionally Islamic society viewed European culture as barbaric and inferior. As early as 1068, Said ibn Ahmad, the chief justice of the Muslim city of Toledo, Spain, had remarked:

> For those of them who live furthest to the north, between the last of the seven climates and the limits of the inhabited world, the excessive distance of the sun in relation to the zenith line makes the air cold and the sky cloudy. Their temperaments are therefore, frigid, their humors raw, their bellies gross, their color pale, their hair long and lank. Thus they lack keenness of understanding and clarity of intelligence, and are overcome by ignorance and apathy, lack of discernment and stupidity . . .[327]

Throughout the Renaissance and Enlightenment, it was the Europeans who sent scholars, scientists, linguists, and merchants to the lands of Islam. Islamic leaders saw little need to reciprocate, since they viewed themselves as the center of an expanding civilization.

But perhaps the greatest impact of European imperialism was the legacy of its collapse. The withdrawal of French and British colonial influence left a disorganized power vacuum that was haphazardly filled by secular Arab regimes and the newly emerging state of Israel. By the end of World War I, the Ottoman Turks were driven out of Palestine by the combined efforts of the British and French, and it was in November 1917 that the British Government issued the now-famous Balfour Declaration, which expressed support for the idea of a national homeland for the Jewish people.[328] After the Treaty of Versailles, the allied powers agreed to settle disputed areas throughout Palestine, Syria, and Trans Jordan under the terms of a political mandate. The mandate, which came into effect in 1922, contained the following provisions:

---

[327]Said ibn Ahmad quoted in Inamdar, xi.
[328]Colin Chapman, Whose Promised Land? *The Continuing Crisis over Israel and Palestine* (Grand Rapids, MI: Baker Books, 2003), 27.

The Mandatory shall be responsible for placing the country under such political, administrative, and economic conditions as will secure the establishment of the Jewish national home, as laid down in the preamble, and the development of self-governing institutions and also for safe-guarding the civil and religious rights of all inhabitants of Palestine, irrespective of race and religion.[329]

Britain took over responsibility for Palestine, and the French were tasked to administer Syria. The interwar period witnessed a growing Zionist influence throughout Palestine as the Jewish Diaspora began to trickle back into the region. Numerous clashes and Arab revolts occurred as the British tried to deal with an increasingly volatile situation. Eventually, the British concluded that the Mandate was no longer workable, and in 1939 suggested that a joint Arab-Israeli state be formed. During Word War II, the region saw continued Jewish immigration and the struggle between the Arabs and the Zionists intensified. By 1947, the British decided to hand the problem of Palestine and the Mandate over to the United Nations, and a special UN commission decided on the creation of two separate states under what became known as the 1947 UN Partition Plan.[330] The Jews in Palestine accepted the plan, but the Arabs rejected it out-of-hand, in part because they believed that it benefited the Zionists. Further armed struggle ensued and "when the British Mandate officially ended on 14 May 1948, Dr. Chaim Weizmann raised the flag of David and proclaimed the new State of Israel."[331]

The British were also key players in the creation of the modern state of Saudi Arabia. Their influence extended throughout the Arabian Peninsula and the Arabian Gulf region, where they administered British protectorates in Saudi Arabia, Kuwait, Bahrain, Iraq, and the United Arab Emirates. The British government had long tacitly supported Ibn Saud and his quest to consolidate the Islamic holy land under his political power and the religious authority of Wahhabi *ulema*. In 1927 the British officially dropped the Saudi state's protectorate status and recognized Saudi Arabia's independence, thereby empowering and legitimizing the royal house of Saud.

---

[329]Chapman, 28.
[330]Chapman, 29.
[331]Chapman, 30.

Abandoned oil fields and slums in Baku, Azerbaijan.

Photo by author.

Throughout the region, boundaries were often haphazardly drawn, sometimes based on personal relationships between the colonial administrators and competing local economic interests. Legend has it that in some cases, national borders were determined by sketches drawn on the backs of napkins after cozy conversations during cocktail parties. Regardless of the accuracy of these claims, the fact remains that the incursion of European colonialism in the region left a muddled wake of Western secularism, arbitrary boundaries, authoritarian governments, and the seeds of the modern day Arab-Israeli struggle—a legacy that is seen to this day as a profoundly negative influence on the Arab Muslim identity.

Secularism. The second notable pressure leveraged against Muslim identity has been secularism. To traditional and nostalgic Muslims, no single event better represents the incursion of secularism than what happened on 24 July1924, when the British government signed the Treaty of Lausanne with the Turkish government. The Treaty of Lausanne formally recognized Turkey's independence. In return, Mustafa Kemal (better known today as Attaturk) officially dissolved the Islamic Caliphate, turned the religious schools over to a civil education ministry, stripped all the religious *ulema* of their authority and deported some of them, and absorbed as property of the state all Islamic religious properties and endowments. The Islamic Caliphate was radically swept aside and Turkey was abruptly secularized. According to Islamic sources, the British Foreign Secretary, Lord Curzon, is rumored to have said: "The point at issue is that Turkey has been destroyed and shall never rise again, because we have destroyed her spiritual power: the Caliphate and

Islam."[332] In the wake of European colonialism and World Wars I and II, secular governments came to power throughout the Muslim world. These governments broadly rejected Islam's historical, political, and religious imperatives. Instead, in order to lend themselves legitimacy, many assumed the mantle of modern nationalism. In Egypt, Gamal Abdel Nasser became the leading proponent of Pan-Arab nationalism. In Syria and Iraq, Ba'thism became the new official state dogma. In Libya, Muammar Quadafi came to power in 1969 after displacing the ruling monarch, and advocated an anti-Western approach. The Gulf Kingdoms, led by Saudi Arabia, were characterized by monarchical, anti-Soviet regimes that were supported by the West in the fight against Communism. Though not openly secular, these ruling families were privately but unabashedly drawn to the modern technological and social allures of Western culture. Taken as a whole, the secularization of the Arab Muslim world was deeply underway by the 1950s and 60s.

Yet this secularization did not produce open and democratic governments. Instead, police states, dictatorial power, and corruption seemed to be the rule. Even with semi-popular and charismatic leadership, as was the case in Nasser's Egypt, the pervasive presence of the state security apparatus still dominated the political culture. This inevitably produced tension as anti-secularists and proponents of traditional Islamic politico-religious collusion clashed against the new order. It gave birth to organizations such as the Muslim Brotherhood in Egypt, which in many ways formed the ideological base for today's Islamic revolutionaries. Thus the intrusion of secularism into Islamic polities introduced a persistent dialectic, whereby the contest between the proponents of a secular state and those favoring an Islamic polity produced conflict and tension.[333] The tension grew out of the fact that proponents of Islamic polity did not respond favorably to either authoritarianism or charisma. To them, the ruler was not to be obeyed because of his own personhood; his legitimacy was based only on the virtue of holding his position through the law of Allah and the prophet. According to this perspective, the ruler's right to obedience was derived from his own personal observance of that law and from no other thing. Hence, if he departed from the law, as secularized Islamic government inherently did, he no longer was entitled to obedience and his orders were no longer to be obeyed.[334] Thus, as Karen Armstrong points out, faithful Muslims abhorred the secular influences of Western society on their political systems, specifically because they separated religion from politics and church from state. They would rather see their societies governed according to

---

[332]Abdul Qadeem Zallum, *How the Kilafah was Destroyed* (London: Al-Khilafah Publications, 1998), 183.

[333]Dekmejian, *Islam in Revolution*, 19.

[334]Qutb, *Social Justice in Islam*, 121.

shariah, the sacred law of Islam, because in this way, governments would both derive their legitimacy from, and be held accountable to, that same law.[335]

Modern Muslim governments have faced thorny challenges posed by these historical Islamic imperatives about political and religious culture. As a result, Muslim leaders "have often lacked the requisite 'political capital' to generate effective policies that constitute the building blocks of stable public order."[336] That kind of political capital comes from a tradition of consensual and contractual government. However, as Bernard Lewis has written, in the history of Islam

> There are no parliaments or representative assemblies of any kind, no councils or communes, no chambers of nobility or estates, no municipalities . . . nothing but the sovereign power, to which the subject owed complete and unwavering obedience as a religious duty imposed by the Holy Law . . . [T]he political thinking of Islam has been dominated by such maxims as "tyranny is better than anarchy" . . .[337]

Half a century of modernity has not changed this status quo. Practically speaking, most Arab Muslim governments continue to uphold their authority by means of a police state apparatus and other means of overt and covert repression. This is certainly the case in Egypt, Algeria, and Tunisia. Elsewhere, corrupt and often repressive monarchies are the rule of the day in countries such as Saudi Arabia, Yemen, Oman, the United Arab Emirates, and Jordan. In other cases such as Syria, Libya, and until recently Iraq, authoritarian regimes oppress their populations. To the Islamic faithful, the effects of secularism are pervasive, persistent, and painful. As a recent editorial in the London Islamic daily *Al-Hayat* put it, "governments continue to be run by a single leader under the banner of a single political party, with no guarantees to individuals or groups that they will be part of the political process, unless they are an integral part of the leadership. This political, economic, and social oligarchy has resulted in a poisonous fallout that is manifested in the lack of transparency in government practices and institutions, including the judiciary."[338] One can argue that the preceding list of maladies stems not only from secularist influences but also from the extensions and imperatives of Islamic traditions.

---

[335]Armstrong, 36.

[336]Dekmejian, *Islam in Revolution*, 27.

[337]Bernard Lewis, "Communism and Islam," in The Middle East in Transition, Walter Praeger, ed. (New York; Frederick A. Praeger, 1958), 318-319.

[338]Nizar Abdel-Kader, "Promoting Reform Efforts in the Middle East," *Dar Al Hayat*, online ed., 21 June 2004, URL: www.daralhayat.net/actions/print2.php, accessed 21 June 2004.

Impotency. The third major assault on Islamic identity has been the painful self-perception of impotency vis-à-vis the West. The recent history of successive military defeats is a searing reality to the psyche of the Islamic identity, whose history exalts the exploits of a proud desert warrior class and Islam's initial and dramatic 100-year military expansion. Since 1948, Islamic armies have been roundly defeated at least seven times by Western militaries. In 1948,

> within hours of the creation of the State of Israel, Arab forces from Jordan, Syria, Egypt, Lebanon and Iraq launched an attack. In the fighting which followed during the next seven months, the Jewish forces defeated the Arab armies and took over large areas in the north (Galilee) and the south (the Negev) . . . between 700,000 and 800,000 Palestinian Arabs left or were driven from their homes . . . By the time of the ceasefire in January 1949, Israel occupied seventy-seven per cent of the land (i.e., one third more than it would have if the Arabs had accepted the UN [Partition] plan).[339]

In the Suez Crisis of 1956, President Nasser fomented a war by nationalizing the Suez Canal and denying access to Israeli and some Western shipping. Israel invaded the Sinai on 29 October 1956, and took the entire peninsula in less than a week, after which Britain and France launched an airborne assault to recover the Suez Canal. After strong international pressure, Israeli, British, and French forces withdrew.[340] In the Six-Day War of 1967, Nasser again instigated hostilities, this time by closing the Gulf of Aqaba to shipping and by requesting that the United Nations withdraw its forces from the border between Israel and Egypt. Israel conducted a devastating air strike that destroyed virtually the entire Egyptian air force while it was still on the ground. In less then a week, Israeli armor was victorious against combined Arab Muslim armies and occupied the entire Sinai, the Gaza Strip, the West Bank, and the Golan Heights.[341] In the Yom Kippur War of 1973, the Egyptian army successfully launched a surprise attack across the Suez Canal. However, eventually and with the help of American aid, the Israeli military again was able to first repel, and then encircle and destroy, a large part of the Arab armies before a cease-fire came into effect. Between 1978 and 1982, the Israeli army pushed into Lebanon in order to root out Palestinian forces that were conducting cross-border attacks into Israel. The Israelis pushed as far as West Beirut before finally withdrawing after a prolonged occupation. In the 1990-1991 Gulf War, a coalition of military forces, the preponderance of which came from the United States and the United Kingdom, dramatically expelled the armies of Saddam Hus-

---

[339]Chapman, 30-31.
[340]Chapman, 32.
[341]Chapman, 32.

sein from Kuwait, effectively vanquishing the largest Arab Muslim army in the world. For over ten years, the coalition held the Iraqi military at bay, striking at will whenever Saddam Hussein decided to test UN resolutions and sanctions against him. Finally, in the 2003 Iraq war, Western armies led by the United States and the United Kingdom conquered Saddam's Iraq, taking the capital city of Baghdad in a dramatically short time. The Muslim world watched in stunned and schizophrenic silence, unsure whether to applaud the demise of a brutal secular dictator, or to bemoan yet another humiliating defeat at the hands of a Western army.

But the perception of impotency is not limited to the military sphere alone. It also applies to science and technology. Muslims sit down and work on Dell and Apple computers, drive Chevrolet, Ford, Mercedes, and Lexus automobiles, fly in Boeing, Airbus, and Gulfstream aircraft, drive on roads built by Western machinery, and go to work in high rises designed by Western architects. They get their Starbucks Coffee in the morning and go to McDonalds, Kentucky Fried Chicken, and Pizza Hut for lunch. Wealthy Muslims fly to the Mayo Clinic in the United States when they are seriously ill, shop in shopping malls filled with Western couture and electronic merchandise, and buy their food in Western-style supermarkets stocked with imported fine foods from Europe and America. In the Gulf States, the oil from which they have obtained their national wealth is pumped out of the ground by Western workers and engineers, and the petroleum infrastructure is designed, maintained, and operated by Western experts. In an ironic note, even the helicopters, tanks, and fighter jets that many Muslim militaries use to try to defend themselves are designed and produced in the West. In short, there are no Muslim computers, cars, aircraft, electronics, or hospitals in the Western world. The discrepancy—the impotence of collective Muslim modernity vis-à-vis the superiority of Western-dominated science, engineering, industrial production, and medicine is not lost on the average Muslim. As a result, Muslims have looked elsewhere to sustain their core identity. Islam turns backward toward, as Karen Armstrong puts it, its "sacred beginnings" or the primordial events and glorious historical foundations of its past.[342] It is through performance of Islam's ritualistic practices and the deep consciousness of the *ummah* that the faithful attempt to restore their sense of meaning in the face of this overwhelming Western influence.

Successes. It is only within the context of the previous three factors—colonialism, secularism, and impotence—that this fourth and last one begins to take shape. Islam and the Islamic identity constitute an all-encompassing life system that includes religion, state, and the law. Therefore, finding a substitute identity framework—in the face of Western military might and secularist influence—

---

[342]Armstrong, 35.

has proven to be, in the words of one scholar, "difficult if not impossible."[343] The 1967 Six-Day war symbolized the final failure of Nasser's Pan-Arabist nationalism. But it also signaled an end to the legitimacy of the secularist experiment. To the extent that the Muslim identity ever received legitimacy from the secularist model, the defeat in 1967 signaled its demise. Instead, the faithful began to rescue their identity with a deliberate and steady revival of Islam. The revival is broadly transnational, and signifies the failure and rejection of alternative secularist models. As John Esposito has stated, "modernization has not led to the triumph of secular political and economic ideologies. Liberal nationalism, Arab nationalism and socialism, capitalism and Marxism have, in fact, come to be viewed as the sources of Muslim political and economic failures."[344]

The old fortress city of Rabat, Morocco.

Photo by author.

In a general sense, the Islamic revival is neither stridently spiritual nor ardently militant. In other words, the 1979 Iranian Revolution or the 1981 assassination of Anwar Sadat should not be seen as symbolic of the broader and transnational Islamic revival. John Obert Voll, the noted Islamic scholar, advises that the original militancy of the Iranian revolution has faded as "the revival of activist Islam moved from the periphery of society and politics to the mainstream," reflecting a broader, global trend in the revival of Islam.[345] The focus here is on the broader

---

[343]Dekmejian, *Islam in Revolution*, 25.

[344]John L. Esposito, *Islam and Politics*, 3d ed. (Syracuse, NY: Syracuse University Press, 1991), 271-72.

[345]Voll, 375.

Islamic identity and milieu, and not on the narrower band of revolutionaries and militants.

The broad-based transnational Islamic revival is in part sustained by what many Muslims see as Islam's successes in dealing with challenges from the West. In fact, Islam *itself* is seen as a means of status and recognition vis-à-vis the West. In the words of one observer, "Arabs become a significant people *with* Islam."[346] That the West is forced to deal with a religion—something that post-modern secular society has studiously avoided—seems to elicit a certain amount of *Schadenfreude* from Muslims throughout the world. In addition, the growing leverage afforded to Muslims by petrodollars and energy politics is viewed as an effective counter to Western influence. The preponderance of Muslim influence within OPEC, the world's most powerful energy cartel, lends credibility to the weight of Muslim identity. Finally, Muslims view their own independence as a successful end to European colonial and imperial influence. Even though many Muslim societies are beset by the challenges of modernity, they nevertheless take pride in asserting their independence. They rightly perceive that they can exert pressure and influence in the game of international politics.

Women students at American University Cairo.
Photo by author.

---

[346]Woodberry, interview with the author.

Yet the "regeneration of the Islamic ethos in the contemporary setting is a complex phenomenon that is at once spiritual, economic, and political in nature."[347] In many ways, it is a middle class phenomenon. Newly educated and moderately enfranchised Muslims are reaching back to resurrect their Islamic heritage. It might manifest itself through increased interest in ritualistic prayer, a renewed emphasis on Islamic scholarship, a display of Islamic symbols, or the wearing of religious clothing. The revival is evident in the renewed emphasis of young Muslim women in Cairo on wearing the veil, in Muslim men growing beards or wearing thin mustaches, or in the nightly lighting of mosques, something that was far less prevalent just a few decades ago. Interestingly enough, the increased access to higher education throughout the region has also amplified this revival. As Dekmejian notes, "while a college education has not brought the expected betterment in economic status, it has contributed to a historically unprecedented sharpening of social consciousness among large segments of the Arab middle class. Hence, the acute sensitivity of its members to socioeconomic injustice and the Western cultural assault on their Islamic identity."[348] The faithful thus equate the successful revival of the principles of Islam with the restoration of their own Muslim identity. The Islamic revival offers an alternative to the Western paradigm and seems to be popular on the mass level for the following reasons:

1. It restores the Islamic identity to a multitude of alienated individuals who had lost their social and spiritual bearings.
2. It defines, for the faithful, an unambiguous worldview by clearly identifying the sources of good and evil.
3. It offers the faithful alternative cognitive modalities to deal with the harshness of their own environments.
4. It provides a protest mechanism against the established order.
5. It restores a sense of dignity and belonging and grants a spiritual refuge from uncertainty.[349]

To summarize, the political and social crisis brought about by the intrusion of Western colonialism, secularism, and military and technological dominance has over time produced what one scholar has called "an indigenous response—a return to Islam and its fundamental precepts. Since the onset of Islam's fifteenth century (A.D. 1980), the movement back to Islamic roots has assumed a powerful self-propelling dynamic with significant religious, political, economic, and strategic implications."[350] The response is pervasive.[351] Islamic groups and movements

---

[347]Dekmejian, *Islam in Revolution*, 6.

[348]Dekmejian, *Islam in Revolution*, 48.

[349]This is a slight adaptation and modification of the benefits listed by Dekmejian, whose book was published in 1995. For further reference, see Dekmejian, *Islam in Revolution*, 49.

have sprung up in virtually every part of the Muslim world with the goal of defending their core Islamic identity. It is, in keeping with the nature of the Islamic ummah, a truly transnational phenomenon. It is also polycentric,[352] for it possesses neither a single leader nor an organizational center. It provides Muslims with a cultural anchor in a world awash with multi-culturalism and globalism. It is a broad-based and reactionary phenomenon best described as a transnational Islamic revival.

Ressentiment and the Transnational Islamic Revival

Having discussed the phenomenon of Muslim identity, and the trauma visited on that identity by European colonialism, modern secularism, military and technological impotency, and the distorting influences of recent successes, we now turn to what seems to perplex Western observers most—namely, the apparent schizophrenia of "the mind of the faithful." Why do many Muslims on the one hand celebrate the downfall of the Taliban regime in Afghanistan or of Saddam Hussein in Iraq, and on the other hand, rejoice in the streets after events like 9/11 or the frequent homicidal bombings in Iraq? This is, in many ways, a question of psychology—of understanding the patterns and passions of the soul, and of probing what appears to be a deep psychosis of the collective Muslim identity. Max Scheler's concept of ressentiment provides a surprisingly valuable tool to begin to approach this difficult and sensitive question.

The Phenomenon of Ressentiment. Scheler (1874-1928) was a German philosopher who studied the non-rational, emotive depths of the human mind. In contrast to some of his contemporaries, whose work focused on analytic philosophy, the question of being, phenomenology, existentialism, and post-modern deconstruction (for example, Edmund Husserl and Martin Heidegger), Scheler conducted a penetrating study of the psychology of tragic human experiences, delving into human feelings and emotions such as love and hate.[353] His primary work, originally entitled *Über Ressentiment und moralisches Werturteil* (Ressentiment and Moral Value-Judgment), was first published in 1912.[354]

---

[350]Dekmejian, *Islam in Revolution*, 3.

[351]Dekmejian, *Islam in Revolution*, 3.

[352]Dekmejian, *Islam in Revolution*, 3.

[353]For a more substantial introduction to Scheler and the impact of his work, please see Manfred Frings' introduction in Scheler, 1-7.

[354]Though Friedrich Nietzsche wrote extensively about ressentiment, Scheler did not agree with his characterization of the "flower of ressentiment" in the concept of Christian love. In fact, Scheler dedicates an entire chapter of his book (Christian Morality and Ressentiment) to refute Nietzsche's ideas on the subject. Please also see Manfred Frings' introduction, Scheler, 3.

Manfred Frings, perhaps the foremost authority on Max Scheler's thoughts and writings, summarizes the concept of ressentiment in the following way:

> Ressentiment is an incurable, persistent feeling of hating and despising which occurs in certain individuals and groups. It takes its root in equally incurable impotencies or weaknesses that those subjects constantly suffer from. These impotencies generate either individual or collective, but always negative, emotive attitudes. They can permeate a whole culture, era, and an entire moral system. The feeling of ressentiment leads to false moral judgments made on other people who are devoid of this feeling. Such judgments are not infrequently accompanied by rash, at times fanatical claims of truth generated by the impotency this feeling comes from.[355]

In Scheler's own words, ressentiment is a "self-poisoning of the mind," a "lasting mental attitude" which "leads to the constant tendency to indulge in certain kinds of value delusions and corresponding value judgments."[356] This emotive upwelling tends to come in the form of "revenge, hatred, malice, envy, the impulse to detract, and spite." According to Scheler, it is the "thirst for revenge that is the most important source of ressentiment."[357] The function and dynamic of revenge within ressentiment is important. Scheler explains that "revenge is distinguished by two essential characteristics. First of all, the immediate reactive impulse, with the accompanying emotions of anger and rage, is temporarily or at least momentarily checked and restrained, and the response is consequently postponed to a later time and to a more suitable occasion."[358] The suspended reaction is caused by "the reflection that an immediate reaction would lead to defeat, and by a concomitant pronounced feeling of 'inability' and 'impotence.'" Thus, the postponement of revenge is not voluntary, but rather occurs because of a pronounced lack of capability. This suspension of revenge creates, over time, a festering psychosis. In Scheler's words, "there is a progression of feeling which starts with revenge and runs via rancor, envy, and impulse to detract, all the way to spite," ultimately leading to ressentiment.[359] This chain reaction is amplified by a painful consciousness of impotency—or the inability to effectively respond to the offending outside impulse or incursion. This "pronounced awareness of impotence" is a critical component of ressentiment. As Scheler notes, "ressentiment can only arise if [the original] emotions are particularly powerful yet must

---

[355]Manfred Frings in his introductory remarks in Scheler, 5.
[356]Scheler, 25.
[357]Scheler, 25.
[358]Scheler, 25.
[359]Scheler, 25.

be suppressed because they are coupled with the feeling that one is unable to act them out—either because of weakness, physical or mental, or because of fear."

Ressentiment is a particularly dangerous and insidious phenomenon because it acts as a "psychological contagion." Scheler writes that "the spiritual venom of ressentiment is extremely contagious"—the suppression of the original revenge impulse leads to an embittering and poisoning of the individual or collective personality. If the individual or group is able to act out its impulse for revenge, then this purges ressentiment from the individual or collective identity. The acting out of revenge is a powerful psychological antidote or therapy for ressentiment. It tends to restore damaged feelings of personal value and injured honor, or brings satisfaction for the perceived wrongs that have been endured. However, it is precisely when this quest for satisfaction is repressed, especially over a prolonged period of time by a collective identity, that the phenomenon of ressentiment begins to establish itself.

But ressentiment is not simply about a repressed desire for revenge that leads to a festering hatred. It is more than that. Eventually, the individual or collective painful tension that is caused by ressentiment—what Frings has called the "psychic venom of ressentiment" that "seeps into all walks of life"—demands some form of relief. Scheler explains that in attempting to relieve this tension, the individual or collective victim of ressentiment "seeks a feeling of superiority or equality" vis-à-vis "the other" and attains this by means of an illusory devaluation of "the other's" qualities or by a specific blindness to those qualities.[360] In other words, ressentiment begins to produce negative value judgments about "the other." It drives a perpetual and self-sustaining comparison of "me" versus "him" or "us" versus "them." It evolves into an "emotional response reaction" and the resultant comparative cycle sinks, over time, more deeply into one's center of personality. The essential quality of this emotion is negative and tends to contain deeper movements of hostility. The cycle, with its tendency to continually devalue or diminish "the other," is important because of its ability to bring an illusory easing of the tension caused by ressentiment.

Certain conditions seem to be conducive to producing the phenomenon of ressentiment. They include, according to Scheler, "lasting situations which are felt to be 'injurious' but beyond one's control."[361] These situations incorporate not only a sense of hopelessness, but also profound and strong feelings of injustice. Another condition or source lies in what Scheler characterizes as "envy, jealousy, and the competitive urge." This is especially relevant in the case when an individual or group's identity is connected to historical imperatives. When those impera-

---

[360]Scheler, 34.
[361]Scheler, 28.

tives clash with present-day realities, the resulting tension can lead to envy, flare up into hatred, and result in the urge for revenge against the imposing reality—against the individual or group that is blocking the achievement of those historical imperatives. As Scheler explains, these conditions seem to be especially potent when there is a "romantic nostalgia for some past era."[362] In this case, historical imperatives not only fuel ressentiment in the face of a current denial of those imperatives, but ressentiment coupled with a praising of the past results in a purposeful downgrading of the present-day reality. Scheler summarizes the formal structure of this process in the following way (where A = the historical imperative, B = the offending reality): "A is affirmed, valued, and praised not [only] for its own intrinsic quality, but [also] with the unverbalized intention of denying, devaluating, and denigrating B. A is 'played off' against B."[363]

Ressentiment, Identity, and Transnational Islamic Revival. As outlined in Part II of this work, the Islamic world has inherited an undeniable political and historical imperative. The combined and powerful legacies of the Qur'an and the prophet bequeathed to the identity and faithful of Islam a decidedly deterministic theological perspective. The all-encompassing unity of Allah, the righteous truth in the Qur'an, the model life of the prophet, and the rightly guided way of Islamic law historically inspired an unprecedented political and military expansion of Islam's sacred geography. This sacred space was expected to bring justice, equality, and peace to all of mankind. For the first millennium of Islam, the growing and expanding kingdom of Allah seemed to be fulfilling its original mandate. However, modernity and Western secularism brought that historical advance to a grinding halt. In 1924, the political manifestation of that sacred geography, the Islamic Caliphate, was officially dissolved. Simultaneously, Western influences brought heretofore-unparalleled pressures to bear on the Islamic *ummah*. The effects of Western secular incursion, the inability to defeat European colonialism, the succession of military defeats at the hand of Western powers, and the perception of technological and scientific backwardness, combine to form a prevailing undercurrent of helplessness and impotency. The extent to which Islam is, in the minds of the faithful, the irreducibly, final, and ultimate truth, makes this Western incursion even more injurious.

The inability to effectively respond to these challenges has resulted in a collective phenomenon of ressentiment in the minds of the faithful, and its powerful tonic is sustained by ongoing frustration and perceived hopelessness. In a recent and surprisingly frank article, the Tunisian intellectual Al-'Afif Al-Akhdar addresses the passion for revenge within Islam's ressentiment phenomenon:

---

[362]Scheler, 42
[363]Scheler, 42.

This deep-rooted culture of tribal vengefulness in the [Islamic] collective consciousness is a fundamental driving force. [It] has transmuted this consciousness into a fixated, brooding, vengeful mentality, instead of transforming [it] into a [source of] farsighted thought and criticism . . . The culture of tribal vengeance . . . haunts not only in our relations with the other but also our relations with each other . . . [It is] a cult of armament and violence aimed at salvaging the injured face of this collective narcissism through martial victory, hoping that this will wash out the disgrace of military defeats.[364]

The Cairo skyline from Al-Azhar Mosque, Cairo.
Photo by author.

The surges of passion, the fiery Friday sermons, the spiritual fervor of the Muslim street, the slogans of "my religion today, your religion tomorrow," the graffiti of "first the Saturday people, then the Sunday people," the mutilating and dragging of bodies through the streets, the spontaneous celebrations of Western casualties, the absence of widespread condemnation of acts like 9/11 and the gruesome spate of decapitations, the appeal and growth of overtly

---

[364] Al-'Afif Al-Akhdar, "Why does the Arab Sisyphus lift the heavy rock only to drop it on his own feet?" trans. *The Middle East Media Research Institute Special Dispatch* No. 499, 4 May 2003, URL: www.memri.org/bin/articles.cgi?Page=archives&Area=sd&ID=SP49903, accessed 14 December 2004.

anti-Western media, and the diffuse financial support of the Islamic revolutionaries, all powerfully contribute to, and are evidence of, the phenomenon of ressentiment. As noted earlier, according to Manfred Frings, ressentiment generates a smoldering current of hostility, "an incurable, persistent feeling of hating and despising" which generates widespread "negative emotive attitudes" and permeates the whole culture, era, and moral system with "false moral judgments" and "rash, at times fanatical claims of truth generated by the impotency this feeling comes from."[365]

The Cairo skyline from Al-Azhar Mosque, Cairo.
Photo by author.

The current transnational Islamic revival is evidence of what Scheler referred to as a "romantic nostalgia of the past," the "wish to escape from the present," and the desire to alleviate ressentiment's tensions by using the glorious past to downgrade present-day realities.[366] In the Qur'an and the *hadiths* of the prophet, the faithful have ample access to supporting materials, and most knowledgeable observers are more than aware of the plethora of current Islamic commentary aimed at accomplishing what Scheler called the "illusory devaluation of the present." The following three examples represent the style of argument that only

---

[365]Manfred Frings in Scheler, 5.
[366]Scheler, 42.

serves to bolster Islamic ressentiment. Sheikh Abd-Rahman al-Sudayyis, the Imam of the Al-Haraam mosque in Mecca, Saudi Arabia, recently remarked:

> The most noble civilization ever known to mankind is our Islamic civilization. Today, Western civilization is nothing more than the product of its encounter with our Islamic civilization in Andalusia and other places. The reason for [Western civilization's] bankruptcy is its reliance on the materialistic approach, and its detachment from religion and values. [This] approach has been one reason for the misery of the human race, for the proliferation of suicide, mental problems . . . and for moral perversion . . . Only one nation is capable of resuscitating global civilization, and that is the nation [of Islam].[367]

Students taking a break at American University Cairo.

Photo by author.

At the Al-Nabawi mosque in Medina, Saudi Arabia, Sheikh Sallah Bin Muhammad Al-Budeir told the faithful:

---

[367]Sheikh Abd-Rahman al-Sudayyis quoted in "Friday Sermons in Saudi Mosques: Review and Analysis," *The Middle East Media Research Institute Special Report* No. 10, 26 September 2002, URL: www.memri.org/bin/articles.cgi?Page=archives&Area=sr&ID=SR01002, accessed 14 December 2004. Hereafter referred to as *Friday Sermons*.

What is the use of [Western] culture, in which the value of man has shrunk to the level of slavery to anything but Allah? Man becomes a slave to his money and his desires . . . It is distressing that some of our people who speak our own language [serve] as procurers of the West, glorifying and extolling it, and calling for its imitation. . . [Only] Islam is worthy of delivering the human race from its misery and despair. Only Islam is capable of bringing happiness to the human race.[368]

Finally, Saudi Arabia's Grand Mufti Sheikh Abd al-'Aziz Aal Al-Sheikh, the most influential voice of Islam in the country responsible for the holiest of Islamic shrines, reserved the following comments for the West:

Those who attack Islam and its people—what have they given to the human race? What have they to be proud of? They gave a false, contemptible culture; they gave various kinds of damage to [human] freedoms and rights on the pretext of preserving these values; they gave discrimination among people by color, gender, language, and race; they gave technology to create weapons of mass destruction for the destruction of the human race; they gave forms of deceit and falsehood . . .[369]

Jamal al-Din al-Afghani, a nineteenth century Muslim intellectual, provides an example of how the Islamic faithful have steadily sought refuge from ressentiment by returning to Islam and by fostering a revival of their religion. Afghani frequently referred to the apparent backwardness of Islam vis-à-vis the West, and used it to "set up the tension of self-pity, which he exacerbated by the call to Islam."[370] His volatile and emotional writing alternatively swings between unhappy nostalgia and fierce assertion. In 1884 he wrote the following:

It is amazing that it was precisely the Christians who invented Krupp's cannons and the machine gun before the Muslims . . . The Europeans have now put their hands on every part of the world. The English have reached Afghanistan; the French have seized Tunisia. In reality this usurpation, aggression, and conquest have not come from the French or the English. Rather it is science that everywhere manifests its greatness and power. Ignorance [meaning Islam] had no alternative to prostrating itself humbly before science and acknowledging its submission.[371]

---

[368] Sheikh Sallah Bin Muhammad Al-Budeir quoted in *Friday Sermons.*
[369] Sheikh Abd al-'Aziz Aal Al-Sheikh quoted in *Friday Sermons.*
[370] David Pryce-Jones, *The Closed Circle* (Chicago, IL: Ivan R. Dee, 2002), 87.
[371] Afghani quoted in Price-Jones, 88.

A Turkish poet summed up the growing helplessness of the Islamic faithful in the following way in 1912:

> Look at Morocco, Tunisia, Algeria—
> They are all gone!
> Iran—they are dividing it too!
> This is most natural, the field is the runner's
> The right to live was given to the strong by God.
> Muslims! A nation afflicted with factional dissent,
> Will civilized Europe not eat them in three bites?
> O community, if only for God's sake, awake![372]

Another Turkish poet of the same period revealed the turbulent passions of the faithful:

> To take revenge, we shall adopt the enemy's science.
> We shall learn his skill, steal his methods.
> On progress we will set our heart.
> We shall skip five hundred years
> And not stand still. Little time is left.[373]

It was Afghani who presaged the Islamic revival when he wrote that "every Muslim is sick, and his only remedy is the Qur'an."[374] A return to Islam, especially in the wake of the failure of Nasser's Pan-Arab nationalism, was broadly seen as a means to restore the health and well being of the Muslim identity. Throughout history, it was argued, Islam made its peoples unique. Thus, as the historian Albert Hourani wrote, "Backwardness in science and civilization is admitted, but it derives from loss of the truth of Islam, and then [also] from bad, that is to say impious, rulers. Islamic civilization was created out of nothing but the Qur'an and this can be repeated."[375] At the same time, Islamic preachers were crying out: "If only we had honored the Book of God nobody would ever have humiliated us, and the banner of Islam would be all over the world."[376]

It is important to note that while the phenomenon of ressentiment applies to the broadly transnational Islamic identity, it does not manifest itself in the mind of the Islamic revolutionaries. These combatants are fulfilling their psychological passion for revenge. As Frings notes, "whenever a prosaic resentment-feeling

---

[372]Mehmed Akif quoted in Price-Jones, 90.
[373]Zia Gokalp quoted in Price-Jones, 90.
[374]Afghani quoted in Price-Jones, 369.
[375]Hourani quoted in Price-Jones, 371.
[376]Price-Jones, 372.

finds satisfaction by way of, say, a successful revenge and retaliation, there is no resentment proper at hand." Therefore, "throughout terrorism resentment is prone to be found among those who do not place bombs to kill, etc., but among those who stay behind such acts. Thus, ressentiment subjects are often to be found among sympathizers of violence rather than among the criminals themselves doing the violence [emphasis in the original]."[377]

Bedouin children in southern Jordan.
Photo by author.

In conclusion, the puzzling schizophrenia in the mind of the Islamic faithful—and in contemporary Islamic identity—is best explained by Scheler's concept of ressentiment. The significant trauma inflicted on that identity by Western secularist incursions spawned enduring and contrarian reactions. The inability to respond in kind, to satisfy the desire for reciprocity and revenge, has fostered a smoldering, subterranean ressentiment—in Scheler's words, "a venomous mass which begins to flow whenever con-

---

[377]Manfred Frings' introduction in Scheler, 7-8.

sciousness becomes momentarily relaxed."[378] This is what explains the spontaneous releases of passion, the celebrations and dancing at the news of an event like 9/11 or the strange state of shock at the rapid fall of the regime of Saddam Hussein. This is the visceral, "spiritual" emotion of hatred or envy, suppressed by the inability to respond, but nevertheless evident when death or destruction befalls the enemy. This is what Scheler referred to as the "psychical dynamite" in the phenomenon of ressentiment. Yet it is also revealed in the suspended hopelessness of the following thoughts from the Algerian writer Kateb Yacine:

> We are in a train which is rolling but we have little or no idea where it came from or where it is going. A people fortified by its history is a strong people. But we have lost our way in our history.[379]

---

[378]Scheler, 44.
[379]Kateb Yacine quoted in Pryce-Jones, 379.

IV. In the Mind of the Enemy

The Revolutionary Islamic Vanguard

Islam is a revolutionary ideology which seeks to alter the social order of the entire world and rebuild it in conformity with its own tenets and ideals. "Muslims" is the title of that "International Revolutionary Party" organized by Islam to carry out its revolutionary program. "Jihad" refers to the revolutionary struggle and utmost exertion which the Islamic Nation/Party brings into play in order to achieve this objective . . . There is no doubt that all the Prophets of Allah, without exception, were Revolutionary Leaders, and the illustrious Prophet Muhammad was the greatest Revolutionary Leader of all.

— **Abul A'la Mawdudi**[380]

Allah has blessed a group of vanguard Muslims, the forefront of Islam, to destroy America. May Allah bless them and allot them a supreme place in heaven.

— **Osama bin Laden**[381]

We are not fighting so the enemy recognizes us and offers us something. We are fighting to wipe out the enemy.

— **Abbas Mussawi**, *Hizbollah leader*[382]

The establishment of an Islamic State and the reintroduction of the Caliphate were (not only) already predicted by the Apostle of God— God's peace be upon him— (but they) are, moreover, part of the Command of the Lord-Majestic and Exalted He is— for which every Muslim should exert every conceivable effort in order to execute it.

— **Muhammad Abd al-Salam Faraj in** *The Neglected Duty*[383]

---

[380]Abul A'la Mawdudi quoted David Zeidan, "The Islamic Fundamentalist View of Life as a Perennial Battle," *Middle East Review of International Affairs* (December 2001), URL: www.meria.idc.ac.il/2001/issue4/jv5n4a2.htm, accessed 29 January 2004.

[381]Text of Statement from Osama Bin Laden," Los Angeles Times (7 October 2001), URL: www.latimes.com/news/nationworld/world/la-100701binladen_text.story, accessed 10 December 2004.

[382]Abbas Mussawi, a leader of Hizbollah quoted in Walter Laqueur, "The New Face of Terrorism," The Washington Quarterly, Autumn 1998.

[383]Translation of Muhammad Abd al-Salam Faraj's text entitled *Al-Faridah al Gha'ibah* [The Neglected Duty] in Johannes Jansen, *The Neglected Duty* (New York: MacMillan Publishing Co, 1986), 162.

The confrontation that we are calling for with the apostate regimes does not know Socratic debates . . . Platonic ideals . . . nor Aristotelian diplomacy. But it knows the dialogue of bullets, the ideals of assassination, bombing, and destruction, and the diplomacy of the cannon and machine gun. Islamic governments have never and will never be established through peaceful solutions and cooperative councils. They are established as they (always) have been by pen and gun, by word and bullet, by tongue and teeth.

- from an al Qaeda training manual entitled Declaration of Jihad[384]

Therefore, when ye meet the Unbelievers (in fighting)—Smite at their necks . . . [decapitate them].

—from the Qur'an (Sura Al Qital —**"The Fighting"-4:47)**

Religious Revolutionary Warfare

The enemy is a revolutionary—not a terrorist. The war he is engaged in is an epochal struggle between his ideas about the affairs of mankind and our ideas about the affairs of mankind. As the enemy has told us, "here we have a clash of two visions of the world and the future of mankind. The side prepared to accept more sacrifices will win."[385] He has not hijacked his religion and he is not its nominal follower—rather, he is an Islamic purist, and passionately follows the example of his Prophet Mohammad. He desperately seeks to restore the preeminence of Islam—to purify the Muslim world of corrupt and apostate rulers, and to bring the entire world under the Islamic rightly guided way of life. He does not represent or fight for a particular nation, class, political state, or region, nor does he seek to represent a local ethnicity or group. Instead, he is an ideologue, fueled by a utopian vision of a worldwide sacred geography, called the Islamic Caliphate—a unique and historical fusion of politics and religion. As a result, he is engaged in a tectonic struggle to change the world as we know it, and will use every means available—including mass genocide—to fulfill his fantasy. He is the lead agent in this transnational revolutionary and religious phenomenon. He views himself as the elite vanguard—a front-line fighting force drawn from the

---

[384]Source is an al Qaeda training manual found by Manchester Metropolitan police (England) during a search of an al Qaeda member's home. The manual was part of a computer file described as "the military series" related to the "Declaration of Jihad." The manual was translated into English and was used by U.S. prosecutors as Government Exhibit 1677-T during legal proceedings held in New York against the perpetrators of the 1998 embassy bombings in Kenya and Tanzania. Hereafter referred to as al Quada training manual (Government Exhibit 1677-T).

[385]Amir Taheri, "Al-Qaida's Agenda for Iraq," *United Press International* (6 September 2003), URL: www.upi.com/print.cfm?StoryID=20030906-105644-1203r, accessed 8 September 2003.

broader Islamic milieu. The ressentiment phenomenon that prevails throughout the global Islamic community ensures that he has a sympathetic audience — if not actively, then at least passively supportive. He also draws tacit and illicit support from regimes and governments who share his passion to humble the secular West. He wields a diverse arsenal and is skilled not only in killing and destruction, but also in political propaganda and religious manipulation. He is driven by historical imperatives, a millennial tradition of Islamic doctrine, and the supererogatory promises of his eschatological foundation — which offer him an afterlife in exchange for martyrdom. In life, he gains great approbation as a religious warrior in the cause of Allah. In death, he gains paradise. Worst of all, he has nothing to lose. He will not yield, he will not negotiate, and he will not compromise. This is the enemy — the revolutionary Islamic vanguard.

A Revolutionary Struggle

The enemy is not a terrorist. The enemy's goals are nothing less than a revolutionary transformation of the status quo. Though the enemy employs terror as part of his strategy, his goal is not to terrorize but to revolutionize the world. There is no spirit of accommodation or compromise. Rather the goal of the revolutionary Islamic vanguard is to change the world as we know it. Abul A'la Mawdudi, a Pakistani Islamic revolutionary, once described the goal in the following manner:

> Islam is not only a set of theological dogmata and a collection of ceremonies and rites, as nowadays the word religion seems to be understood. In fact, it is an all-embracing order that wants to eliminate and to eradicate the other orders which are false and unjust, so as to replace them by a good order and a moderate program that is considered to be better for humanity than the other orders and to contain rescue from the illnesses of evil and tyranny, happiness and prosperity for the human race, both in this world and in the Hereafter. The call of Islam for this cause . . . does not concern only one nation with the exclusion of others, or one group with the exclusion of others, for Islam calls all people to its Word . . . Whosoever believes in this call and accepts it in a proper way, becomes a member of the "*Islamic party*" [italics in the original].[386]

There seem to be some parallels between the writings of today's Islamic revolutionaries and that of the anti-colonialist writer and leader of the Algerian Front,

---

[386]Abul A'la Mawdudi quoted in Peters, 107-08.

Frantz Fanon. In his popular work *The Wretched of the Earth*, Fanon described the revolutionary struggle in the following way:

> To wreck the colonial world is . . . a mental picture of action which is very clear, very easy to understand . . . To break up the colonial world does not mean . . . that lines of communication will be set up between two zones [of colonized and colonizer]. The destruction of the colonial world is no more and no less than the abolition of one zone and its burial in the depths of the earth.[387]

The revolutionary Islamic vanguard has an outlook similar to that of Fanon, who taught that "revolution can never accomplish its goals through negotiation or peaceful reform." Instead revolutionary leaders "regard terror as good in itself, a therapeutic act . . . the willingness to kill is proof of one's [religious] purity."[388] The powerful religious imperative resident within the revolutionary ideology is unavoidable. It was Mawdudi who wrote: "Islam wants the whole earth and does not content itself with only a part thereof. It wants and requires the entire inhabited world . . . Islam wants and requires the earth in order that the human race altogether can enjoy the concept and practical program of human happiness, by means of which God has honored Islam and put it above the other religions and laws."[389]

The revolutionaries use identity as a valuable ideological tool. As discussed previously, first colonialism and then secularism ruptured the social fabric and identity of Islam. The West's secularist bias against religion and faith has created a vacuum that is being exploited by the Islamic revolutionaries. They fill that vacuum with an identity ideology. In a sense, they have turned identity into a religion—the concept of the *ummah* has become synonymous with Islam itself. The transnational *ummah* becomes the vehicle through which the self-appointed, elitist vanguard rises to power. According to Dr. Abdallah Schleifer, the argument goes as follows: "First there is a special people. That special people is the *ummah*. Then the *ummah* needs to be purified and protected from the influences of the secular world. That requires a special and committed group of elites. That group of educated elites becomes the vanguard of the *ummah*. Ultimately, the mission of the vanguard becomes totalitarian and exclusivistic."[390] In its totalitarian quest for purity, revolutionary ideology focuses its attack physically against "the other" as well as contesting the philosophies and ideas of "the other." History, of course, has witnessed the destructive and revolutionary impact of similar

---

[387]Frantz Fanon, *The Wretched of the Earth* (New York: Grove Press, 1963), 40.

[388]Newell, "Postmodern Jihad."

[389]Abul A'la Mawdudi quoted in Peters, 128.

[390]Schleifer, interview with the author.

phenomena. Dr. Schleifer, himself a practicing Muslim, long-time correspondent for NBC throughout the Middle East, and the director of the Adham Center for Journalism in Cairo, draws the following parallels between utopian revolutionary ideologies: "The National Socialists wanted to get rid of the Jews, the Communists wanted to get rid of the bourgeoisie, and revolutionary Islam wants to get rid of all infidels."[391] The revolutionaries are well aware that the focus on identity, the division of the world between "Islam" and "the other," and the divine predeterminism of Islam's historical imperatives have "guaranteed for fourteen centuries that wars waged by Muslims against external enemies will always be perceived by meaningful segments of the polity as having a transcendental dimension closely interwoven with the foundation 'myths' of the culture to which this society belongs."[392]

This amalgam of politics and religion in Islam provides a fertile revolutionary medium for the vanguard to draw from. Dr. Dan Tschirgi, Professor and Chairman of the Department of Political Science at the American University in Cairo, notes that "the role of religion within revolutionary ideology is to both reaffirm the fundamental and changeless tenets of identity, as well as to justify demands for far-reaching change in the socio-politico-economic status quo."[393] Thus religion becomes the basis for—and the vehicle of—revolutionary transformation. The vanguard views the battle on a trans-historical, cosmic plane. The outcome of the struggle is predetermined, because it is ultimately not in the hands of men, but in the hands of the divine. Therefore, compromise with "the other" is inconceivable, because Allah has predetermined ultimate victory. Once again, there is nothing to lose for the combatants—in life they look forward to victory on earth; in death they expect paradise.

According to the revolutionary Islamic vanguard, the struggle has been ongoing ever since the beginnings of Islam. They picture Islam and its past and present leaders as a modern-style revolutionary party engaged in a struggle to reshape the world.[394] In the words of Mawdudi, the Pakistani Islamic revolutionary, "Islam is a revolutionary ideology which seeks to alter the social order of the entire world and rebuild it in conformity with its own tenets and ideals . . . There is no doubt that all the Prophets of Allah, without exception, were Revolutionary Leaders, and the illustrious Prophet Muhammad was the greatest Revolutionary Leader of all."[395] Yet, even as the revolutionaries see their struggle for sacred geography on

---

[391] Schleifer, interview with the author.

[392] Emmanual Sivan, "The Holy War Tradition in Islam," *Orbis* 42 (Spring 1998).

[393] Dr. Dan Tschirgi Professor and Chairman of the Department of Political Science, American University in Cairo, Egypt, interview with the author, 22-23 March 2004.

[394] David Zeidan, "The Islamic Fundamentalist View of Life as a Perennial Battle."

a trans-historical plane, they also assert that their ultimate aim is peace and not war. Once again, it was the Egyptian Islamic scholar Sayyid Qutb who explained what "peaceful" means to Islam's revolutionaries:

> When Islam strives for peace, it does not want a cheap peace, a peace that does not mean more than that one is safe in that particular territory where people embrace Islamic faith. No, it wants a peace wherein all religion belongs to God, which means that all people worship God alone and that they do not take each other as objects of worship to the exclusion of God.[396]

The "peace" that the revolutionary Islamic vanguard talks about is, as discussed earlier in this work, the equality that comes from the submission of all of mankind to one religion—Islam, one God, Allah, and one law—the Islamic law.

In their revolutionary ardor, the vanguard is trying to draw the West into what Paul Schulte has called a spiral of *engrenage* (a French term for becoming enmeshed like cogs in interlocking gears in a repetitive cycle of atrocity and revenge).[397] The revolutionary Islamic vanguard expects an overwhelming military response. One might argue that it is their strategy to purposefully target the West in such a way as to draw out massive military responses. They anticipate the loss of entire cadres of fighters, even while celebrating their martyrdom and heroic warrior status. Schulte explains that, much as depicted in the classic film *The Battle of Algiers*, the spiral of *engrenage* will over time: (1) increase their determination, (2) recruit new warriors and supporters, (3) gain political support, (4) delegitimize so-called moderate or secular regimes, and (5) bring about (eventually) war weariness, division, and self-disgust in the enemy population.[398] The revolutionary Islamic vanguard is convinced that ultimately the cycle of engrenage will lead to a disengagement of the enemy. This will enable the revolutionaries to "impose a true religious order far beyond [their] original base, liberate Palestine and the Muslim Holy Places and settle accounts with corrupt traitors there. [They] will reconstruct a potent supra-national Caliphate that will return Islam at least to its original boundaries before the long Judeo-Christian counter-attack began."[399]

---

[395] Abul A'la Mawdudi quoted in Zeidan.

[396] Sayyid Qutb quoted in Peters, 131.

[397] Paul Schulte, "I am Osama bin Laden: A Strategic Warning and Challenge to the West," *RUSI Journal*, June 2002, 21.

[398] Schulte, 21.

[399] Schulte, 21.

Islamic Revolutionary Theology

Shiite mosque in Baku, Azerbaijan.
Photo by author.

The revolutionary Islamic vanguard is not an isolated group of so-called radicals that have hijacked a religion. Instead, it represents historical continuity bequeathed to it from the Prophet and the origins of Islam. The lineage begins most fundamentally with the Qur'an and the *hadiths* of the Prophet, the Hanbalite school of jurisprudence, and the writings of scholars like Ibn Salamah (1032), Ibn Hazm al-Andalusi (1064), Qadi Musa Iyadh (1149), Nawawi (1277), the monumental Ibn Taymiyyah (1328), Ibn al-Qayyim (1350) Ibn Kathir (1373), Ibn Abd al-Wahhab 1792), and more recently Sayyid Qutb, and Abul A'la Mawdudi.[400] Ibn Hanbal, the foremost champion of strict orthodox Islamic interpretation and originator of the Hanbalite school of Islamic jurisprudence, founded the Islamic revolutionary purist's doctrine. Ibn Hazm al-Andalusi, who lived in eleventh century Muslim Spain, combined Ibn Hanbal's stress on doctrinal purification and simplicity with a militant advocacy of *jihad*. Imam Ibn Salamah's pugnacious conception of *jihad* and Qadi Musa Iyadh's strict traditionalism (of the Maliki school of jurisprudence) are used by the revolutionary Islamic vanguard to advocate *jihad* not simply as a collective obligation but also as an individual duty. Al-Nawawi was a

---

[400]The following descriptions are taken from *Islam in Revolution* (37-40). For further and more detailed elaboration, please see Dekmejian, *Islam in Revolution*, 37-40.

preeminent Shafi advocate of *jihad*. He apparently possessed an amazing knowledge of the traditions of the Prophet Mohammad and was uncompromising in his quest for traditional purity. The collected thoughts and works of the fourteenth century Muslim jurist ibn Taymiyyah are revered among today's revolutionaries. Ibn Taymiyyah sought to defend Islam against the incursion of the Mongols. He "was the embodiment of the militant theoretician and activist defender of the faith. He recognized no authority except the Qur'an, the Sunnah [sayings of the prophet], and the practices of the early Islamic community; he violently opposed 'heretical' beliefs and practices."[401] Taymiyyah was an activist, attempting to build moral solidarity amongst the warrior faithful by means of a reinvigorated Islamic ideology and its strict implementation in society. His teachings were perpetuated by his disciples, including Ibn Qayyim and Ibn Kathir. But the direct descendant of Ibn Taymiyyah's purist theology was Muhammad Ibn Abd al-Wahhab, who was responsible for reinvigorating Hanbalism after a period of decline. The Wahhabi doctrines bore the clear imprints of Ibn Taymiyyah and ensured their propagation into the modern period. Ibn Abd al-Wahhab formed the link between his predecessors and the group of modern Islamic revolutionaries, including the following group of revolutionaries: Abul A'la Mawdudi (Pakistan), Sayyid Qutb (Egypt), Shukri Mustafa (Egypt), and Abd al-Salam Faraj (the Egyptian who wrote what is considered by some to be the Communist Manifesto of Revolutionary Islam, *The Neglected Duty*).

As Dekmejian explains, these men represent a fourteen-hundred-year revolutionary legacy in Islam. In that sense, their modern protégés have hardly hijacked Islam for their own revolutionary purposes—rather they have assumed the mantle of predecessors with whom they share the following characteristics: (1) a commitment to renewing and purifying the *ummah* by returning to Islam's roots; (2) a revolutionary advocacy of militancy and *jihad* in defense of the sacred geography of Islam; (3) a personal commitment to political, military, and social activism; and (4) a readiness to challenge religious and political authority and to be martyred for the sake of revolutionary Islam.[402]

By means of comparison, in Christianity, Protestantism traces its roots from Jesus Christ, the Pauline ministry, and the impact of early church fathers like St. Augustine to the events of the Reformation and the writings of Martin Luther and John Calvin—to name a few. Just as few would argue today that Protestantism represents a radical hijacking of Christianity, so it would be equally inappropriate to say that the revolutionary Islamic vanguard represents a hijacking of Islam. This misunderstanding results from haphazard scholarship produced by a social science

---

[401]Dekmejian, *Islam in Revolution*, 38.
[402]Dekmejian, *Islam in Revolution*, 40.

community that is profoundly uncomfortable with the phenomenon of religion. Much of this contemporary analysis liberally interjects terms such as "radical" and "fundamentalist," and the ill-defined political and ideological baggage associated with these terms tends to obfuscate the importance of the theological doctrines involved. What is "radical" to one individual might be mundane to another. The term "fundamentalist" is especially unhelpful, because in the case of Islam, the great majority of practicing Muslims faithfully subscribe to the "fundamental" doctrines of the faith, including the *Shahadah*, the five orthopractical pillars, and Islam's eschatological and supererogatory mechanisms. As such, Sunni and Shia agree on the so-called "fundamentals," notwithstanding their extreme differences about leadership succession. A more fruitful approach is to categorize the so-called "moderates" as *nominal*, and the "fundamentalists" or "radicals" as *purists*. In this sense, the broader transnational Islamic revival is populated by mostly nominal Muslims who, to varying degrees, practice regular mosque attendance and perhaps abide by some or most of the pillars of the faith, thereby striving to appear to live a religious life that gives them renewed meaning in the face of modern secularism. In the same sense, the revolutionary Islamic vanguard is populated by purists who scrutinize in detail the origins of the faith and the writings of ancient scholars, as the foundation for their revolutionary agenda. They strictly abide by all the core tenets and beliefs and practices of Islam, and pay careful attention to the model life lived by the prophet. As demonstrated previously in this work, there are ample political and historical imperatives in Islam to support their vision.

Today's revolutionary Islamic vanguard represents Islam's millennial challenge to resolve its political imperatives against the conflicting realities and philosophies of the surrounding world. They are following the example of their Prophet, who told them, while fighting against the Jews of the Quraysh tribe:

> By Allah, if they were to put the sun in my right hand and the moon in my left on condition that I relinquished this matter, until Allah had made it triumphant or I perish therein I would not relinquish it. By Allah, I shall not cease to fight for the mission with which Allah has entrusted me until he makes it triumphant or this Salifah [my neck] gets severed.[403]

They are responding to the call of the prophet when he said: "God showed me all corners of the earth. I saw its East and its West, and (I saw) that my Community will possess of it what he showed me from it."[404] And they are carrying forward the prophet's determinism when he said: "This matter will be [as certain] as the day

---

[403]The Prophet Muhammad quoted in Zallum, 203.
[404]The Prophet Muhammad quoted in Jansen, The Neglected Duty, 162.

and the night: God will make this religion [Islam] enter into every house of every inhabitant of the deserts, of villages, of towns, of cities, with glory or with disgrace. God will give glory to Islam, and God will bring disgrace upon Unbelief."[405] They bring their message of "peace" to the rest of the world, in the same vein as the prophet Muhammad did, when he addressed the Christians of Najran:

> In the Name of the God of Abraham, Isaac, and Jacob. From Muhammad, the Prophet and Apostle of God to the Bishop and the people of Najran. Peace upon you. I praise the God of Abraham, Isaac, and Jacob. I call upon you to serve God, and not to serve men. I call upon you to let yourself be ruled by God [Allah], and not by men. When you refuse, then a head tax. When you refuse this too, be apprised of war. A greeting of Peace.[406]

Finally, today's revolutionaries look to the prophet to hear of the benefits of martyrdom: "A martyr has six virtues in the eyes of God. He will be forgiven upon the first drop of blood. His seat will be in Paradise. He will be free from the punishment of the grave. He will be safe from the Great Fright. He will be dressed in the garb of faith. He will marry the heavenly dark-eyed virgins. He will intercede for 70 of his relatives."[407] For nominal Muslims as well as non-Muslims, it is ultimately and cynically paradoxical that all of this is presented under the pretext of "peace" and "freedom," for as Sayyid Qutb wrote:

> [We do this] to establish God's authority on the earth; to arrange human affairs according to the true guidance provided by God; to abolish all the Satanic forces and Satanic systems of life; to end the lordship of one man over others, since all men are creatures of God and no one has authority to make them his servants or make arbitrary laws for them. These reasons are sufficient for proclaiming Jihad. However, one should always keep in mind that there is no compulsion in religion; that is, once the people are free from the lordship of men, the law governing civil affairs will be purely that of God, while no one will be forced to change his beliefs and accept Islam.[408]

Passionate Indiscriminate Slaughter: Genocide and Decapitation

James Billington, the Librarian of Congress, wrote the following about revolutionary faith: "The heart of revolutionary faith . . . is fire: ordinary material trans-

---

[405]The Prophet Muhammad quoted in Jansen, 162.
[406]The Prophet Muhammad quoted in Jansen, 194.
[407]The Prophet Muhammad quoted in Jansen, 205.
[408]Qutb, *Milestones*, 127.

formed into extraordinary form, quantities of warmth suddenly changing the quality of substance. If we do not know what fire is, we know what it does. It burns. It destroys life; but it also supports it as a source of heat, light, and—above all—fascination."[409] The fires of revolutionary passion know no boundaries in the pursuit of ultimate victory. There should be little doubt that given the opportunity, the vanguard would not hesitate to inflict genocidal casualty rates on the West. One of Al-Qa'ida's spokesmen, Suleiman Abu Gheith, made this clear in a statement released in June 2002: "We have the right to kill 4 million Americans—2 million of them children—and to exile twice as many and wound and cripple hundreds of thousands. Furthermore, it is our right to fight them with chemical and biological weapons, so as to afflict them with the fatal maladies that have afflicted the Muslims because of American chemical and biological weapons."[410]

The revolutionary Islamic vanguard claims legitimate authority to indiscriminately employ weapons of mass destruction against its enemies. Sheikh Nasser ibn Hamed, a well-known Saudi cleric, is the author of "A Treatise on the Ruling Regarding the Use of Weapons of Mass Destruction Against the Infidels." In it, he argues that it is "permissible to use weapons of mass destruction against 10 million Americans specifically, and against infidels in general, and that support for their use could be found in Islamic religious sources."[411] Hamed cites the Qur'an (2:194 and 42:40) to argue that "it is permissible to strike America with weapons of mass destruction in order to repay it in kind." He also presents "the general evidence for the legitimacy according to Islamic law for an inclusive operation of this kind, in the event that *Jihad* for the sake of Allah requires it."[412]

Questions regarding the legality of killing women and children were resolved by referring to the hadiths of the prophet. According to the traditions, under general circumstances, the Prophet Mohammad forbade the killing of women, children, and old men. However, when asked about killing the dependents of polytheists at night,

---

[409]James H. Billington, *Fire in the Minds of Men: Origins of the Revolutionary Faith* (New York, NY: Basic Books), 5.

[410]What the author of this communiqué was referring to with "the fatal maladies that have afflicted the Muslims because of American chemical and biological weapons" is unclear. The United States has not employed WMD in any military operations in the Middle East. For further comments, please see Suleiman Abu Gheith, "In the Shadow of Lances," trans. *Middle East Media Research Institute, Special Dispatch* No. 388, 12 June 2002, URL: www.memri.org/bin/opener.cgi?Page=archives&ID=SP38802, accessed 29 January 2004.

[411]Sheikh Nasser ibn Hamed quoted in "Contemporary Islamist Ideology Permitting Genocidal Murder," *Middle East Media Research Institute*, Special Report No. 25, 27 January 2004, URL: www.memri.org/bin/opener_latest.cgi?ID=SR2504, accessed 29 January 2004.

[412]Sheikh Nasser ibn Hamed quoted in "Contemporary Islamist Ideology Permitting Genocidal Murder."

the prophet responded: "They are part of them." In other words, it is permissible to kill them because women and children are part of the polytheist enemies. The prophet further clarified his opinion by adding: "They are part of their fathers"—which has been interpreted as meaning that "there is no objection to it because the rules applying to their fathers pertain to them as well, in inheritance, marriage, retaliation, blood-money, and other things." It is therefore argued that if it is not done on purpose, it is allowed to kill dependents during the course of *jihad*.[413]

Another Muslim revolutionary writer presents a detailed set of circumstances under which it is permissible to kill women, children, and so-called "inviolable infidels." He bases his deductions on the conduct of the Prophet Muhammad himself: "This is what the Messenger of Allah did with [the infidels]: he abducted them like he did with the Banu 'Uqail; he plundered their merchant caravans as he did with the Quraysh; he assassinated their leaders as he did with Ka'ab Ibn Al-Ashraf and Salamah bin Abi Al-Huqaiq; he burned their land as he did with Banu Al-Nadhir; he destroyed their fortifications as he did in Taif."[414] He continues by writing that "the sanctity of the blood of women, children, and the elderly from among the people of Dar Al-Harb [land of war] is not absolute" and it is permitted to kill them:

- in order to repay them in kind;
- in the event that they cannot be differentiated from the warriors or fortifications that are being attacked (so long as their death is not premeditated);
- if they are aiding the fighting in deed, word, opinion, or any other way;
- if there is a need to burn the enemy fields or fortifications in order to weaken the enemy's strength, to breach the ramparts, or topple the country [in other words, if victory demands the application of massive force against the enemy's resolve];
- if there is a need to use heavy weapons [weapons of mass destruction] that cannot differentiate between combatants and non-combatants;
- if the enemy uses women and children as human shields; and
- if the enemy has an agreement with Muslims, and the enemy violates that agreement, non-combatants may be killed to make an example of them.[415]

---

[413]Evidence for the previous paragraph is taken from Section 121 "The Permissibility of Attacking the Infidels at Night and Firing at Them Even if it Leads to Killing Their Dependents" in Jansen, *The Neglected Duty*, 217.

[414]"Contemporary Islamist Ideology Permitting Genocidal Murder."

[415]"Contemporary Islamist Ideology Permitting Genocidal Murder."

Some might argue that this list reveals a commitment to establishing rules of war that protect non-combatants. However, the list is not a set of rules restricting the killing of non-combatants—indeed, it is an extensive set of conditions which authorize their killing.

On the whole, the ideology of the revolutionary Islamic vanguard perpetuates the notion, as Paul Schulte has pointed out, "that hopeless disparities in conventional military capability entitle the weaker side to use asymmetric methods which indiscriminately target the stronger side's civil population."[416] As a consequence, most observers would immediately predispose their thinking toward the threat of weapons of mass destruction, yet no practice demonstrates this idea in a more egregious fashion than the passion toward decapitation. It should be said, from the outset, that this is not something new in Islamic revolutionary warfare. Once again, it is the Prophet Mohammad who set the example for the faithful when, according to Ibn Ishaq, he single-handedly beheaded between 600 and 700 men from the Jewish tribe of the Qurayza in Medina. Muhammad had their corpses thrown into a long trench that was especially dug for the occasion down the middle of the market in Medina. During the golden age of the Abbasid-Baghdadian Caliphate, the jurist al-Mawardi declared that the first choice, when dealing with infidel captives of *jihad* campaigns was to put them to death by cutting their necks.[417] The great Muslim leader Saladin, admired for his chivalrous and generous treatment of defeated enemies during the fight against the Crusaders, continued the tradition in 1182 when he defeated the forces of Reynald of Chatillon. The Arab historian Ibn al-Athir chronicles how Saladin separated Reynald of Chatillon out from the rest of the prisoners and beheaded him with his own hands.[418] While it is not the purpose of this work to document every act of decapitation in the fourteen-hundred-year history of Islam, it is clear that this practice dates back to the earliest Islamic leaders, and has direct links to the prophet and the Qur'an. According to the Qur'an, Allah directs Muslims to stike the necks of those who deny Islam whenever the faithful encounter them (Sura *Al Qital*—"The Fighting"—4:47). Today's Islamic revolutionaries follow that mandate. Videos of these barbaric acts are circulated among the vanguard in order to encourage and motivate the faithful. Indeed, according to reports obtained by the U.S. Embassy in Rabat, Morocco, "screenings have been arranged in both private homes and, often after prayers, in mosques. Many showings have been timed so that young people, students, and school

---

[416]Schulte, 21.

[417]Jascha Kessler, "The West's Barbarity is Islam's Law," *Financial Times*, 19 May 2004, 12.

[418]Bernard Lewis, "License to Kill," *Foreign Affairs* (November/December 1998), URL: www.web.archive.org/web/20011218022957, accessed 29 January 2004.

children can attend." [419] Videos often display the shocking footage of acts perpetrated in Iraq, Afghanistan, Chechnya, and Bosnia.

According to the report, "one video called *The Mirror of the Jihad* showed Taliban forces in Afghanistan decapitating Northern Alliance soldiers with knives." Another video, this one from a revolutionary Muslim group from Algeria (the Salafist Group for Preaching and Fighting, or GSPC), starts with "a flickering screen of Arabic script: an injunction to 'Fight them until the sentence of God is carried out on Earth.' Then, with a soundtrack of chanted verses from the Qur'an, more commands scroll across the screen. 'You have to kill in the name of Allah until you are killed,' the viewers are told. 'Then you will win your place forever in Paradise.'" The video then shifts to the scene of an obvious ambush where government soldiers and their convoy have been blown up by a roadside bomb. The voyeuristic blood lust continues as the Muslim revolutionaries discover a live government soldier. A revolutionary calmly bends down and runs his knife across the conscript's throat. The images of the blood pumping out from his severed carotid artery are shown numerous times during the rest of the video. The throats of the dead soldiers are also cut. Later, in the same video, the commentator says the following as the camera pans across the carnage: "God loves people who kill in his name. The enemies of Islam are scared. The Jews and the Christians know that they have lost [the war] and want to stop us from spreading the truth." Several Westerners have recently suffered similar fates, decapitated by Islamic revolutionaries, with the pictures and videos of their deaths spread by modern media throughout the Islamic world.

The following offers a unique glimpse into the mind of a leader within the revolutionary Islamic vanguard. Fawwaz bin Muhammad Al-Nashami, the commander of the Al-Quds Brigade, led the 29 May 2004 operation against the Western oil company compounds at Khobar, Saudi Arabia, during which 22 non-Muslims were slaughtered. Below are excerpts of an interview published online by *Sawt Al-Jihad*, in which Al-Nashami describes some of the actions he and his fellow revolutionaries took during the raid. *Sawt Al-Jihad* is a journal published by the Islamic revolutionaries and has ties to Al Qa'ida. The revolutionaries forced their way into the Western oil compound, and proceeded to separate the "infidels" from the "Muslims" in order to methodically execute them.

---

[419]The following information comes from a report provided to the author by the U.S. Embassy in Rabat, Morocco. It describes in detail the contents of a videotape being circulated by the Algerian Salafist Group for Preaching and Fighting (GSPC). The report was obtained by the author in March 2004.

As soon as we entered, we encountered the car of a Briton, the investment director of the company. We tied the infidel by one leg [behind the car]. The infidel's clothing was torn to shreds, and he was naked in the street. The street was full of people, as this was during work hours, and everyone watched the infidel being dragged, praise and gratitude be to Allah.

We entered one of the companies' [offices], and found there an American infidel who looked like a director of one of the companies. I went into his office and called him. When he turned to me, I shot him in the head, and his head exploded. We entered another office and found one infidel from South Africa, and our brother Hussein slit his throat. We asked Allah to accept [these acts of devotion] from us, and from him. This was the South African infidel.

And I saw the skull of the soldier standing behind the machine gun explode before my eyes. Allah be praised.

We entered and in front of us stood many people. We asked them their religion, and for identification documents. We used this time for *Da'wa* [preaching Islam], and for enlightening the people about our goal. We spoke with many of them.

At the same time, we found a Swedish infidel. Brother Nimr cut off his head, and put it at the gate [of the building] so that it would be seen by all those entering and exiting.

We continued in the search for the infidels, and we slit the throats of those we found among them.

We began to comb the site looking for infidels. We found Filipino Christians. We cut their throats and dedicated them to our brothers the *Mujahideen* in the Philippines. [Likewise], we found Hindu engineers and we cut their throats too, Allah be praised. That same day, we purged Muhammad's land of many Christians and polytheists.

Afterwards, we turned to the hotel. We entered and found a restaurant, where we ate breakfast and rested a while. Then we went up to the next floor, found several Hindu dogs, and cut their throats.

We utilized the time for [teaching] the Qur'an to the Muslims who remained. We taught them how to read [Surat] Al-Fatiha properly. They were amazed by us, [and said], "How are you able to do this in such an inflamed atmosphere?" Thanks be to Allah for enabling us.

Then I phoned Al-Jazeera television, and they conducted an interview with us, that they did not release. I told them I was speaking with them from the compound, and that only the infidels were our targets.[420]

It seems clear that the revolutionary Islamic vanguard is at war with "anyone who opposes its program for the restoration of a unified Muslim *ummah*, ruled by a new Caliphate, governed by reactionary Islamic *shariah* law, and organized to wage *jihad* on the rest of the world."[421]

Revolutionary Islam as a Fantasy Ideology

The notion of consolidating a transnational, global Islamic sacred geography and of restoring the Islamic Caliphate is not just revolutionary—it is a fantasy. It is the collective fantasy of the revolutionary Islamic vanguard supported by the ressentiment phenomenon of the broader, world-wide Islamic *ummah*. Yet, as Lee Harris asserts, such collective fantasies are not new.[422] "Certain groups," according to Harris, "do not seem to have the knack for a realistic appraisal of themselves: they seem simply incapable of seeing themselves as others see them or of understanding why other groups react to them the way they do . . . Classical examples of this are easy to find: the Jacobin fantasy of reviving the Roman Republic; Mussolini's fantasy of reviving the Roman Empire; Hitler's fantasy of reviving German paganism and the thousand-year Reich."[423] As previously discussed in this work, a romantic notion of history, of reaching back to the hoary beginnings of an idea, seems to be important to understanding fantasy ideologies. As Harris rightly summarizes, "fantasy ideologies tend to be the domain of those groups that history has passed by or rejected—groups that feel that they are under attack from forces that, while more powerful perhaps than they are, are nonetheless inferior to them in terms of virtue; they themselves stand for what is

---

[420]"Commander of the Khobar Terrorist Squad Tells the Story of the Operation" in Sawt Al-Jihad, Issue 18, June 2004, trans. Middle East Media Research Institute, Special Dispatch 731, 15 June 2004, URL: www.memri.org/bin/articles.cgi?Page=archives&Area=sd&ID=SP73104, accessed 28 June 2004. The original Arabic transcript may be found at URL: www.hajr.ws/forum/showthread.php?p=404390047. The words enclosed by brackets [ ] signify text added by the translator for clarity of meaning.

[421]Paul Marshall, "War Against the Infidels," *The Weekly Standard* 9, no. 41 (26 June 2004), URL: http://www.theweeklystandard.com/check.asp?idArticle=4279&r=kvtyq, accessed 26 April 2004.

[422]Harris, 8.

[423]Harris, 8.

pure."[424] Hence, again, the previous suggestion that "purist" is a better descriptive than "fundamentalist" or "radical."

Fantasy ideologies, in this case revolutionary Islam, are fueled by intense passions and beliefs, the goal of which is not gradual transformation, but radical, tectonic, revolutionary change. As Harris adroitly notes, these beliefs "cannot be demonstrated logically and scientifically—[they are] beliefs that are therefore irrational if judged by the hard sciences."[425] Indeed, modern social science is profoundly challenged by the fires of religious revolutionary passion—typically anti-religious, quantitative approaches yield anemic explanations when confronted with the seemingly irrational fervor of revolutionary violence. The "terrorist" label is equally tepid in its power to penetrate the mind of the enemy. Harris writes, with irony, that "the purpose of 9/11 was not to create terror in the minds of the American people, but to prove to the Arabs [and other Muslims] that Islamic purity . . . could triumph over the West. The terror, which to us seems the central fact, is, in the eyes of Al-Qaeda, merely an incidental by-product, an irrelevancy." Indeed, numerous sources have documented the fact that the leaders of the attacks on 9/11 were transfixed by its spectacular success. They did not expect the buildings to collapse, yet what could be more demonstrative of Allah's divine presence than to have the attack be so dramatically effective.

Instead of thinking of acts like 9/11 as "terrorism," these acts of war should be seen as chapters in a strategic narrative, composed by the revolutionary Islamic vanguard to expose the weaknesses of Western secularism, and magnify the great, all-encompassing unity of Allah and Islam. Their relentless persistence should be seen as evidence of the deterministic perspective inherent in the collective Islamic fantasy—Allah has determined that they will eventually win. Within this context, martyrdom takes the stage of Islam's trans-historical narrative as a primary supporting act" in all its transcendent glory and accompanied by the panoply of magical powers that religious tradition has always assigned to it."[426] Thus, martyrdom is best seen as what Emile Durkheim once called "altruistic suicide." The men and women who regularly blow themselves up, at the direction of the vanguard and in support of their fantasy ideology, do so not because they are crazed radicals or fanatics that are recruited from the depressed and huddled masses of the Muslim world. Instead, the vanguard is skimming the simmering ressentiment surface of the collective Muslim identity for individuals predisposed toward self-sacrifice and "absolute subordination of self to the greater cause."[427]

---

[424]Harris, 8.

[425]Harris, 9.

[426]Harris, 13.

[427]Harold Gould, "Suicide as a Weapon of Mass Destruction," *Counterpunch* (25 November 2003), URL: www.counterpunch.org/gould11282003.html, accessed 1 December 2003.

The revolutionary Islamic vanguard has created a pool of men and women who willingly and eagerly serve as weapons of war, as guided missiles indiscriminately aimed at Western infidels wherever they exist.[428] As Durkheim described them, they are individuals who "are almost completely absorbed in the group"; who "completely [discard] their [individual] personalities for the idea of which they [have] become the servants."[429] In this sense, they are true believers, "the product of a socio-religious system which successfully motivates persons who are culturally enmeshed in it to altruistically commit suicide for the greater glory of the doctrines that it espouses."[430]

The revolutionary Islamic vanguard itself is not composed of individuals who were the victims of the so-called "root" causes of conflict—poverty, unequal resource distribution, lack of education, and disparities of wealth concentration, to name a few. Rather, as Harris points out, the revolutionaries who propel this Islamic fantasy ideology have "historically been produced by members of the intelligentsia, middle-class at the very least, and vastly better educated than average."[431] Many Islamic revolutionaries were educated in the West, owned profitable professional businesses or commercial trading companies, and lived comfortable to luxurious lives before joining the ranks of the diffused vanguard. Their Western educations notwithstanding, these individuals are compelled by a passionate, deeply historical religious belief that runs completely contrary to modernity's assertions. They are a product of their Semitic, Bedouin, tribal past.[432] In the words of T.E. Lawrence, their intensive religion "stresses the emptiness of the world and the fullness of God."[433] The revolutionary arrives at an "intense condensation of himself in God by shutting his eyes to the world, and to all the complex possibilities . . . which only contact with wealth and temptations could bring forth."[434] Instead, he attains a powerful trust in the divine, the deterministic nature of which robs him of compassion, and manifests itself in finding luxury in abnegation, renunciation, and self-restraint.[435] It is the ancient faith of the desert—now in the domain of the vanguard in the mountains of Afghanistan, the hinterlands of Pakistan, and the desert landscape stretching across North

---

[428]Gould, "Suicide as a Weapon of Mass Destruction."

[429]Emile Durkheim quoted in Gould, "Suicide as a Weapon of Mass Destruction.

[430]Emile Durkheim quoted in Gould, "Suicide as a Weapon of Mass Destruction."

[431]Harris, 15.

[432]While Islamic revolutionaries in Asia (such as Indonesia and the Philippines) do not share the same Arabic Bedouin tribal past, they nevertheless identify with this type of ethos.

[433]T.E. Lawrence, 41.

[434]T.E. Lawrence, 41.

[435]T.E. Lawrence, 41.

Africa from Sudan across to Morocco. It is the ethos and mystery of the caves, the tunnels, and the vanishing hideouts.

Camel traders/drivers in southern Jordan.

Photo by author

The vanguard operates across this transnational space without a formal structure or organizational model. Imaginary maps, transnational identities, and transparent borders allow for a dispersal of resources and a decentralized organizational structure.[436] The diffused nature of the vanguard "reduces costs of entry. It allows amateurs easily to replicate casual organizational forms and to adapt them to locale and circumstance. Ideas and practice diffuse by a kind of capillary action," one that is proving difficult to track, control, or destroy.[437] In addition, the dispersed nature and absence of vertical organizational structures among many revolutionary groups contribute to their survival. As Rudoph and Eickelman have written, "the amorphousness of many activist groups, formed from networks of trusted neighborhood and school acquaintances and devoid of complex hierarchies, makes them difficult for security services to even monitor."[438]

---

[436]Rudolph and Eickelman, 13.
[437]Rudolph and Eickelman, 13.
[438]Rudolph and Eickelman, 35.

In this, their "real" world, the Islamic revolutionaries postulate a universe which, to use Harris' philosophical language, is thoroughly *occasionalist*.

> That is to say, event A does not happen because it is caused by a previous event B, with both events occurring on the same ontological plane. Instead, event B is simply the occasion for God to cause event A, so that the genuine cause of all events occurring on our ontological plane of existence is God—God and nothing else. If this is so, then the "real" world that we take for granted simply vanishes, and all becomes determined by the will of God. Thus the line between realist and magical thinking dissolves.[439]

After all, for the revolutionary Islamic vanguard, God has predetermined that his religion will, in the words of Sayyid Qutb, "inevitably rule." It is this religious determinism, along with the indiscriminate genocidal passion, and Islam's historical imperatives, that collectively yield the gravest military threat confronting the United States today:

> The greatest threat facing us—and one of the greatest ever to threaten mankind—is the collision of this collective fantasy world of Islam with the horrendous reality of weapons of mass destruction, for weapons of mass destruction are unlike any other previous military threat.[440]

---

[439]Harris, 17
[440]Harris, 31

Conclusion

Seven Propositions for Recovering Strategic Insight

Our aim is victory—victory at all costs, victory in spite of all terror, victory, however long and hard the road may be; for without victory, there is no survival.

—**Winston Churchill**[441]

One man with beliefs is equal to ninety-nine with only interests.

—**John Stuart Mill**[442]

In 1946, the United States, seeking a peaceful world after the collective pain and toil of two world wars, faced a new threat it had never encountered before. This threat was both ideological and totalitarian. Winston Churchill famously described the new challenge in his Iron Curtain speech in Fulton, Missouri, in March 1946:

> We are now confronted with something quite as wicked but in many ways more formidable than Hitler, because Hitler had only the *Herrenvolk* pride and the anti-Semitic hatred to exploit. He had no fundamental theme. But these thirteen men in the Kremlin have their hierarchy and a church of Communist adepts, whose missionaries are in every country as a fifth column, obscure people, but awaiting the day when they hope to be absolute masters of their fellow countrymen and pay off old scores.[443]

U.S. policymakers and strategists reluctantly turned toward Communism with an uneasy concern, one that was reinforced by war weariness, a national desire to refocus on domestic agendas, the promises of resurgent capitalism, and the international jurisprudence of the United Nations. Yet it was the analysis by George F. Kennan that infused American perspectives with strategic insight and became the foundation for U.S. doctrine and strategy for the next 50 years. In his visionary 1947 article "The Sources of Soviet Conduct," Kennan issued a call for containment of the Soviet threat, based upon his penetrating and strategic analysis of the Communist ideology.[444] His scholarship reverberated throughout the policy community and

---

[441]Winston Churchill quoted in Stephen Mansfield, *Never Give In: The Extraordinary Character of Winston Churchill* (Harding, TN: Cumberland House, 1996), 73.

[442]This quote is generally attributed to John Stuart Mill.

[443]Winston Churchill quoted in Stephen Mansfield, 79.

[444]Kennan, *American Diplomacy.*

down the halls of academia, provoking a necessary discussion at the strategic level. The debate focused on penetrating the ideological core of Soviet Communism in an attempt to first understand—and then counteract—its growing threat.

In the early 1990s, the United States, again seeking a peaceful world after the collective pain and toil of the Cold War, faced a new threat it had not encountered before. This time, the threat was a revolutionary and religious ideology. The United States had never fought a religious war before. At best, the existence of the threat was not recognized. At worst, it was ignored or relegated to the realms of criminal or terrorist activity. The Enlightenment pedigree of modern philosophy had taught American policy and academic elites that religion was no longer a variable to be contended with in the modern world. Instead, postmodern academia looked for "root" causes to explain the apparent visceral passions displayed by the enemy's actions. Even after the first World Trade Center bombing in 1993, the embassy bombings in Kenya and Tanzania in 1998, the attack on the USS *Cole* in 2000, and an outright declaration of religious war in 1998, policymakers and strategists were blind to strategic realities. The 23 February 1998 statement issued by the World Islamic Front "Jihad Against Jews and Crusaders" was signed by five men calling for a united war against the enemies of Islam. The five men were: Usamah Bin-Ladin (amir of al Qaeda), Ayman al-Zawahiri (amir of the Jihad Group of Egypt), Abu-Yasir Rifa'i Ahmad Taha (leader of the Egyptian Islamic Group), Mir Hamzah (Secretary of the Jamiat-ul-Ulema-e-Pakistan), and Fazlur Rahman (amir of the Jihad Movement of Bangladesh).[445] The *fatwa*—or religious ruling—stated that to "kill Americans and their allies—civilian and military—is an individual duty for every Muslim who can do it in any country in which it is possible to do it."[446] Their exhortation ended with an appeal to Allah and the Prophet: "O ye who believe, give your response to Allah and His Apostle, when he calleth you to that which will give you life . . . So lose no heart, nor fall into despair. For ye must gain mastery if ye are true in faith."[447]

Eventually—just as in the late 1940s—policymakers and strategists in the United States reluctantly and uneasily turned toward the new threat, their concern undermined by Cold War weariness, a national desire to focus on domestic agendas, the promises of global capitalism, the authority of international law, and the jurisprudence of the United Nations. But this time, both the strategic analysis and the strategic consensus have failed to emerge. Politicians and strategists alike

---

[445]"Jihad Against Jews and Crusaders," World Islamic Front Statement, 23 February 1998, hosted by the Federation of American Scientists, URL: www.fas.org/irp/world/para/docs/980223-fatwa.htm, accessed 29 January 2004.

[446]"Jihad Against Jews and Crusaders."

[447]"Jihad Against Jews and Crusaders."

seem blinded by their own intellectual pedigree—the combined effects of post-Enlightenment philosophy, an anti-Socratic mentality, and an obfuscating Wilsonian idealism. The cumulative effect of these blinders is to conceal the ideological and religious imperatives driving the threat.

Most significantly and most detrimentally, the current context lacks the strategic insight of George Kennan's 1947 analysis. Indeed, a rigorous and penetrating analysis of the threat is not permitted by the standards of today's political and policy landscape. *To put it bluntly, we are not permitted to enter the mind of the enemy because we are not permitted to critically analyze his religion.* Dr. Christopher Melchert, a Lecturer of Arabic and Islam at Oxford University, poignantly reminds us that "modern social science hates to study Protestant fundamentalism, and Islam reminds them of that too much."[448] Islam, in the minds of the postmodern American political and academic elites, is thus simply "just another religion," something that is individually practiced, compartmentalized, separate from politics and the affairs of the state, and therefore not a suitable element of public discussion or debate. In such religious and anthropological ignorance, we "assume that religion means the same for Muslims as it has meant in the Western world . . . that is to say, a section or compartment of life reserved for certain matters, and separate, or at least separable, from other compartments of life designed to hold other matters."[449]

Yet this is not the case in the Muslim world. In classical Arabic, there are "no pairs of words corresponding to spiritual and temporal, to lay and ecclesiastical, religious and secular," and "even in modern usage, there is no Muslim equivalent to 'the Church,' meaning 'ecclesiastical organization.'"[450] Instead, as Bernard Lewis concludes, "the very notion of a secular jurisdiction and authority—of a so-to-speak unsanctified part of life that lies outside the scope of religious law and those who uphold it—is seen as an impiety, indeed as the ultimate betrayal of Islam."[451] Western academic and policy elites, profoundly uncomfortable with the concept of religion, thus seek answers to the current conflict in the so-called "root causes" of "terrorism," typically raising to the forefront arguments of unequal resource distribution, poverty, and lack of education.

Chronically and dangerously absent is George Kennan's strategic insight, the ideologically penetrating analyses that provided practical guidance to policymakers in the face of Soviet Communism. Yet it is in Kennan's words that we find an

---

[448]Dr. Christopher Melchert, Lecturer in Arabic and Islam, The Oriental Institute, Oxford University, England, interview with the author, 12 February 2004.

[449]Bernard Lewis, *The Political Language of Islam*, 2.

[450]Bernard Lewis, *The Political Language of Islam*, 3.

[451]Bernard Lewis, *The Political Language of Islam*, 3.

arresting similarity between two very different realities—the predeterminism of Soviet Communism and the divine imperatives of revolutionary Islam:

> For ideology [*religion*] taught them that the outside world is hostile, and that it was their duty eventually to overthrow the political forces beyond their borders. The powerful hands of Russian [*Islamic*] history and tradition reach up to sustain them in this feeling. Finally, their own aggressive intransigence with respect to the outside world began to find its own reaction . . . It is an undeniable privilege of every man to prove himself right in the thesis that the world is his enemy; for if he reiterates it frequently enough and makes it the background of his conduct he is bound eventually to be right.[452]

> In the light of the above, it will be clearly seen that Soviet [*revolutionary Islam's*] pressure against the free institutions of the Western world is something that can be contained by the adroit and vigilant application of counter-force at a series of constantly shifting geographical and political points, corresponding to the shifts and maneuvers of Soviet policy [*of the Islamic vanguard*], but which cannot be charmed or talked out of existence. The Russians [*revolutionary Islamic vanguard*] look forward to a duel of infinite duration, and they see that already they have scored great successes.[453]

The illustration above is meant to advocate a strategic perspective, one that can only come about after an honest debate about the core truths of the enemy's religious ideology. We have not engaged in that discussion, because the political and policy elites have effectively removed Islam from public comment and criticism. Yet, as Thomas Jefferson wrote, it is when human interposition disarms the truth of her natural weapons-free argument and debate that errors become prevalent and dangerous. The simple and Socratic elegance of rigorous debate is that contradictory ideas are freely permitted to compete in order for the participants to elevate their understanding and knowledge. But our postmodern philosophy inclines away from free and open debate. The nihilistic concept that says that all ideas are of equal merit, and therefore there is no idea with more inherent value or truth than another, also tells us that all religions are of equal value and are best consigned to private life. In short, our intellectual pedigree stops us from engaging in meaningful debate, thereby stripping us of the strategic insight required to deal with the religious ideologies of our enemies. Instead, as Kennan wrote in 1947,

---

[452]Kennan, 111-112. Brackets with my interpretation added.
[453]Kennan, 120.

exhibitions of indecision, disunity and internal disintegration within this country have an exhilarating effect on the whole Communist [*revolutionary Islamic*] movement. At each evidence of these tendencies, a thrill of hope and excitement goes through the Communist [*Islamic*] world; a new jauntiness can be noted in the Moscow tread [*Friday sermons*]; new groups of foreign supporters [*Islamic revolutionaries*] climb on what they can only view as the band wagon of international politics [*revolutionary Islam*].[454]

Today's policy and academic elites seem to lack "the aptitude and inclination to penetrate the mind of adversary cultures."[455] As one observer recently remarked, the message from all our top officials is abundantly clear: "'The 19 suicide terrorists hijacked a great religion . . . That's that; Islam off the table; no need to go deeper.'"[456] This is not the way to recover strategic insight. Andrew McCarthy, the chief assistant U.S. attorney who prosecuted Sheik Omar Abdel Rahman, the mastermind of the first World Trade Center bombing, puts it more directly:

> We have taken the ostrich routine way too far. A commitment in favor of toleration is not the same as a commitment against examination. We have been so paralyzed by fear of being portrayed as an enemy of Islam—as an enemy of a creed practiced by perhaps a billion people worldwide—that we've lost our voice . . . we need to understand that we are fighting a religious, political, and social belief system—not a method of attack, but a comprehensive ideology that calls for a comprehensive response.[457]

Strategic insight will only be recovered when the policy and academic elite (1) rediscover the reality of religious identity; (2) reinvigorate public discourse with rigorous debate aimed at critically examining all alternative ideas in the pursuit of truth, knowledge, and public policy; and (3) question whether foreign and anthropologically diverse cultures are truly receptive to the American experiment with democracy.[458] A renewed emphasis on the classical disciplines of history, anthropology, and theology will facilitate an unvarnished assessment of Islam—as a religion, a culture, and an identity phenomenon. This would bring about what

---

[454]Kennan, 127.

[455]"How America can win the intelligence war," *Asia Times Online Edition*, 15 June 2004, URL: www.atimes.com/atimes/Front_Page/FF15Aa01.html, accessed 15 June 2004.

[456]Andrew McCarthy, "The War that Dare Not Speak Its Name," *National Review Online*, 13 May 2004, URL: www.nationalreview.com/mccarthy/mccarthy200405130837.asp, accessed 18 May 2004.

[457]Andrew McCarthy, "The War that Dare Not Speak Its Name."

[458]John W. Kingdon, *America the Unusual* (Boston, MA: Bedford/St. Martin's, 1999).

Adda Bozeman, the late strategic thinker, advocated, namely to accentuate assessment of cultural and religious boundaries rather than official territorial frontiers, or to think more geopolitically rather than juristically.[459]

The following seven propositions are suggested as markers to reinvigorate the strategic perspective. They begin to address the difficult "why" questions discussed in the introduction. Although the decades-long struggle against Soviet Communism was fundamentally different from today's emerging conflict, these propositions are nevertheless intended to uncover the core ideas that fuel the enemy's mind, in the same way that Kennan's 1947 analysis laid bare Soviet Communist ideology.

---

[459]Bozeman, 254.

Proposition #1

Islam's theological foundations yield expansionist imperatives

It is Islam's theological foundations that provide the basis for its political and historical imperatives. These theological doctrines are held to be fundamentally true across the entire spectrum of Islam—from Sunnis to Shia to Sufis. Islam's anthropological outlook sees mankind's essential nature as neutral—the concept of *fitra* predisposes man neither toward good nor evil. In Islam, it is man's immediate environment—the family and the society—that act as a corrupting or edifying influence. Thus, Islam demands that the family and society be structured in such a way as to facilitate a positive influence on the individual believer. Since its eschatology dictates that paradise is only gained if one's good works outweigh one's evil deeds, Islam therefore also established an orthopractical system of works that allows the individual believer to meritoriously gain access to paradise. This system consists of the ritualistic observances, such as daily prayer, the fast, alms-giving, and the pilgrimage, as well as supererogatory deeds—including martyrdom during *jihad*. The concepts of martyrdom and *jihad* are deeply resident in the sacred history of Islam, in the Qur'an, in the sayings of the Prophet Muhammad, and in the dramatic post-Mohammedan expansion of Islam's sacred geography. There is no concept of divine redeeming grace in Islamic soteriology as there is in the foundations of Christian religion; rather, it is a doctrine of deeds that enables the believer to gain access to paradise. This places the burden squarely on the backs of individual believers, whereas in Christian doctrine, that burden was borne by Jesus Christ.

As a result, Islam emerged as an activist phenomenon. From the outset, the Prophet Mohammad arranged the *ummah* in such a way as to facilitate Islam's orthopractical requirements. As a prophet, a soldier, and a statesman, he set the Islamic precedent and permanently fused the realm of religion and the realm of politics. Karen Armstrong explains that "by ordering the whole of life so that God was given priority and his plans for humanity were fully implemented, Muslims would achieve a personal and societal integration that would give them intimations of the unity which was God. To fence off one area of life and declare it to be off-limits to this religious 'effort' would be a shocking violation of this principle of unification (*tawhid*), which is the cardinal Islamic virtue. It would be tantamount to a denial of God himself."[460]

Thus Islam evolved as a unitary kingdom—the divine kingdom of Allah was co-existent with the earthly kingdom of man. Muslims viewed the Caliphate as

---

[460]Armstrong, *The Battle for God*, 37.

this unitary kingdom—a broad sacred geography that was ever-expanding under the predeterministic will of Allah. Within that sacred geography, Islamic jurisprudence and Shari'ah law enabled the faithful to fulfill their religious requirements. They came to see themselves as endowed with a broader, transnational identity—undoubtedly with local textures and variances, sometimes with rifts and bloody feuds—but nevertheless unified by the fundamental doctrines of the religion. Islam has bequeathed this fusion between religion and the state as its fourteen-hundred-year legacy, perpetuating theocratic governments even as it has periodically expanded politically and militarily. The grandeur of the early Caliphate left an indelible impression on the Islamic ummah. Combined with the determinism of the prophet and his message of Allah's ultimate and final revelation in the Qur'an, it formed an historical expectation of future greatness—one that would inevitably put it into conflict with other ideas and belief systems. Eventually, the most significant challenge came from Western modernity and its new religion—secularism. The modern age inaugurated by the West—with its Enlightenment resentment of all things metaphysical, its religion of secularism, its powerful predominance in science, technology, and warfare, and its imperial designs throughout the Muslim sacred geography—has brought severe trauma to the collective Muslim identity.

Proposition #2

The Islamic ummah is traumatized and suffers
from a ressentiment phenomenon

Today, Muslims throughout the world may understandably be consumed by humiliation and resentment because of the contrast between their past cultural and religious grandeur and their current relative decline. The combined effects of Western secularism, European colonialism, military and scientific impotency, and the distorting influences of modern Arab successes have generated a broad emotive reaction throughout the Islamic *ummah*. This reaction is best characterized as a simmering ressentiment, which manifests itself in the visceral hatred, malice, envy, and spite that periodically boils to the surface in the "Muslim street." Ressentiment is, as Max Scheler noted, a "psychological contagion" leading to an embittering and poisoning not only of the individual, but more importantly the collective personality. It is a powerful emotive force because it is amplified by feelings of helplessness, or an inability to attain revenge for perceived injustices. The surges of passion, the fiery Friday sermons, the spiritual fervor of the Muslim street, slogans like "my religion today, your religion tomorrow," graffiti declaring "first the Saturday people, then the Sunday people," the gruesome decapitations, the spontaneous celebrations of Western casualties, the absence of widespread condemnation of acts like 9/11, the appeal and growth of overtly anti-Western media, and the diffuse financial support of the Islamic revolutionaries, all powerfully contribute to, and are evidence of, the phenomenon of ressentiment. Ressentiment in the Islamic identity generates a smoldering current of hostility, "an incurable, persistent feeling of hating and despising" which generates widespread negative attitudes and permeates the whole culture, era, and moral system with false moral judgments and "rash, at times fanatical claims of truth generated by the impotency this feeling comes from."[461] Most importantly, the ressentiment phenomenon generates a fertile recruitment medium for the Islamic vanguard. They have a receptive worldwide audience from which to select future members of their revolutionary ranks.

Proposition #3

The United States is fighting against
a revolutionary Islamic vanguard

The enemy is a revolutionary—not a terrorist. While the phenomenon of ressentiment applies to the broadly transnational Islamic identity, it does not manifest itself in the mind of the Islamic revolutionaries. These combatants are fulfilling their psychological passion for revenge. The revolutionaries are engaged in an epochal struggle between their ideas and our ideas about the affairs of mankind. They have not hijacked their religion and they are not its nominal followers—instead, they are Islamic purists, who passionately follow the example of their beloved Prophet Mohammad. According to them, Mohammad inaugurated their revolution fourteen hundred years ago. It is Mohammad whom they imitate when they engage in an apocalyptic predeterministic struggle against unbelievers. It is Mohammad whom they emulate when they decapitate the infidels. It is Mohammad whom they emulate when they call upon every believer to personally and individually engage in the struggle that they call *jihad*. It is Mohammad's vision which they endorse as they desperately seek to restore the preeminence of Islam—to purge the Muslim world of corrupt and apostate rulers, and to bring the entire world under the Islamic rightly guided way of life.

Their ideology is not evolutionary, but rather revolutionary, calling for a complete rejection of the status quo. The Director of the Middle East Centre at Oxford University assesses the overarching goal of the revolutionary Islamic vanguard: "They are in a fight against globalization and their goal is

---

[461]Manfred Frings in Scheler, 5.

to undo the Westphalian system and establish an Islamic Caliphate."[462] It is fueled by a utopian vision of a worldwide sacred geography, called the Islamic caliphate—a unique historical fusion of politics and religion. As a result, they are engaged in a tectonic struggle to change the world as we know it, and they will use every means available—including mass genocide—to fulfill their fantasy. They view themselves as the lead agents of revolutionary change and the vanguard of a religious revival. The ressentiment phenomenon that prevails throughout the worldwide Islamic community ensures that they have a sympathetic audience that is at least passively supportive. The broader Islamic revivalist fervor has produced a hospitable environment for the revolutionaries. As one sociologist recently noted, "[L]ike Mao's fish swimming in a sea, a relatively small cadre of revolutionaries, a revolutionary subculture, passes through and comes to be sustained by a larger subculture of revolution."[463]

Yet the revolutionaries also draw tacit and illicit support from a few regimes and governments who share their passion to humble the secular West. They wield a diverse arsenal and are skilled not only in killing and destruction, but also in political propaganda and religious manipulation. They are driven by historical imperatives, a millennial tradition of Islamic doctrine, and the supererogatory promises of their eschatological foundation—which offer them an afterlife in exchange for martyrdom. In life, they gain approbation as religious warriors in the cause of Allah—in death, they gain paradise. Worst of all, they have nothing to lose. They will not yield, negotiate, or compromise.

Proposition #4

The United States is engaged in a religious war

The United States has never before fought a religious war. Religious wars have throughout history been among the bloodiest, most visceral and indiscriminate conflicts known to man. But the statement that "the United States is engaged in a religious war" demands clarification. This is not a clash of civilizations. If anything, this is a clash between Western civilization and the revolutionary religion of Islam. It is not a war between Christianity and Islam—mainly because the United States and other Western countries do not represent *pax Christiana*. To the contrary, the predominant "religion" of the West today is secularism. It is not

---

[462]Dr. Eugene Rogan, Director, Middle East Center, Oxford University, England, interview with the author, 13 Feburary 2004.

[463]Mark Gould, *Eschatology and Soteriology: Religious Commitment and Its Consequences in Islam and Christianity*, 26.

Clausewitzian war, in which war is said to be the extension of politics. It is religious war, initiated by the historical, religious imperatives of Islam. The conflict is a war between the ideas of Western democracy and those of revolutionary Islam. The enemy is the revolutionary Islamic vanguard, and it obtains its support from the ressentiment felt among followers of transnational Islam. The enemy is driven and sustained by an ideology rooted in the historical doctrines of Islam, is certain of Allah's divinely pre-ordained victory, and is imbued with an ideology that begins and ends with the Qur'an and the Prophet Mohammad. In other words, this is a religious war.

In terms of a net assessment of the two sides of the conflict, the anti-Socratic pathology prevalent in the West is highly damaging because it precludes the conduct of an open and honest debate about Islam, thereby preventing a meaningful and strategic understanding of the threat. Only with that understanding can we "level the playing field." The U.S. can reasonably well seek out answers to all the who-what-when-where-how questions and can attempt to execute pin-point military strikes against the enemy's assets and diffused infrastructures. But this will not win the war, principally because it does not answer the most important question—the question of why. The strategic question concerns ideas and convictions. The United States and its allies need to defeat the ideas of revolutionary Islam, marginalize its leaders, and talk about their religion openly. "It means," in the words of one astute observer, "making people take clear positions: making them stand up and be counted—and be accountable—not letting them hide under murky labels like 'moderate.'"[464] Most critically, policy elites in the United States must realize that the West's secular democratic paradigm is not only completely unacceptable to the revolutionary Islamic vanguard, but also has little or no legitimacy among the broader Islamic *ummah*. Western secular democracy and its commitment to the divided kingdom—the separation between the kingdom of this world and the kingdom of heaven embodied in the parallel separation of state and church—are in utter conflict with Islam's unitary kingdom—Allah's earthly sacred geography and the historical fusion and complex interdependence between the rightly guided religion, society, and state.

Proposition #5

Strategic victory involves winning the war of ideas

The United States is losing the strategic battle. Its long-term support of corrupt Islamic regimes has rendered it illegitimate in the eyes of the Islamic *ummah*. The United States turned a blind eye to the internal policies of Cold War allies in the

---

[464]Andrew McCarthy, "The War that Dare Not Speak Its Name."

Islamic world, so long as their governments could be counted on to support the United States against Communism. These "allies" have traditionally included Saudi Arabia, Egypt, Jordan, the Gulf kingdoms, Pakistan, and others. Today, Saudi Arabia remains a theocratic police state governed by the corrupt house of Saud. As has been well documented elsewhere, Saudi Arabia is perhaps the most egregious example of self-serving, theo-monarchical rule. The House of Saud, which owes its current power to a Faustian bargain made between the original Saudi ruler and the Wahhabi *ulema*, continues to encourage worldwide propagation of revolutionary Islam while simultaneously lending a façade of official support to Western attempts to fight the Islamic revolutionaries. The Saudis continue to fund "'the largest worldwide propaganda campaign ever mounted'—dwarfing the Soviets' propaganda efforts at the height of the Cold War."[465] The Saudi weekly *Ain al-Yaqeen* has noted that $70 billion in Saudi funding has produced "some 1,500 mosques, 210 Islamic centers, 202 colleges, and nearly 2,000 schools in non-Islamic countries."[466]

Observers from across the Islamic world testify to persistent meddling in foreign internal affairs by Saudi-funded Wahhabist revolutionaries. Dr. Mohammad Tozi at the University of Casablanca explains that "the Saudis shrewdly worked to take over the mantle of Pan-Islamic leadership, infusing the Islamic *ummah* with a political identity and permeating educational systems throughout the Islamic world with their closed-minded Wahhabi concepts."[467] Daoud Casewit, at the Moroccan-American Commission for Educational and Cultural Exchange, laments that "for decades, the big dollars have been coming out of Saudi Arabia, and now we are reaping the rewards. They have traditionally had the resources, logistics, and means to fund their ideas throughout the Islamic world."[468] According to Dr. Fatiha Benlabbah at the University of Rabat, "the Saudis exploit the fact that they 'own' the *hajj* and the two holy places of Islam and they use this to fuel their Wahhabi doctrines and its demonization of modernity, the West, and globalization. They realize that the mosques are the best way to get out their messages, especially to the uneducated masses."[469] These sentiments are echoed by Dr. Mustafa Zekri, also at the University of Rabat, who asserts that "Saudi Arabia's rigid vision and singular, narrowly focused perspectives about Islam have been successfully propagated to the Islamic masses on a worldwide scale."[470]

---

[465]Frank Gaffney, "Waging the War of Ideas," *Washington Times*, 9 December 2003, A19.

[466] Frank Gaffney, "Waging the War of Ideas."

[467]Dr. Mohammad Tozi, interview by the author.

[468]Daoud Casewit, interview with the author.

[469]Dr. Fatiha Benlabbah, Professor of Literature, University of Rabat, Morocco, interview with the author, 18 March 2004.

[470]Dr. Mustafa Zekri, interview with the author.

Woman walking past the mausoleum in Rabat, Morocco.
Photo by author.

The director of the Middle East Studies Program at the American University of Cairo provides evidence of another type of Saudi influence. The Arabian Gulf oil boom fostered a need for imported cheap labor from foreign countries. According to Elmusa, generations of young Egyptians were indoctrinated by Saudi clerics and the Saudi religious educational system while employed by Saudi Arabia's oil industry. Now, those workers are returning to Egypt as adherents to Saudi Arabia's Wahhabi Islamic doctrines.[471]

Finally, Dr. Fares Braizat, Director of the public polling unit at the Center for Strategic Studies at the University of Jordan, has expressed with no small amount of frustration the physical evidence of Saudi influence within the Jordanian Kingdom. As Braizat pointed out to the author, the numerous mosques and schools that were built by Saudi aid societies epitomize what many educated and secularized Muslims assert throughout the region: "We can't compete with these people—they have the money, they have the resources, and because of their social welfare approach, they have the hearts of the people."[472]

But the regime in Saudi Arabia does not stand by itself. Egypt, democratic in name only, is essentially a police state, undergirded by a strictly controlled government security apparatus and billions of dollars of U.S. aid designed to subsidize basic consumer prices and to forestall economic collapse. The entire Persian Gulf region is populated by kingdoms ruled by royal families—benevolent when they have reason to be—and tightly controlled by internal security organizations whose primary function is to protect the ruling families. In Pakistan, the government survives only by delicately balancing Islamic revolutionaries and secular interests, and by securing itself with a ruthless intelligence organization whose primary purpose is to ensure the survival of the central government. Other examples of these types of regimes abound throughout the Islamic world. They exist today, to no small extent, due to their erstwhile propped-up status as client states during the Cold War. Now that the bipolar world has faded, the corrupt nature of many of these governments grates on Muslims who connect the very existence of those governments to support from the U.S. government.

If the United States is to win the strategic war of ideas, it must begin by standing true to its own core ideas throughout the Muslim world. This will inevitably involve making some very difficult and challenging policy decisions. It will require moving away from the Cold War era Machiavellian support of corrupt police states. It will involve, in Kennan's words, vigilantly asserting pressure at a series of constantly shifting geographical and political points throughout the Islamic world—in the same manner as the United States did in its efforts to effect change in the Eastern Bloc countries. This war of ideas must be pursued through bold political, diplomatic, and economic means. The objective of the war of ideas

---

[471]Dr. Sharif Elmusa, Director, Middle East Studies Program, American University, Cairo, interview with the author, 22 March 2004.

[472]Dr. Fares Braizat, Director, Public Polling Unit, Center for Strategic Studies, University of Jordan, Amman, Jordan, interview with the author, 28 March 04.

is not to "make the world safe for democracy," nor to forcibly change the regimes of other countries, but rather to demonstrate to the populations of those countries the value of American ideas about the affairs of mankind, to explain the benefits of these ideas to individuals, families, and society at large, and to show how these ideas transcend official government-to-government relationships. The U.S. can begin to influence Muslim populations by arguing strongly for their holding corrupt governments accountable to widely disregarded international norms, such as the UN's Universal Declaration of Human Rights. Ultimately, however, lasting domestic change in the Muslim world will only come about if it is propelled by indigenous leadership. It seems hopelessly naïve to assert that change can be compelled by outside influences.

Proposition #6

The Palestinian movement is fundamentally different from revolutionary Islam

No other issue seems to find the same resonance among Muslims as what is perceived by the Muslim world to be the so-called "unqualified" or "unbalanced" support the United States provides to the state of Israel. The chorus of criticism echoes throughout the Islamic world, often coming from corrupt regimes and monarchies who seek legitimacy in the eyes of their own populations by moralistic finger pointing about the Palestinian issue. That this often amounts to nothing more than Pan-Islamic band-wagoning or feigned sympathy seems irrelevant in the eyes of the political elites—they tend to use this propaganda for their own purposes. These hypocrisies notwithstanding, the United States stands to gain potential allies throughout the region if it can do more to ensure the appearance and reality of impartiality in resolving this decades-old issue.

Strategically speaking, there are fundamental differences between the Palestinian Liberation Organization (PLO) and its military elements, and the revolutionary Islamic movement and organizations such as al Qaeda. The Palestinian movement is local, composed of Palestinians, and deeply rooted ethnically to the Palestinian people as a whole. Their military tactics notwithstanding, Palestinian militant groups are welfare organizations, providing practical services to the people they represent. Those services include schools, medical clinics, and other similar support structures. The military wing's tactics, violent and gruesome as they are, are focused against a single target—the state of Israel. It has rarely, if ever, struck targets outside of tight, self-imposed parameters, taking care to avoid increasing the number of its potential enemies. Of course, militant Palestinian groups do this for the purposes of self-preservation, mainly out of fear that out-of-area escalations will likely draw a direct response from the United States. Nevertheless, their targets remain predominantly

Israelis. Indeed, as difficult as it sometimes seems to imagine, the notional goal of one day attaining Palestinian statehood is relatively realistic and pragmatic, when compared to satisfying the fanatical goals of the Islamic revolutionaries.[473] Because the Palestinian militant's goals are politically bounded and rational, their military strikes are concomitantly limited and in a sense, Clausewitzean—designed to put political pressure on the Israeli government.

Palestinian goat herd at a Roman historical site in northern Jordan.
Photo by author.

The revolutionary Islamic vanguard, with al Qaeda in the forefront, is altogether a different phenomenon. The Islamic revolutionary ranks comprise individuals from across the Muslim world. There are Algerians, Tunisians, Moroccans, Saudis, Egyptians, Pakistanis, Yemenis, and even some Westerners—to name a few. There is no ethnic commonality and there are no representative functions or local connections. They are, essentially, a group of misfits. To the extent that they claim to represent anybody, they do so in the name of the greater Muslim ummah as a whole. Their goal is fanciful. The establishment of a global sacred geography called a caliphate is neither realistic nor pragmatic. Their methodology is therefore also fanciful and non-Clausewitzean—and includes their stated aim of mass indiscriminate genocide

---

[473]This remains true even though many of the Palestinian-associated groups advocate the elimination of the state of Israel. Even though this is a radical goal, it still does not compare to the global aspirations of the revolutionary Islamic vanguard. It is not certain whether Palestinian militant groups might some day have wider global aspirations.

against Western populations as a whole. Thus, while the Palestinian movement comes from Gaza and the West Bank, has local ties, and is connected to the community, the Islamic revolutionaries belong to no one and are accountable to no people or non-revolutionary group. The violence that Palestinian militants propagate is focused on attaining political recognition and power in the form of a Palestinian state. The mass genocidal violence propagated by the Islamic revolutionaries is focused on achieving a complete religious revolution of the global status quo.

It is in the national interest of the United States to politically acknowledge these differences and to exploit them strategically. Instead of crudely encompassing all groups under the broad umbrella of the "Global War on Terror," U.S. policy and academic elites should begin to marginalize and isolate the Islamic revolutionaries by politically highlighting the differences between the Palestinian cause and the Islamic revolutionary phenomenon. In doing so, U.S. policy should focus on the comparatively limited, political aims of the Palestinian cause, by contrasting them with the fantastical, genocidal, apocalyptic nature of the Islamic revolutionaries. Conversations with educated Muslims in Amman, Baku, Cairo, Dubai, and Rabat suggest that Muslims would be prepared to show a great deal of pragmatism with respect to potentially collaborative efforts to fight the revolutionaries—if the U.S. would be willing to expend political capital to lend greater legitimacy to the Palestinian cause. Based on the present analysis and the stark differences between the two movements, it seems reasonable to assert that this type of policy would have considerable grounding. As a minimum, it could remove the Palestinian rallying cry from the propaganda toolbox of corrupt regimes throughout the region, as well as from the recruitment rhetoric of the Islamic revolutionaries.

Proposition #7

Consider Sufism as a strategic alternative to revolutionary Islam

The final proposition is enticing but admittedly anecdotal in nature. It emerged after an evening of conversation between the author and Adnane Raiss in Rabat, Morocco. Mr. Raiss is the national coordinator for Morocco of the U.N. International Labor Office in Rabat. He is a Muslim, but of greater significance is the fact that he is a devout Sufi. Most Westerners know little about Sufism. According to Raiss, Sufism, "far from being a doctrine, represents an experience or a state of being that is accessible to each and every individual by means of inward cleansing and purification."[474] As is perhaps apparent from this statement, Sufism is an aesthetic as well as ascetic application of Islam, focused on inner purification,

---

[474]Mr. Adnane Raiss, National Coordinator, U.N. International Labor Office, Rabat, Morocco, interview with the author, 16 March 2004.

and attaining harmony both with Allah as well as the brotherhood of believers. It is intensely experiential and personal, and often involves serious meditation, sometimes evolving into extended trances. While Sufism incorporates the five traditional pillars and basic doctrines of Islam, its focus is more properly understood to be *ihsan*—directly translated as "doing what is beautiful"—something which the Angel Gabriel, according to the traditions, is said to have described as the innermost dimension of true Islam.[475] In a scholarly paper Raiss describes *ihsan* as "beneficence, performance of good deeds, but in the religious sense it implies the doing of good deeds over and above what is just and fair. It is indicative of the intense devotion of man to his Creator and Master and his enthusiasm for virtue and piety. The aim of *ihsan* is to create a sense of inner piety in man and to train his sensibilities in a way that all his thoughts and actions flow from the fountainhead of the love of God."[476] What seems dramatically different in comparing Sufism to the rest of Islam is that the former is focused on mankind's experiencing and living in the realm of divine love.

Christian cathedral in downtown Rabat, Morocco.
Photo by author.

---

[475]Mr. Adnane Raiss, interview with the author.

[476]Adnane Raiss, *The Contribution of Sufism in Promoting a Culture of Peace*, unpublished scholarly paper, Spring 2002.

Sufis traditionally meet in a *turuq*, a congregation formed around a Sufi master, who leads the faithful in *majalis*, or spiritual sessions. Over time, Sufism has come to represent a form of Islamic asceticism, a retirement from the world, and a spiritual devotion to divine worship, sometimes culminating in an ecstatic experience. Sufis are known for *dhikr*, or long repetitions of sacred phrases. This method is used as a form of spiritual exercise—it is focused on opening what Sufis call the "eye of the heart," an emotional, metaphysical experiencing of divine mercy, grace, beauty, kindness, and love.[477]

The Sufi path of education also includes *jihad*, but unlike the meaning propagated by Islamic revolutionaries, to Sufis *jihad* is the internal effort or struggle toward unity with the divine. In this sense, it is like the general Islamic concept of the greater jihad, or the struggling against one's lower, sinful self—more popularly known as one's *nafs*. For Sufis, the lesser or outward jihad involves struggles against social injustice. Sufis often characterize the struggle against one's nafs by explaining that the heart is owned mutually by evil forces and by angels. The struggle is therefore to allow the impulses of the angels to assume preeminence in one's personal life.[478]

Perhaps the most profound statement by Raiss was the following comment regarding soteriology in the Sufi tradition: "Deeds will not save you, but rather God's mercy and grace. God wants the creation to be detached from its deeds and instead to be attached to him."[479] This is significant—to the extent in which this statement tends to de-emphasize the traditional orthopractical requirements of Islam—for if there is even a small relaxation of those requirements in Sufism, this also means that Sufis are more likely to require less structure in their societies and less form in their worship. Indeed, Raiss explains that "Sufis are the sons of their time," meaning that one has to adapt to the context and era in which one lives. This is in dramatic contradistinction to the Islamic revolutionaries, who are emphatically bound to rigid, orthopractical formalism. Raiss concludes that "God does not look at one's deeds, but at one's heart. On the day in which neither wealth nor family nor children will be of any benefit, God will favor those who come to him with a pure heart. This is what we work on."[480] Again, the focus on inner purity versus outer formalism and ritualism is significant in Sufism. It tends to alleviate the traditional and revolutionary Islamic demand that society be strictly structured based upon religious law and Islamic jurisprudence. One gets the sense in talking with

---

[477] Adnane Raiss, interview with the author.
[478] Adnane Raiss, interview with the author.
[479] Adnane Raiss, interview with the author.
[480] Adnane Raiss, interview with the author.

Sufis that perfecting one's faith is less a factor of external ritual, and more a pursuit of spiritualism—of a search for internal, metaphysical purity and unity with the divine. Ignaz Goldziher, the well-known Islamic scholar, wrote that "Sufism appears, first of all, as an important spiritual liberation, an expansion of the constricted religious horizon, over against the legal and doctrinal system of official Islam developed by the jurists and *mutakalimun* [scholars]. Painstaking, blind obedience is replaced by self-education through asceticism . . . by a mystical immersion in the essence of the soul and by its liberation from the dross of materiality."[481]

What does this all mean for U.S. strategy? Sufis are considered apostates and heretics by most of revolutionary Islam. Indeed, in the history of Islam, they have often been the persecuted minority. A traditional Islamic scholar once said of the Sufis: "I never knew until now that filth is part of religion."[482] Goldziher writes that "their doctrines, and perhaps too their religious attitudes, their indifference to the explicit laws of Islam—indifference that frequently reached the point of rejecting all observances—drew upon them severe attacks from the representatives of established theology."[483] Today's Islamic revolutionaries, especially the Saudi Wahabbist ulema, still consider Sufis a heretical element of Islam. The Sufi way stands in relatively stark contrast to the predominant ideology of revolutionary Islam. Daoud Casewit, also a practicing Sufi, explains that "the aim of Sufism is not to mobilize people for specific worldly goals or aims—it is not a political movement nor is it religious propaganda—the raison d'être of Sufism is not correcting the world, but correcting yourself."[484] Dr. Abdallah Schleifer at the American University of Cairo, another intellectual Sufi, put it most succinctly when he said "Islam without Sufism is monstrous!"[485] Indeed, Sufism, along with proselytization by non-revolutionary Muslim clerics, may represent an exploitable fissure in the bulwark of Islam. It may provide the means to penetrate a religious ideology that otherwise seems impenetrable. At the least, as the United States struggles to find allies in the war against revolutionary Islam, it may well have a silent partner in Sufism.

---

[481]Goldziher, 150.
[482]Goldziher, 155.
[483]Goldziher, 155.
[484]Daoud Casewit, interview with the author.
[485]Dr. Abdallah Schleifer, interview with the author.

Final Thoughts

In the end, the struggle that the United States, and more begrudgingly the rest of the Western world, are faced with will not be won by solely kinetic means. The application of military force is certainly necessary to combat the global insurgency propagated by Islamic revolutionaries, but it is not nearly sufficient for victory. Ultimately, defeating revolutionary Islam requires winning the strategic war of ideas. Victory will entail now, just as it did during the Cold War, that the enemy's core ideology be defeated and discredited. The battle of ideas against the principles of Marxism-Leninism was carefully and deliberately waged throughout the Cold War. Indeed, it seems reasonable to assert that rather than détente, it was the West's persistent and aggressive pressure against the Communist ideology that acted in concert with internal weaknesses of the Communist regime and persistent resistance from internal groups like the Solidarity movement in Poland that spelled the Soviet Union's ultimate demise. This so-called Cold War of ideas was a drumbeat that reached warlike intensities during the Reagan administration. Reagan wrote in an essay entitled "Communism, the Disease," that "Communism is neither an economic nor a political system—it is a form of insanity—a temporary aberration which will one day disappear from the earth because it is contrary to human nature. I wonder," Reagan wrote, "how much more misery it will cause before it disappears."[486]

But perhaps more poignant, and also directly relevant to the current struggle, is the comparison that Reagan drew in a speech entitled "The Two Worlds," which captured the fundamental ideological divide between Communism and American democratic values. In his characterization, Reagan contrasted the differences between the philosophies of the West and those of Communism by drawing attention to the words of the Soviet Union's founding father. Apparently, V. I. Lenin once wrote that "It would not matter if 3/4 of the human race perishes; the important thing is that the remaining 1/4 be communist . . . The communist party enters into bourgeois institutions not to do constructive work but in order to direct the masses to destroy from within the whole bourgeois state machine and the parliament itself."[487] Reagan, who would go on to characterize the Soviet Union as the "evil empire," reminded reticent, détente-era Americans that the struggle was ultimately a strategic, ideological competition about how to organize the affairs of society and of mankind as a whole.

---

[486]Ronald Reagan from a speech entitled "Communism, the Disease," in *Reagan: In His Own Hand*, ed. Kiron Skinner, Annelise Anderson, and Martin Anderson (New York: The Free Press, 2001), 12.

[487] Cited from Ronald Reagan from a speech entitled "Two Worlds," in Reagan: *In His Own Hand*, 14.

Unfortunately there is no Western equivalent in today's conflict. Instead, as Western policy elites nervously fidget with the religious nature of the struggle, the revolutionary Islamic vanguard has seized the initiative in the battle of ideas. They articulate a vision that is propelled by the historical and political imperatives of their religion. They comprehend that this is as much a kinetic fight as a metaphysical one. Furthermore, they envisage a struggle of infinite duration. As Abdul Qadeem Zallum wrote in his book *How the Khilafah was Destroyed*,

> It will continue this way—a bloody struggle alongside the intellectual struggle—until the Hour comes and Allah inherits the Earth and those in it. This is why Kufr is an enemy of Islam, and this is why the Kuffar will be the enemies of the Muslims as long as there is Islam and Kufr in this world . . . This is a decisive and a constant fact.[488]

The Islamic revolutionaries paint grand strategic themes as they stoke the fires of fervor with younger believers. Young Muslims throughout the global Islamic *Ummah* hear these messages from *Imams* and *Akhunds* in their Friday Sermons, from teachers in their *madrassas*, and from a proliferating revolutionary Islamic publishing industry that distributes books, pamphlets, videotapes, and increasingly electronic media via the global Internet. Their message, while sometimes driven by local context, is an all-encompassing doctrine of divine empowerment. An al Quada training manual, which places primacy in the ideological elements of the struggle, contains the following in its preface:

> The young men returning to Allah realized that Islam is not just performing rituals, but a complete system: Religion and government, worship and Jihad (holy war), ethics and dealing with people, and the Koran and the sword . . . The young men came to prepare themselves for Jihad (holy war), commanded by the Majestic Allah's order in the holy Koran. [Koranic verse:] "Against them make ready your strength to the utmost of your power, including steeds of war, to strike terror into (the hearts of) the enemies of Allah and your enemies, and others besides whom ye may not know, but whom Allah doth know."[489]

The revolutionary Islamic vanguard understands the significance of the battle of ideas and the deeply ideological nature of the struggle, and leaves no doubt as to its ultimate goals. Today's revolutionaries are individuals like Yussuf al-Ayy-

---

[488]Zallum, 1.

[489]al Quada training manual (Government Exhibit 1677-T). All parenthesis and comment in the original document.

eri, who believe as Lenin did, that the final objective is to bring about a worldwide regime that conforms to Islamic (or in the case of Lenin, Communist) ideology. Al-Ayyeri was one of Osama bin Laden's closest associates and a Saudi citizen who was killed in a gun battle with Saudi security forces in Riyadh in June 2003. Lenin believed that his opponents—the capitalists, imperialists, and bourgeoisie—would eventually "wither away" or be defeated. Perhaps the Islamic revolutionaries incline toward an even more radical solution. Al-Ayyeri wrote regarding religious belief that Islam "annuls all other religions and creeds;" Islam's final solution involves, in the words of Ayyeri, "effacing the final traces of all other religions, creeds and ideologies."[490]

The struggle with revolutionary Islam will only be won when the West begins to methodically analyze the ideological religion that empowers it and forms its basis. Just as Marxism-Leninism had to be understood to defeat the Soviet Union during the Cold War, so too ideological Islam has to be understood in order to defeat the revolutionaries in the current struggle. Scholars and policymakers in the West often wonder why the so-called moderate Muslims do not speak out against the religious ideology of the revolutionaries. It may be because these moderates confront two rather thorny challenges. Not only do they face the difficulty of refuting the legal-religious arguments advanced by the radical worldview of the revolutionaries, but they also have to deal with the broader Islamic aversion to—or even prohibition of—inciting an internal Islamic schism that would split the ranks of the *ummah*.[491]

It is likely that Western policymakers will forever be disappointed if they continue to hope for a spontaneous internal "transformation" or "reformation" within Islam. Instead, as one scholar has recently noted, the West must be prepared to engage in a comprehensive strategy in the war of ideas, based on (1) "an acceptance of the fact that for the first time since the Crusades, Western civilization finds itself involved in a religious war" and (2) "that the conflict has been defined by the attacking side . . . with the eschatological goal of the destruction of Western civilization."[492] Indeed, "this conflict began at the religious-ideological level" and therefore the true roots of the conflict—the cultural and religious sources of

---

[490]Yussuf al-Ayyeri quoted from a book entitled *The Future of Iraq and the Arabian Peninsula After the Fall of Baghdad*, in Amir Taheri, "The Future of Iraq and The Arabian Peninsula After The Fall of Baghdad," 5 September 2003, URL: www.townhall.com/columnists/GuestColumns/Taheri20030905.shtml, accessed 8 September 2003.

[491]This description and wording of the twin dilemma is described by Shmuel Bar, The Religious Sources of Islamic Terrorism, *Policy Review*, no. 125 (June & July 2004), URL:www.policyreview.org/jun04/bar.html, accessed 9 February 2005.

[492]Shmuel Bar.

radical Islamic ideology—must be confronted in order to develop a long-range strategy for winning this war.[493]

This ideological struggle against the revolutionaries will not be simple to conceptualize, nor easy to conduct and win. Thoughtful circumspection will inevitably reveal that the West has several serious disadvantages. Western notions about freedom of religion are likely to come in conflict with a strategy aimed at questioning the enemy's religious ideology. As one observer has noted, "The danger here is not only that you might be seen as attacking one religion, but also as proposing to put the U.S. government in the business of deciding which religious beliefs are acceptable and which ones constitute risks to America's political and social order."[494] Indeed, as the same observer continues, "someone raised in the Enlightenment approach of tolerance and hands-off skepticism about religious disputes (an after-effect in some ways of the wars of religion in Europe in the sixteenth and seventeenth centuries) recoils at the thought of getting the government involved in judgments about the accuracy or social merits of metaphysical beliefs, doctrines of revelation and salvation, and so on."[495] Others amplify the dilemma by drawing attention to the fact that "Western concepts of civil rights along with legal, political, and cultural restraints preclude government intervention in the internal matters of organized religions."[496]

It is precisely because the Islamic revolutionaries are empowered and propelled by a religious ideology—or perhaps an ideological religion—that this threat is so challenging to the standard security mechanisms and mindsets of the largely secularized West. An important point of departure would be to critically examine the elements of the Islamic faith that are being exploited by the revolutionaries, and especially to conduct an exhaustive study of the life of the prophet Mohammad, whom Muslims universally uphold as their ideal role model. Furthermore, analysis and debate should address fundamental theological principles and assumptions (including Islamic anthropology, soteriology, and eschatology as discussed in the previous chapters of this work) in order to attempt to clarify the core differences between Judeo-Christian and Islamic imperatives.

Whether this is even possible in a secularized society that increasingly disregards or even disparages the metaphysical and religious elements of the human experience seems to be the most crucial question. Perhaps, as Julien Benda once wrote in *La Trahison des Clercs* (*The Treason of the Intellectuals*), today's West-

---

[493]Shmuel Bar.

[494]Notes and comments provided by Dr. David Yost, Senior Research Fellow, NATO Defense College, Rome, in conversations with the author in January/February 2005.

[495]Dr. David Yost.

[496]Shmuel Bar.

ern society has determined that there is no good beyond the secular world, and that in this world, there is no god except society itself.[497] Perhaps this society, driven by its own vanity, no longer recognizes knowledge beyond the scope of science, rationality, and logic. Perhaps this society is dominated by a haughty sense of its own power, its own greatness, and its own achievements—beyond and in direct contradistinction to any divine presence or intervention. And as Benda poignantly muses about the prevailing mood of modern Western society,

History will smile to think that this is the species for which Socrates and Jesus Christ died.[498]

---

[497]Julien Benda, *La Trahison des Clercs* (Paris: Grasset, 1927), trans. Richard Aldington as *The Treason of the Intellectuals* (New York: William Morrow & Company, 1928), 203.
[498]Benda, 203.

Bibliography

Abdel-Kader, Nizar. "Promoting Reform Efforts in the Middle East." *Dar Al Hayat*, online edition, 21 June 2004. URL: <www.daralhayat.net/actions/print2.php>. Accessed 21 June 2004.

Abu Gheith, Suleiman. "In the Shadow of Lances." Trans. *Middle East Media Research Institute*, Special Report No. 25, 27 January 2004. URL: <www.memri.org/bin/opener.cgy?Page=archives&ID=SP38802>. Accessed 29 January 2004.

Al-Akhdar, Al-'Afif. "Why does the Arab Sisyphus lift the heavy rock only to drip it on his own feet?" Trans. *Middle East Media Research Institute* in MEMRI Special Dispatch No. 499, 4 May 2003. URL: <www.memri.org/bin/articles.cgi?Page=archives&Area= sd&ID=SP49903>. Accessed 14 December 2004.

American Heritage: A Reader. 2d rev. ed. Ed. History Department Hillsdale College. Acton, MA: Tapestry Press, 2001.

Anderson, Norman. *God's Law and God's Love: An Essay in Comparative Religion*. London: Collins, 1980.

—. *Islam in the Modern World*. Leicester: Apollos Press, 1990.

Armstrong, Karen. *The Battle for God*. London: Harper Collins Publisher, 2000.

Bell, Daniel. *The Winding Passage*. Lanham, MD: Rowman & Littlefield, 1984.

Benda, Julien. *Les Trahison des Clercs*. Paris: Grasset, 1927. Trans. Richard Aldington as *The Treason of the Intellectuals*. New York: William Morrow & Company, 1928.

Benlabbah, Fatiha. Professor of Literature, University of Rabat, Morocco. Interview with the author, 18 March 2004.

Berkhof, Louis. *Summary of Christian Doctrine*. Grand Rapids, MI: William B. Eerdmans, 2000.

Billington, James H. *Fire in the Minds of Men: The Origins of Revolutionary Faith*. New York, NY: Basic Books.

Bobbitt, Philip. *The Shield of Achilles*. New York: Alfred A. Knopf, 2003.

Bozeman, Adda B. *Strategic Intelligence and Statecraft*. Washington D.C.: Brassey's (US), 1992.

Braizat, Fares. Director, Public Polling Unit, Center for Strategic Studies, University of Jordan, Amman, Jordan. Interview with the author, 28 March 04.

Brooks, David. "Hooked on Heaven Lite." *New York Times*, 9 March 2004, A27.

—. "The C.I.A.: Method and Madness." *New York Times*, 2 February 2004, A27.

—. "The Rise of Global Christianity: A Conversation with Philip Jenkins and David Brooks." *Center Conversations* no. 23. Washington D.C.: Ethics and Public Policy Center, July 2003.

Builder, Carl. "Keeping the Strategic Flame." *Joint Force Quarterly* (Winter 1996-97).

Casewit, Daoud. Executive Secretary, Moroccan-American Commission for Educational and Cultural Exchange, Rabat, Morocco. Interview with the author, 17 March 04.

Chapman, Colin. *Whose Promised Land? The Continuing Crisis over Israel and Palestine.* Grand Rapids, MI: Baker Books, 2003.

Chetti, Sam. Archbishop of the American Baptist Churches of Greater Los Angeles. Interview by the author, 20 January 2004.

Cole, C. Donald. *Basic Christian Faith.* Westchester, IL: Crossway Books, 1985.

"Commander of the Khobar Terrorist Squad Tells the Story of the Operation." Middle East Research Institute, Special Dispatch 731, 15 June 2004. URL: <www.memri.org/bin/articles.cgi?Page=archives&Area=sd&ID=SP73104>. Accessed 28 June 2004.

"Contemporary Islamist Ideology Permitting Genocidal Murder." Washington D.C.: *Middle East Media Research Institute*, Special Reoprt No 25, 27 January 2007. URL: <www. memri.org/bin/opener_latest.cgi?ID=SR2504>. Accessed 29 January 2004.

The Columbia World of Quotations, online ed., 1996. URL: <www.bartleby.com/66/76/28576.html>. Accessed 10 December 2004.

Cragg, Kenneth and R. Marston Speight. *The House of Islam.* 3d ed. Belmont, CA: Wadsworth Publishing, 1988.

Dekmeijian, R. Hrair. *Islam in Revolution: Fundamentalism in the Arab World.* 2d ed. Syracuse, NJ: Syracuse University Press, 1995.

Denny, Frederick. *Islam and the Muslim Community.* Prospect Heights, IL: Waveland, 1987.

Eickelman, Dale F. "The Coming Transformation of the Muslim World." Templeton Lecture on Religion and World Affairs. Philadelphia, PA: *Foreign Policy Research Institute*, August 1999. URL: <www.fpri.org/fpriwire/0709.199908.eickelman.muslimtransform. html>. Accessed 6 April 2004.

Eickelman, Dale and James Piscatori. *Muslim Politics.* Princeton: Princeton University Press, 1996.

Elmusa, Sharif. Director, Middle East Studies Program, American University, Cairo. Interview with the author, 22 March 2004.

Esposito, John L. *Islam and Politics.* 3d ed. Syracuse, NY: Syracuse University Press, 1991.

Fanon, Frantz. *The Wretched of the Earth.* New York: Grove Press, 1963.

"Friday Sermons in Saudi Mosques: Review and Analysis." MEMRI Special Report No. 10, 26 September 2002. Washington D.C.: *The Middle East Media Research Institute.* URL: <www.memri.org/bin/articles.cgi?Page=archives&Area=sr&ID=SR01002>. Accessed 14 December 2004.

Gaffney, Frank. "Waging the War of Ideas." *Washington Times*, 9 December 2003, A19.

Gaustad, Edwin. *A Documentary History of Religion in America: To the Civil War.* 2d ed. Grand Rapids: Eedrmans Publishing Company, 1993.

Geisler, Norman L. and Abdul Saleeb. *Answering Islam: The Crescent in Light of the Cross.* Grand Rapids: Baker Books, 2002.

Gessus, Mohammad. Political Pundit and Strategist, Rabat, Morocco. Interview with the author, 18 March 04.

Gibb, H. A. R. *Mohammedanism*. London: Oxford University Press, 1970.

Gibbon, Edward. *The History of the Decline and Fall of the Roman Empire*. Norwalk, CT: The Easton Press, 1974.

Gold, Dore. *Hatred's Kingdom*. Washington D.C.: Regnery Publishing, Inc., 2003.

Goldziher, Ignaz. *Introduction to Islamic Theology and Law*. Trans. Andreas and Ruth Hamori. Princeton: Princeton University Press, 1981.

Gould, Harold. "Suicide as a Weapon of Mass Destruction." *Counterpunch* (25 November 2003). URL: <www.counterpunch.org/gould11282003.html>. Accessed 1 December 2003.

Gould, Mark. "Eschatology and Soteriology: Religious Commitment and Its Consequences in Islam and Christianity." Draft paper submitted for publication in August 2003. Philadelphia, PA: Department of Sociology, Haverford College.

Hanson, Victor Davis. *Carnage and Culture: Landmark Battles in the Rise of Western Civilization*. New York: Doubleday, 2001.

Hanson, Victor Davis and John Heath. *Who Killed Homer?* San Francisco: Encounter Books, 2001.

Harris, Lee. *Civilization and its Enemies*. New York, NY: Free Press, 2004.

Hayek, F. A. *The Road to Serfdom*. Chicago: University of Chicago Press, 1994.

History of Political Philosophy. 3d ed. Eds. Leo Strauss and Joseph Cropsey. Chicago: Chicago University Press, 1987.

"How American can win the intelligence war." *Asia Times Online Edition* (15 June 2004). URL: <www.atimes.com/atimes/Front_Page/FF15Aa01.html>. Accessed 15 June 2004.

Inamdar, Subhash C. *Muhammad and the Rise of Islam: The Creation of Group Identity*. Madison: Psychosocial Press, 2001.

Jansen, Johannes. *The Neglected Duty: The Creed of Sadat's Assassins and Islamic Resurgence in the Middle East*. New York: MacMillan Publishing Co, 1986.

Jefferson, Thomas. *Thomas Jefferson: Writings*. Ed. Merril D. Peterson. New York: Library of America, 1984.

"Jihad Against Jews and Crusaders." World Islamic Front Statement (23 February 1998). Washington D.C.: *Federation of American Scientists*. URL: <www.fas.org/irp/world/para/docs/980223-fatwa.htm>. Accessed 29 January 2004.

Kelly, Douglas. *The Emergence of Liberty in the Modern World*. Phillipsburg, N. J.: P&R Publishing, 1992.

Kennan, George F. *American Diplomacy*. Expanded edition. Chicago: University of Chicago Press, 1984.

Kent, Sherman. *Strategic Intelligence*. Princeton: Princeton University Press, 1949. Review by Willmoore Kendall entitled "The Function of Intelligence." In World Politics, July 1949.

Kessler, Jascha. "The West's Barbarity is Islam's Law." *Financial Times*, 19 May 2004.

Khanna, Parag. "Terrorism as War." *Policy Review* (October/November 2003). URL: <www.policyreview.org/oct03/khanna_print.html>. Accessed 23 March 2003.

Kingdon, John W. *America the Unusual*. Boston, MA: Bedford/St. Martin's, 1999.

Laqueur, Walter. "The New Face of Terrorism." *The Washington Quarterly* (Autumn 1998).

Lawrence, T. E. *Seven Pillars of Wisdom*. New York, NY: Anchor Books, 1991.

Leites, Nathan and Charles Wolf, Jr. *Rebellion and Authority: An Analytic Essay on Insurgent Conflicts*. Chicago: Markham, 1970. Review by Kenneth E. Boulding in *The Annals of the American Academy*, November 1970.

Lewis, Bernard. "License to Kill." *Foreign Affairs* (November/December 1998). URL: <www. web.archive.org/web/20011218022957>. Accessed 29 January 2004.

—. *The Political Language of Islam*. Chicago: The University of Chicago Press, 1988.

—. "The Roots of Muslim Rage." *The Atlantic Monthly* (September 1990). URL: <www.theatlantic.com/issues/90sep/rage.htm>. Accessed 20 January 2004.

Mackinder, Halford J. *Democratic Ideals and Reality*. Ed. Anthony J. Pearce. Westport, CT: Greenwood Press, 1962.

—. *Democratic Ideals and Reality*. NDU Press Defense Classic Edition. Washington D.C.: National Defense University Press, 1996.

"Madrid Suspect Was on Police Radar." *The Wall Street Journal Europe*, 19-21 March 2004, A5.

Mamedaliev, Vasim. Chairman of the Department of Arabic Philology and Dean of the Theological Faculty, University of Baku, Azerbaijan. Interview with the author, 23 March 04.

Mansfield, Stephen. *Never Give In: The Extraordinary Character of Winston Churchill*. Harding, TN: Cumberland House, 1996.

Marshall, Paul. "War Against the Infidels." *The Weekly Standard* (26 June 04). URL: <www. theweeklystandard.com/check.asp?idArticle=4279&r=kvtyq>. Accessed 26 April 2004.

Masugi, Ken. "Interview with James V. Schall on Reason and Faith," 23 December 2002. Claremont, CA: The Claremont Institute for the Study of Statesmanship and Political Philosophy. URL: <www.claremont.org/writings/021223/masugi_b.html>. Accessed 13 June 2004.

McCarthy, Andrew. "The War that Dare Not Speak Its Name." *National Review Online* (13 May 2004). URL: www.nationalreview.com/mccarthy/mccarthy200405130837.asp. Accessed 18 May 2004.

The Meaning of the Holy Qur'an. Trans. Abdullah Yusuf 'Ali. In *The World of Islam: Resources for Understanding*. Colorado Springs: Global Mapping International, 2000. CD-ROM.

Melchert, Christopher. Lecturer in Arabic and Islam, Oriental Institute, Oxford University, England. Interview with the author, 12 February 2004.

Mitri, Tarek. Professor of Interreligious Relations and Diaglogue, World Council of Churches, Geneva, Switzerland. Interview with the author, 17 February 04.

Muggeridge, Malcolm. *Jesus: The Man who Lives*. New York: Harper & Row, 1975.

Newell, Waller R. "Postmodern Jihad." *The Weekly Standard* (11 November 2001). URL: <www.weeklystandard.com/Content/Public/Articles/000/000/000/553fragu.asp>. Accessed 26 April 2004.

Noll, Mark A. *Turning Points*. Grand Rapids: Baker Academic Books, 1997.

O'Connell, Kevin and Robert R. Tomes. "Keeping the Information Edge." *Policy Review* (December 2003), URL: <www.policyreview.org/dec03/oconnel>. Accessed 23 April 2004.

Palmer, R. R., and Joel Colton. *A History of the Modern World*. 6th ed. New York: Alfred A. Knopf, 1984.

Peters, F. E. *A Reader on Classical Islam*. Princeton: Princeton University Press, 1994.

Peters, Rudolph. *Jihad in Classical and Modern Islam*. Princeton: Markus Wiener Publishers, 1996.

Pryce-Jones, David. *The Closed Circle*. Chicago, IL: Ivan R. Dee, 2002.

Quasem, Muhammad Abdul. *Salvation of the Soul and Islamic Devotions*. London: Kegan Paul International, 1983.

Qutb, Sayyid. *Islam and Universal Peace*. Indianapolis: American Trust Publications, 1977.

—. *Milestones*. Dheli: Markazi Maktaba Islami, 1996.

—. *Social Justice in Islam*. Trans. John B. Hardie. Oneonta, NY: Islamic Publications International, 2000.

Raiss, Adnane. National Coordinator, United Nations International Labor Office, Rabat, Morocco. Interview with the author, 16 March 2004.

—. *The Contribution of Sufism in Promoting a Culture of Peace*. Unpublished scholarly paper (Spring 2002).

Rauf, Muhammad Abdul. *Islam: Creed and Worship*. Washington D.C.: The Islamic Center, 1974.

Reagan: In His Own Hand. Eds. Kiron Skinner, Annelise Anderson, and Martin Anderson. New York: The Free Press, 2001.

Religion, The Mission Dimension of Statecraft. Eds. Douglas Johnston and Cynthia Sampson. New York: Oxford University Press, 1994.

Rogan, Eugene. Director, Middle East Center, Oxford University, England. Interview with the author, 13 February 2004.

Russell, Richard L. "Intelligence Failures." *Policy Review* (February 2004). URL: <www.policyreview.org/feb04/russell>. Accessed 23 April 2004.

Schaeffer, Francis A. *How Should We Then Live?* Wheaton: Crossway Books, 1995.

Scheler, Max. *Ressentiment*. Trans. Lewis Coser and William Holdheim. Ed. Manfred

Frings. Milwaukee: Marquette University Press, 2003.

Schimmel, Annemarie. *And Muhammad Is His Messenger*. Chapel Hill: The University of North Carolina Press, 1985.

Schleifer, Abdallah. Distinguished Lecturer and Director of the Adham Center for Journalism, American University in Cairo. Interview with the author, 22 March 04.

Schneider, Peter. "Separated by Civilization." *International Herald Tribune*, 7 April 2004, 6.

Schulte, Paul. "I am Osama bin Laden: A Strategic Warning and Challenge to the West." *RUSI Journal* (June 2002).

Schuon, Frithjof. *Understanding Islam*. Trans. D. M. Matheson. London: George Allen and Unwin, 1965.

Schwarz, Karl Peter. "Der Engle der Nationen." *Frankfurter Allgemeine Zeitung*, 7 April 2004, 8.

Sells, Michael. *Approaching the Qur'an: The Early Revelations*. Trans. Michael Sells. Ashland, OR: White Cloud Press, 1999.

Sivan, Emmanual. "The Holy War Tradition in Islam." *Orbis* (Spring 1998).

Smoler, Frederic. "The Shah Always Falls: An Interview with Ralph Peters." *American Heritage* (February/March 2003). URL: <www.americanheritage.com/xml/2003/1/2003_1_feat_0.xml>. Accessed 30 January 2004.

Stephens, Philip. "The unwitting wisdom of Rumsfeld's unknowns." *Financial Times*, 12 December 2003, 19.

Sun Tzu. *The Art of War*. 2d rev. ed. Ed. Michael I. Handel. London: Frank Cass & Co Ltd, 1996.

Taheri, Amir. "Al Qaida's Agenda for Iraq." *United Press International* (6 September 2003). URL: <www.upi.com/print.cfm?StoryID=20030906-105644-1203r>. Accessed 8 September 2003.

—. "The Future of Iraq and The Arabian Peninsula After The Fall of Baghdad." Townhall.com (5 September 2003). URL: < www.townhall.com/columnists/ GuestColumns/Taheri20030905.shtml>. Accessed 8 September 2003.

"Terrorist Targets, Washington Maps found in October Raid." *News Tribune Online Edition*, 21 February 2002. URL: <www.newstribune.com/articles/2002/02/21/export181125.txt>. Accessed 13 December 2004.

"Text of Statement from Osama Bin Laden." *Los Angeles Times* (7 October 2001). URL: <www.latimes.com/news/nationworld/world/la-100701binladen_text.story>. Accessed 10 December 2004.

Tilmann. Shiite Akhund in Baku, Azerbaijan. Interview by the author, 3 April 2004.

Tocqueville, Alexis de. *Democracy in America*. London: David Campbell Publishers, 1994.

Tozi, Mohammad. Professor, University of Casablanca, Morocco. Interview by the author, 16 March 04.

Transnational Religion and Fading States. Eds. Susanne Hoeber Rudolph and James Piscatory. Boulder: Westview Press, 1997.

Tschirgi, Dan. Professor and Chairman of the Department of Political Science, American University in Cairo, Egypt. Interview with the author, 22-23 March 2004.

Voll, John Obert. *Islam: Continuity and Change in the Modern World*. 2d ed. Syracuse: Syracuse University Press, 1994.

Waddy, Chris. *The Muslim Mind*. London: Longman, 1976.

Watt, W. Montgomery. *Islamic Political Thought*. Edinburgh: Edinburgh University Press, 1999.

Wensinck, A. J. *Semietische Studien Uit De Nalatenschap*. Leiden: A. W. Sijthoff, 1941.

Western Heritage: A Reader. 1st rev. ed. Ed. History Department Hillsdale College. Acton, MA: Tapestry Press, 2000.

Wight, Martin. *Power Politics*. Eds. Hedley Bull and Carsten Holbraad. London: Leicester University Press, 1978.

Wilken, Robert Louis. *The Spirit of Early Christian Thought*. New Haven: Yale University Press, 2003.

Woodberry, Dudley. Dean Emeritus and Professor of Islamic Studies, School of International Studies, Fuller Theological Seminary. Interview by the author, 19 January 2004.

Zallum, Abdul Qadeem. *How the Khilafah was Destroyed*. London: Al-Khilafah Publications, 1998.

Zeidan, David. "The Islamic Fundamentalist View of Life as a Perennial Battle." *Middle East Review of International Affairs* (December 2001). URL: <www.meria.idc.ac.il/2001/ issue4/jv5n4a2.htm>. Accessed 29 January 2004.

Zekri, Mustafa. Professor of Anthropology and Religion, University of Rabat, Morocco. Interview with the Author, 18 March 2004.

Index

About the Author

Lt Col (Sel) Stephen P. Lambert is the action officer for Austria, Germany, Slovenia, and Switzerland at the Joint Staff, Strategic Plans and Policy Directorate (J-5), Washington, DC. He is responsible for politico-military affairs, military-to-military contacts, and policy analysis and advice to the Chairman of the Joint Chiefs of Staff. He is a graduate of the U.S. Air Force Academy Class of 1990 and is a senior pilot with 3,000 flying hours from operational assignments involving Special Air Missions, air refueling, and strategic airlift. In 1995, he completed his Master of Arts degree as a distinguished graduate from the Naval Postgraduate School in Monterey, CA. Following graduate school, he taught in the Department of Military Strategic Studies at the U.S. Air Force Academy as a course director, assistant professor, and director of the Academy's War Gaming Center. After returning to Travis AFB, Major Lambert was selected to a special duty flying assignment at Andrews AFB, where he flew Special Air Missions in support of the President and Vice President, as well as numerous members of the President's cabinet and members of Congress. Since 1995, Major Lambert has been involved in extensive research on nuclear strategy, WMD proliferation, and Islamic revolutionary theology and identity mobilization for the Institute for National Security Studies. His work, which was supported by several research grants, culminated in the publication of three occasional papers and several book chapters on national security policy. His research resulted in collaboration with the national security division at Sandia National Laboratories, the Defense Threat Reduction Agency, and the Nuclear Weapons and Counterproliferation Division of the USAF Air Staff. Prior to assuming his current position, he was a Fellow at the Center for Strategic Intelligence Research, Joint Military Intelligence College, Defense Intelligence Agency, Washington, DC.